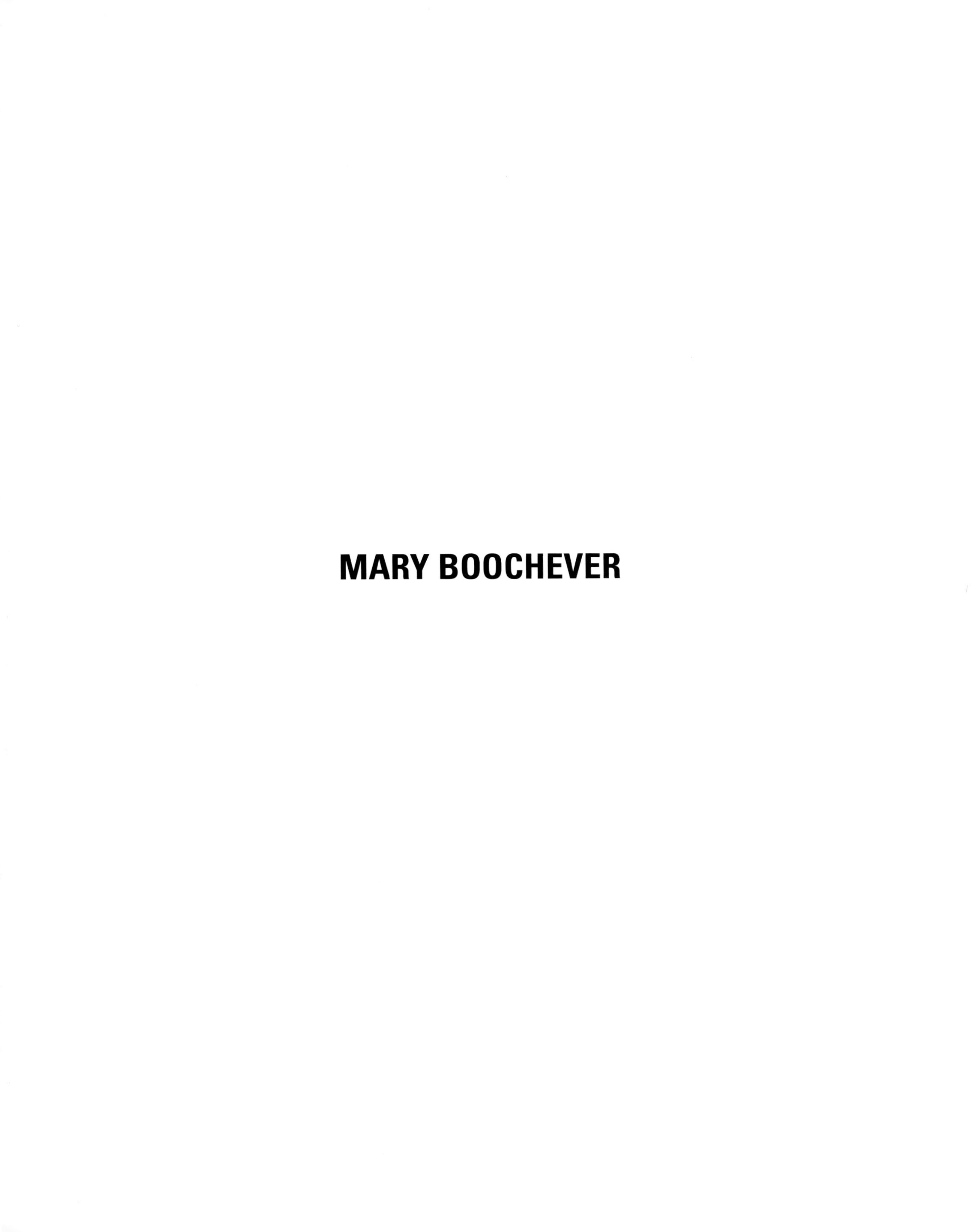
MARY BOOCHEVER

MARY BOOCHEVER

CHARTA

CONTENTS

IN THE PRESENCE OF POSSIBILITY

SUSAN STOOPS

*Every era has to reinvent the project
of "spirituality" for itself.*[1]

At the heart of Mary Boochever's practice is a belief
in art's capacity to engage viewers in a contemplative experience, thereby creating opportunities to
envisage a meaning of "world" that moves beyond
one's immediate physical and historical presence.
Staring into her paintings, one passes into an awareness of endless possibilities, eternities.

Boochever's deft articulation of a multiplicity of spatial experiences is accomplished primarily through
transitions of color, the movements between which
are sometimes so subtly perceptible as to be nearly
indescribable. Her practice communicates an under-
standing of the world as something mutable, specu-
lative, uncertain. The uncertainty inherent in con-
ceiving and reading a painting outside representa-
tion is constantly embraced by Boochever. In the
seventeenth century, Blaise Pascal argued that the
reality of a limitless world lies beyond human con-
structs, that no ideas come near it, and it is this dis-
junction between representations of reality and reality itself that forces us to look beyond our systems,
beyond our representations.[2]

The clarity expressed by Boochever's painting com-
positions (built upon a system of triangles, dia-
monds, and pentagons amid ubiquitous squares and
rectangles) ultimately underscores geometry's own
limits. For within the relative stability of these de-
fined shapes reside interiors that are unquantifiable
and indefinable—elusive states of luminosity, surface depth, hue, emptiness. Aggregates of thinly
painted strata, resulting in chromatic fields that
seem to breathe as they visually expand and con-
tract, together give form to spaces that exist between clarity and obscurity, definition and dissolu-
tion, completeness and possibility.

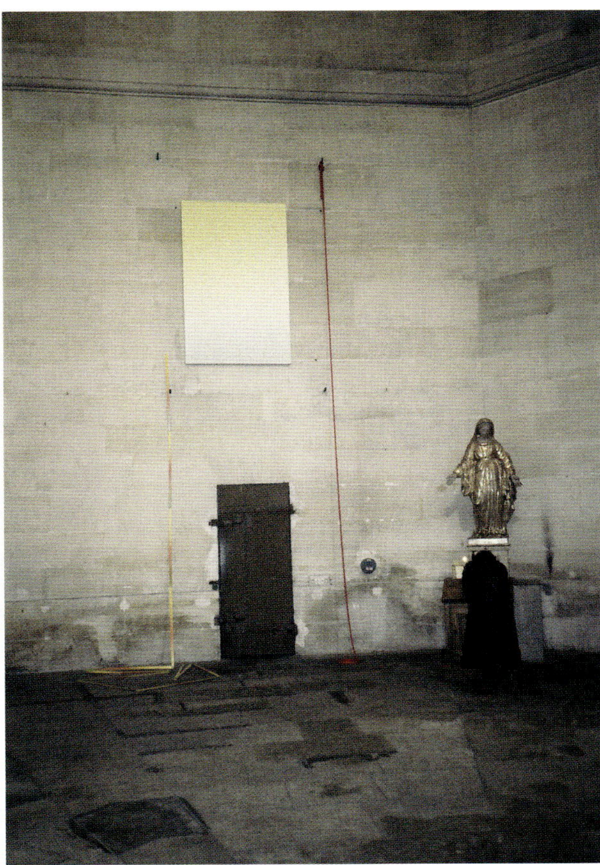

Installation, 1986
Chapelle de la Salpêtrière, Paris, France

Boochever's formal education in painting took place
in Germany in the late 1970s, where she concentrat-
ed on color theory. Her artistic practice since then
shows an intimate awareness of a tradition of radical
(re)visions of abstract painting, including the varia-
tions of geometric abstraction practiced by Piet Mondrian, Josef Albers, Agnes Martin, Robert Ryman,
and Jeremy Gilbert-Rolfe to cite only a few. Boochever's occasional enigmatic sculptures (the leather-
sandaled foot *Prezo*, the landscape-as-apron *Brilo*,
both from 1987, and the glass *Eye*, 1992) and her-
metic installations with painting and sculptural com-
ponents (*Hidden Entrances*, 1994, and *Vertical Minute*, 1995) demonstrate that she also absorbed the
lessons of Joseph Beuys concerning the redemptive

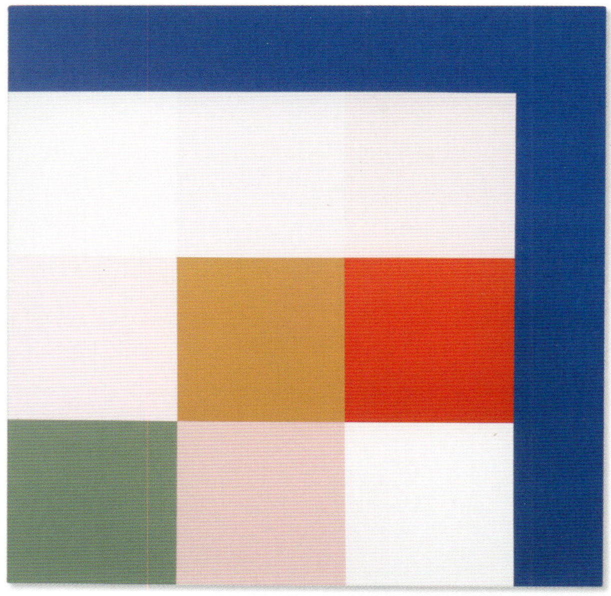

Khar, 2006
23 x 23 inches, pigment, acrylic, canvas

potential of objects. Just as critical to Boochever's aesthetic project have been her decades-long explorations of the historical connections between abstract painting and theorizing of the spiritual as proposed in the literary works of Johann Wolfgang von Goethe, Johannes Itten, and Rudolf Steiner.

As early as 1986, Boochever's absorption in spatial concepts of color found expression in painting projects conceived for architectural environments. An installation in the group show "Distances" at the Chapelle de la Salpêtrière in Paris created a multi-dimensional dialogue: a painted canvas titled *Michael* ("a subtle color gradation from yellow to blue without passing through green"[3]) was sited high above a chapel doorway and flanked by a painted folded yardstick and a suspended red satin rope. A year later in the stairwells of White Columns in New York City, Boochever orchestrated a sensory-rich passageway altered by chromatic shifts and volumes painted across the walls, floors, ceiling, stairs, and railing.

Not surprisingly, the physical shapes Boochever has chosen for the paintings on canvas are central to her explorations into colors' spatial capacities. Vertically oriented rectangles in which color regions sometimes are divided geometrically yet integrated at the surface emphasize connections (rather than divisions) between any sense of "above" and what lies "below." Verticality can also have the effect of colors appearing, only to disappear as they ascend or descend into an ethereal lightness or enveloping darkness. Possibilities awaiting viewers of the luminous *Phthonos* (1996) or the soaring "inverted arch" of *Raphael* (1990) include imagining them as colors/spaces into which one can pass.

I can recall vividly my first encounter with *Raphael* and this phenomenon in a 1991 solo exhibition of Boochever's paintings at Genovese Gallery in Boston. A group of identically sized (95 x 49 inches) and shaped canvases, which the artist says "evolved from the idea of finding a way to combine intelligence (orthogonal shape) above with the subconscious (round shape) below,"[4] hung about one foot above the floor. The chapel-like, symmetrical installation and individual chromatic gradations, so nuanced in each canvas yet richly varied from painting to painting, created a symphonic silence that was both meditative and truly visceral.

Over the years, Boochever has explored the possibilities of the cruciform-shaped canvas, a "mystical conjunction of opposites."[5] Sometimes it contains its own interior geometry, as in *Fourth of July* (1990); elsewhere, as in *Sensible – Super Sensible* (1990), the painting's peripheral reach is countered by its contemplative core. In the quartet of pentagonal paintings *Eurus*, *Zephyr*, *Borus*, and *Notus*

(1986), inspired by the concept of wind ("an invisible force which is materially present"[6]) and named after the four winds in Greek mythology, the multi-directional nature of the support allows Boochever's delicately painted surfaces to dissolve into constantly moving fields of shifting color and light.

Incompleteness in Boochever's paintings suggests possibility; it accommodates doubt in the midst of geometric clarity as in *Gate* (1996) with its diamond-shaped aperture or *Khar* (2006) where a band of blue frames only two sides of a color grid. In the monochromatic *Khet* (1999), the ziggurat-shaped format and skin-like encaustic surface simultaneously give form to the concepts of absence (a once-complete rectangle) and presence (the tactile being of blue).

Among the framing devices Boochever has conceived, the "ladder" format of *Pearl*, *Minium*, and *Iron Glimmer* (all from 1997–1999) acts to hold distinct units of color in place relative to one another in ascending or descending gradations; it also demonstrates a bridge between painting and sculpture that has been of interest to the artist over several decades. While experiences of "unimpeded space"[7] more typically describe the experience of Boochever's canvases over the years, occasionally she has created visual experiences that depend upon an interrupted view (the cinder block wall in *Hidden Entrance*, 1994, may be the most overt). In the recent horizontal canvas *L.A.W.* (2006), Boochever challenges the very idea of a comprehensible space. Here, repeated colors perform seemingly irreconcilable spatial roles; incomplete framing devices (one rectangular, the other curvilinear) define internal (not external) spaces while also serving as quasi-imagistic details.

In the myriad physical forms it has taken over the past three decades, Boochever's art remains purposefully mute; it communicates through a language of metaphysical effects and decision-making possibilities (although consummately confident, Boochever's decision-making embraces intuition and never submits to total control). What is possible by virtue of her process—indicated by the evolution of choices about media, shapes, colors, layers—over time becomes truly tangible.

Susan L. Stoops
Curator of Contemporary Art, Worcester Art Museum

1. Susan Sontag, "The Aesthetics of Silence," *Styles of Radical Will* (New York: Farrar, Strauss and Giroux, 1969), 3.

2. Blaise Pascal, *Pensées*, translated by A.J. Krailsheimer (Harmondsworth: Penguin, 1966), 85.

3. Mary Boochever in correspondence with the author, May 2009.

4. Mary Boochever in correspondence with the author, May 2009.

5. David Shapiro, "Mild Steel: On the Art of Mary Boochever," *Mary Boochever: Vertical Minute* (New York: Annika Sundvik Gallery, 1995), 6.

6. Jeremy Gilbert-Rolfe, "Nonrepresentation in 1988: Meaning-Production Beyond the Scope of the Pious," *Arts Magazine*, May 1988, 33; reprinted in Gilbert-Rolfe, *Beyond Piety: Critical Essays on the Visual Arts, 1986-1993* (New York: Cambridge University Press, 1995), 61.

7. Jeremy Gilbert-Rolfe, "Beyond Absence," *Arts Magazine*, October 1988, 60; reprinted in Gilbert-Rolfe, *Beyond Piety*, 163.

THRESHOLDS

PHILIP VANDERHYDEN

Where we are concerned with my body, the natural world, the past, birth or death, the question is always how I can be open to phenomena which transcend me, and which nevertheless exist only to the extent that I take them up and live them; how the presence to myself which establishes my own limits and conditions every alien presence is at the same time depresentation and throws me outside myself.[1]

Maurice Merleau-Ponty
The Phenomenology of Perception

Just a few steps back from one of Mary Boochever's paintings sat a small object, which looked a little like a pyramid with its top cut off. Since its wood surface resembled the floor on which it perched, one might not notice it at first; or worse, one might back into it as one took in *Location*, the subtly gradated painting it aligned itself with. If that were to happen, one might be relieved (if still a bit unsettled) when one learned its title: *Stool.*

In this 1989 exhibition at Daniel Newburg Gallery, one could be forgiven for wondering about the limited amount of seating space. After all, if it were a gallery bench—whose surface could accommodate multiple viewers—one might linger and converse with someone else, chatting about Boochever's paintings and sculptures from a safe, non-immersive distance. *Stool's* small—almost pointed—profile breaks decisively from the sprawl of a bench.

The lateral form of the bench evokes leisure, social conviviality, and public reflection on one's experiences. In most cases, one withdraws to the bench from the private experience of engaging with objects on the wall. *Stool* is less a place for rest and conversation than it is a realignment of the experience of the painting it faces: its vertically oriented wood grain channels upward toward the

Location, 1989
63 x 63 inches, pigment, acrylic, canvas

small seat. It emphasizes a more singular, solitary, inward-turning and temporary experience.

As a work within that show and as part of Mary Boochever's oeuvre, it opens up a way of thinking about the manner in which her work addresses the viewer. As lush and visually sophisticated as Boochever's work can be, it never compartmentalizes the optical sensory experience. Boochever's work addresses vision as a function of the other senses and clears a space for them to exist in dramatic relation with each other.

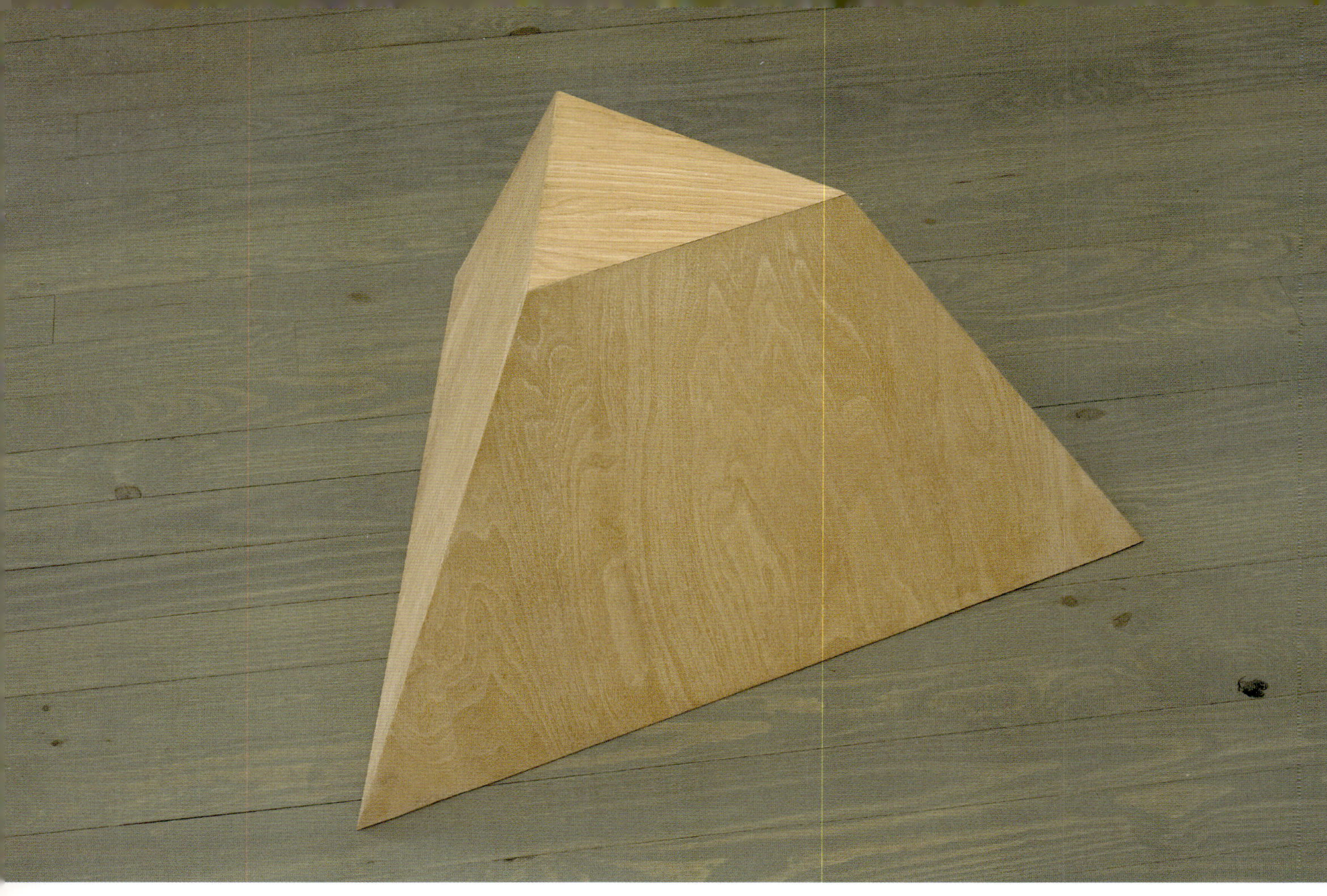

Stool, 1989
24 x 24 x 15 inches, wood

Mary Boochever's work is transitional. In common parlance, that might not sound like a quality that should span a body of work as complete as hers: "transitional" sounds more like a way of describing a work that doesn't fit comfortably into the regular serial pattern of an artist's practice. Quite to the contrary, Boochever's work never looks tentative: the economy and stridency of her paintings, sculptures, and installations evidences a sure-footed and unified approach. The word transitional applies to Boochever in a more broadly historical, existential, and formal sense of the word. Her work thrives in liminal spaces.

Historically speaking, Boochever's work began at a time that is itself hazy and in flux. In the late 1970s, Boochever completed her education at the Akademie der Bildenden Künste in Munich. Outside of the academy, ambitious artists began to see the fruits of the enterprise of modernist painting withering on the vine. What long seemed the future of art, began to look like the past.

Artists who weren't abandoning painting for performance, photography, and installation commenced a decade-long retrenchment around expressionistic and figurative forms. If those who stopped painting did so because of its inability to participate more directly and confrontationally with its audience, the ones that remained gravitated toward more recognizably painterly forms. To many painters, the disappointment over the seemingly predictable and contained radicality of modernist painting led to a belief that it should retrench around picture making, materiality, and other mannerisms that self-evidently assured the audience of the object's inherent sense of purpose.

An alliance with either of these two camps would appear out of step with Boochever's more patient interpretation of the surrounding discourse. While

Fourth of July, 1990

her earliest work from this era began an ongoing relationship with color fields that nod to high modernism, her 1980 installation *Night & Day, Night & Day, Night & Day*—with its literal sculptural forms and immersive physical space—evidences a justifiable restlessness with a faithful, uncritical continuation of modernist painting's frontality and gratuitous opticality. As if to set the tone for future bodies of work, Boochever began to augment her practice of painting with sculptural and installation works that attempt to anchor the lofty ambitions of modernism to the concrete, localized dimensions of sculptural and architectural form.

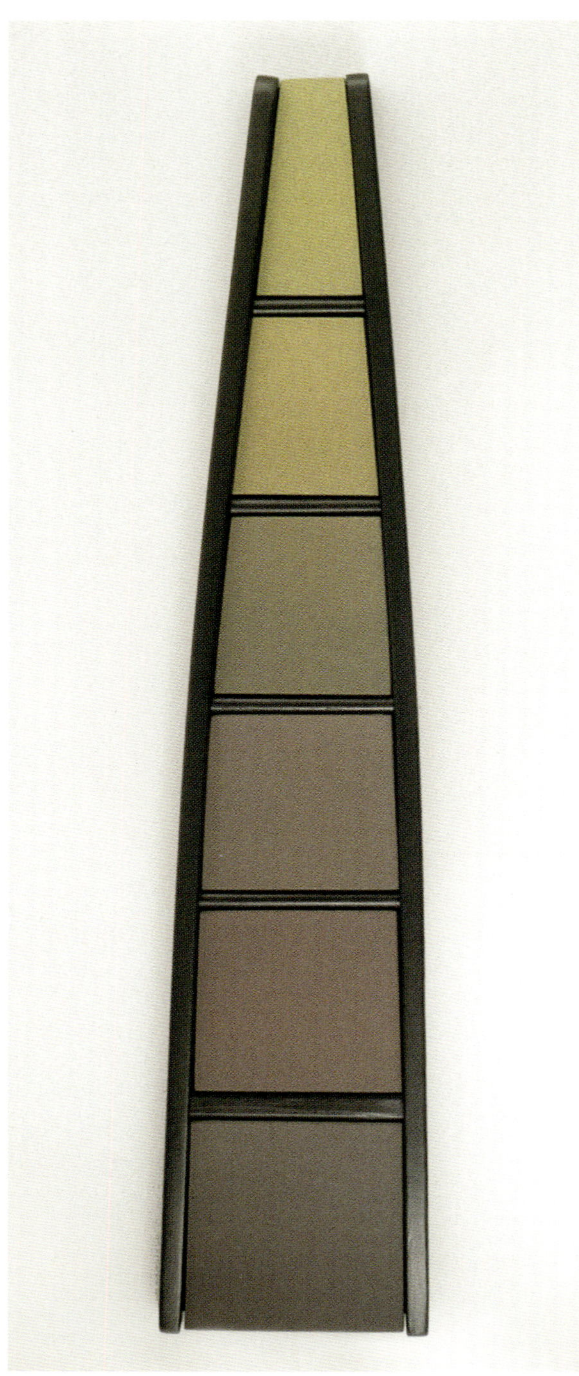

Iron Glimmer, 1997–1999

In a gradual synthesis, the "here and now" conditions of this sculptural work crept into Boochever's more autonomous paintings in terms of the attention they drew towards their framing edge. If framing seems like an afterthought to other genres of painting, in the case of the modernist, few elements hold more importance: for modernist painters it stands as the ultimate arbiter of meaning. It performs the important existential drama of simultaneous connection and separation. The frame connects by figuring a deliberate and therefore meaningful act of marking out, delimiting, focusing, and cognition. This connection not only asserts the object's separateness and singularity, but the contents of the frame express the boundary between viewer and object, causing it to take on metaphoric significance.

For dyed-in-the-wool painters of this tradition, like Barnett Newman, the lateral edges of the stretcher and the surface were not just a cropping or end point, but an agent in a metaphysical event. The viewer's posture in front of the object became mirrored by the vertical "zips" in the composition of the painting itself. Newman's zips echo the uprightness of both the framing edge and viewer, causing the body to linger within the experience of looking. One can never simply *look* at Newman's paintings. Unlike the more purely visual paintings of the late 1970s—such as Larry Poons, Jules Olitski, and Kenneth Noland—in this work, the whole body of the viewer matters.

For Newman and for Boochever, the body never becomes a sensory remainder. The body creates the painting's sense of purpose by providing a foundation from which the eye can be meaningfully reflected upon. In this arena—the passage between the eye and the body—Boochever's most meaningful transitional moments occur.

In order to see how this works, it helps to look at instances where Boochever uses both standardized and non-standardized framing strategies. In some cases, such as Boochever's 1990 show at Daniel Newburg Gallery (the follow-up to the show that included *Stool*), one can find them within the same painting. For this exhibition, she arranged seven large paintings of uniform dimension. Using a slightly larger than human-size (95 x 49 inches) stretcher, Boochever created a somewhat eccentrically shaped frame. On the top two edges of this portrait-orientation format, she used a conventional rectilinear contour. Along the bottom, she rounded the frame downward in an inverted arch, the outermost point of which would come just shy of grazing the gallery floor.

Like most large, narrow vertical canvases, the paintings' framing edges center and orient the viewer in mirror-like opposition to their standing posture, in much the same manner a doorway anticipates the dimensions of its user. But, just as Boochever's inverted arch sculpturally draws viewers into frontal alignment, it pushes attention downward toward the floor, above which the painting appears to hover as though levitating. The painting creates a contrast between the viewer's weighted, worldly presence and the painting's stance on the wall.

These qualities of the frame affect the movement and containment of the color gradations in analogous ways. At the upper rectilinear edges, where the frame plays by more established rules, color moves more flexibly. While Boochever sometimes contains the movement of the gradation within these limits, she also allows it to drift in and out of them. In other words, the format behaves the way a rectangular support most often behaves: it becomes either a boundary or a window.

Not so in the lower inverted arch. More than in the upper rectangle, color collects and concentrates. In *Raphael*, the color's "weight" appears to cause a "sagging" of the framing edge, while that same slackening forms the boundaries within which the color seems held. In other cases, such as *Fourth of July*, the red tip of the arch appears emphasized as it takes on the role of a charged point. While the color gradient can express movement *through* the object, it also animates the earthward momentum of the canvas shape by restating and exaggerating it.

Boochever's 1990 Daniel Newburg show isn't the only instance of canvas shape and color movement working in lockstep to express a connection to the viewer. She struck a similar—if more pared down— tone in an exhibition at the same gallery a few years prior. In this show, she created four pentagon-shaped paintings, each named after a different type of wind: *Borus, Eurus, Notus,* and *Zephyr.* On the wall, the pentagons point downward toward the floor, with a flat edge forming the top. As a way of not only creating a connection between the group of paintings and also reiterating the horizontal plane of the gallery floor, Boochever painted a thin linear band around the perimeter of the gallery walls, just below eye-level, through which the lowermost point of each pentagon crossed.

Compositionally, the works use much subtler gradations than the 1990 show, alluding to colors one might find in the sky of a romantic landscape painting. In this case, the open, unbounded color expresses the more multi-directional pentagon shape. But in spite of the less emphatic direction of the frame and the airy, Venetian color, the paintings still root themselves in the physical space of the gallery. Indeed, the frames' piercing of Boochever's "horizon line" around the gallery brings the paintings back down to earth. The wind runs along the ground as it does through the sky.

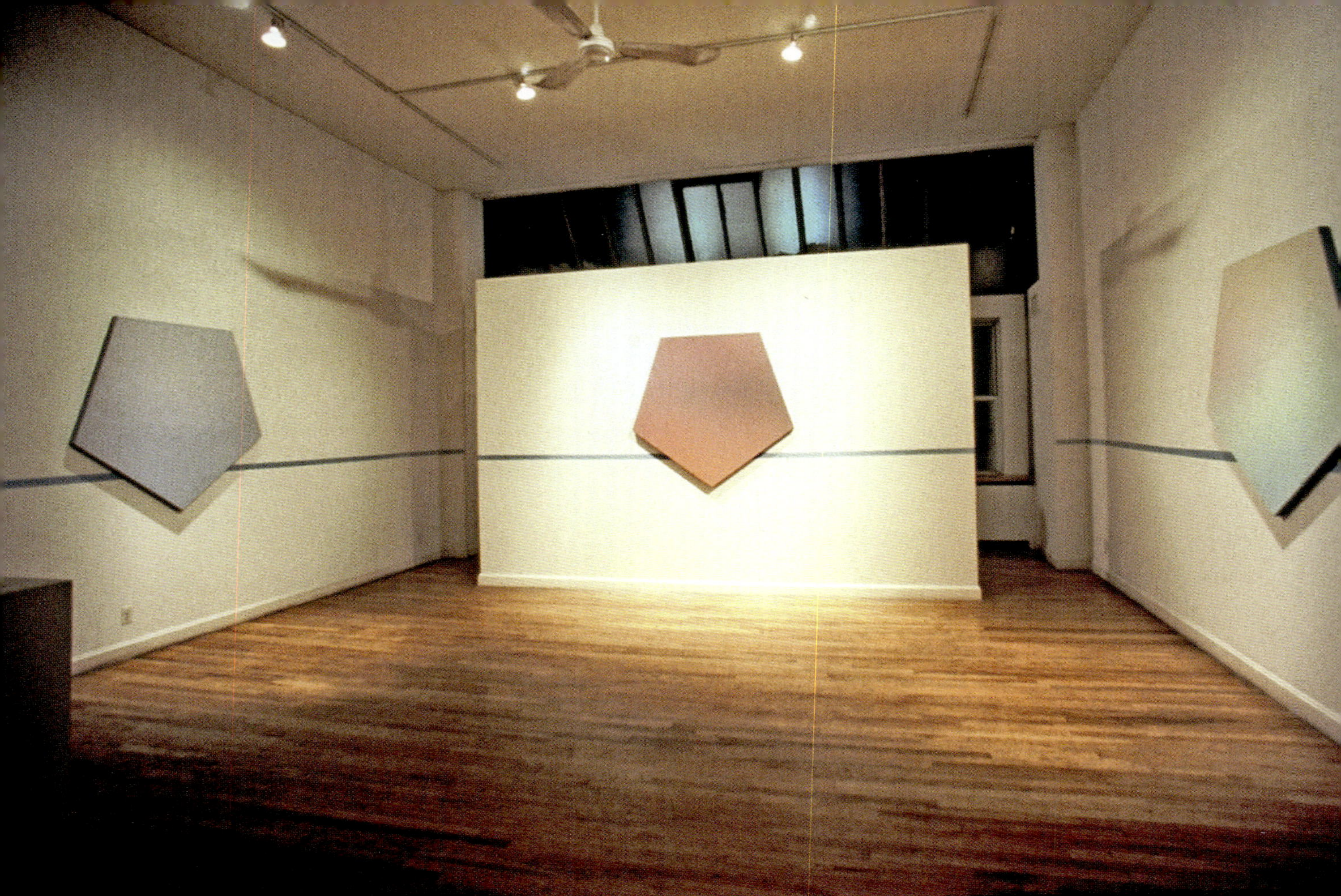

Zephyr, Borus, Notus, 1986
54 x 56 inches each, acrylic, canvas

However, a broader look at Boochever's work over time reveals that the supports of her paintings don't just wrest and localize her ethereal color gradations. The opposite becomes true as the shape of the support becomes more literal. In these instances, Boochever uses color to reference a space beyond the object's physical moorings.

In three works completed in 1999, the contours of Boochever's frame become a more direct image. In *Minium, Pearl,* and *Iron Glimmer,* Boochever uses the five steps on a ladder to frame and unite six separate canvases. In a twist to Boochever's strategy, these paintings create movement by subtly changing color from one canvas to the next, rather than by gradating within the canvas. A step on the ladder becomes a pause within an interval.

As an installed object, she raised the ladder frame off of the floor, creating a transition between two non-specific points in space. Like her previous work, the ladder uses the floor without touching it, to create a more generalized existential place. One then considers its ascending and descending movement more abstractly, as the ladder becomes a way to suspend the action of departure and return.

Boochever's work reminds us that the experience of encountering a painting is neither an escape to another place, nor a negotiation of its local surroundings. Rather, the expression of the transition between them opens up a new set of dimensions. She understands that the flip side to the public spaces that her paintings occupy is the private space that each viewer carries with them. Boochever's work sweeps us away, but this movement always folds back and transforms our consciousness of the space from whence we came.

Her emphasis of this quality, while not common, is common to the more challenging, rewarding, and historically persistent painters. Boochever knows what Barnett Newman knew: a painting's inability to physically remove its observer from their surroundings opens a reflective relationship with that space. The pull of a painting is simultaneously a push against the world.

1. Maurice Merleau-Ponty, *Phenomenology of Perception* (New York: Routledge & Kegan Paul, 1962).

MILD STEEL

DAVID SHAPIRO

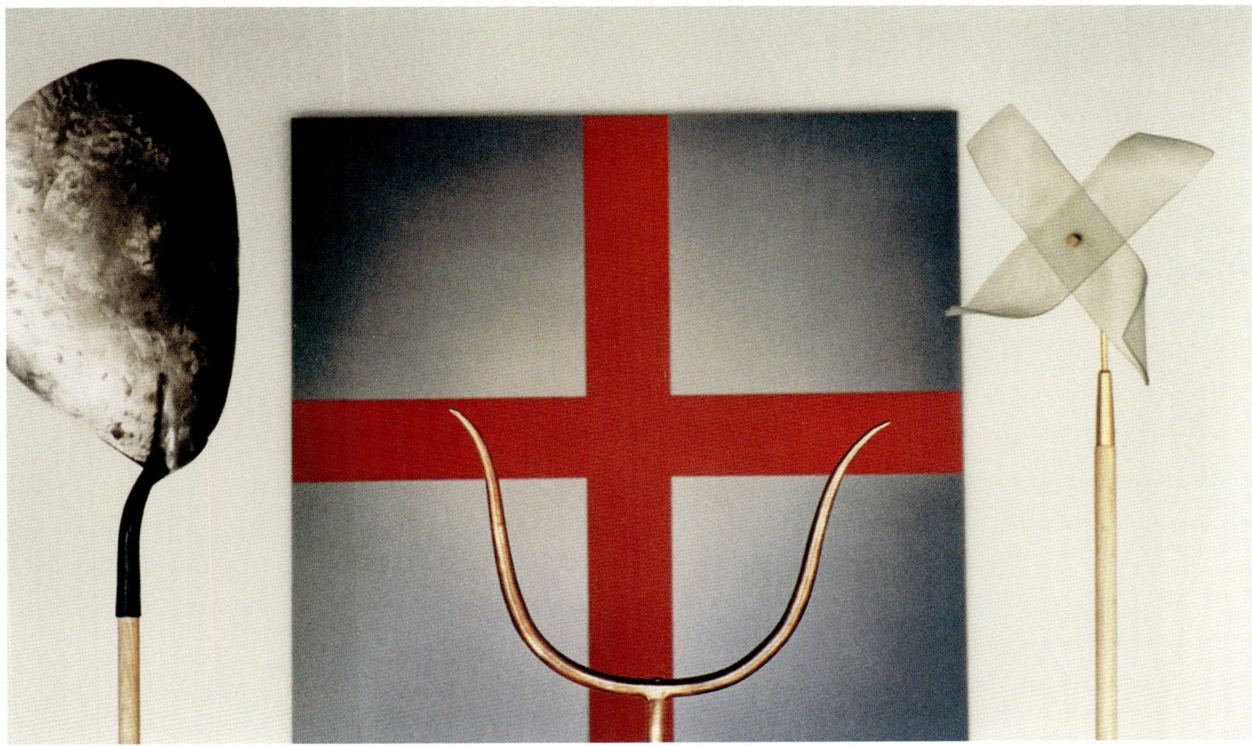

Vertical Minute, 1995, installation view

There exist many ways to reduce the multiplicity of twentieth-century art, and the recent interpretations of Mondrian that tend to suppress the mystical in him in favor of the Cubist and post-Cubist are good examples of one Procrustean whim. There exists, moreover, an influential riptide in modernism, and one that flouts our sense of a rampant secularism, positivism, and materialism. One has to be ideologically blinded to suppress half of Mondrian's career as "nineteenth century" or "Theosophical." The work of Mary Boochever, exquisite, referential, and replete, speaks unembarrassedly of the mystical, or better, permits a variety of readings, including the transcendental. This is not because she misunderstands the shock of abstraction, but because she favors polysemy and a wild indeterminacy in her codes. There is in her the complex synthesis of Duchamp, Beuys, Arte Povera, and Rudolf Steiner, as

she has noted herself. The momentum of her work derives from the permissions guaranteed by this almost uncontrollable overlay of codes.

It is said that Scholem, when prodded to reveal his own bias, one day commented on his affinity for the migration of the sacred into the ordinary, as in Whitman. Boochever's work also has a species of Spinozaistic romance, as when she calculates a landscape from elements of the human body. Here, a pure cube of color presents us at once with the charm of inscape, landscape, manscape, and the work of desire. Spinoza praised the bewildering possibilities of the body, and in her pure pigments, Boochever yields a polarized ode in which the most shocking crystalline abstraction is linked with our seemingly reductive physiology. A positivist chart is turned into a painterly refuge. If God is little, or has shrunk into such ordinariness, the art remains to create a circular grassy garden to accompany such an occultation. The artist has spoken of the garden as a privileged icon, and she recognizes, both in her work as a sculptor, painter, and landscapist, that the garden is also a Paradise of possible individuation. Her sense of art as a meditative region in the Jungian sense is no doubt also part of the reticent power of her sculpture elsewhere of an eye or a foot in sandals. These are not abrupt exceptions in a non-objective artist. They are clearly part of an essay not to be trivially clear. Her own notes reveal that the cross in her work is thought of as a mystical conjunction of opposites, and her book, with its self-lacerating title and exclamation, "The Secret of Youth!," is not merely comical in its exploration of Tantric maps of lucidity. Her ten prints within that book show an intense awareness of the most stringent traditions of abstraction, through Ryman, Marden, and Gilbert-Rolfe, with an insistence on what Blanchot has spoken of as the necessary exoticism of the poetic vocabulary. Even when Boochever uses what seems a low vocabulary in her expanded number *Five,* or stars, or zebra stripes, she is never reductively blank, neutralizing, or laconic. Perhaps installation art is the most appropriate for a vision of the multifoliate. In her work with tools, she is not alluding to the happy facts of Jim Dine, who spent childhood days in his grandfather's hardware store. Nor is she affixing the real to the unreal, in the ways in which Johns has mesmerized us with the melancholy additions and subtractions of brooms, prisms, and flashlights. The instruments here, with their careful triple presentation in steel, copper, and glass, and with their "ordinary" handles in wood, are an ambiguous trio of "unemployed" spoon, pitchfork, and fan. The artist

has spoken of a "zebra" painting as a science fiction, and I admire the fiction here, in which the human body and work is translated, as in her "hourglass" rendition of elements, into Giacometti-like verticalities. A reductive critic has perseverated that only the horizontal in that master's work is adventurous. But that is to delete the exhausting numinosity of Giacometti's almost suicidal audacity in the dessications of portraiture. I see Boochever's dignity as a portraitist among non-representational artists as the paradox of her spiritual bias. She has spoken of her fondness for the zebra as an animal said to be "disguised as what it is." Her installation, with its radical diversity of themes and materials, and with its insistence not only on the subtle gradations of the cross but its full symbolism of ascent and descent, of the human in trouble, and of the sacred in occultation, performs for us the work of mourning. As in the theologian Dodd's sense of the subversive rhetoric of the parables of the Kingdom, something grand and ordinary is accomplished here.

Some quotes and allusions derive from an interview with the artist and her unpublished notes from August 1995.

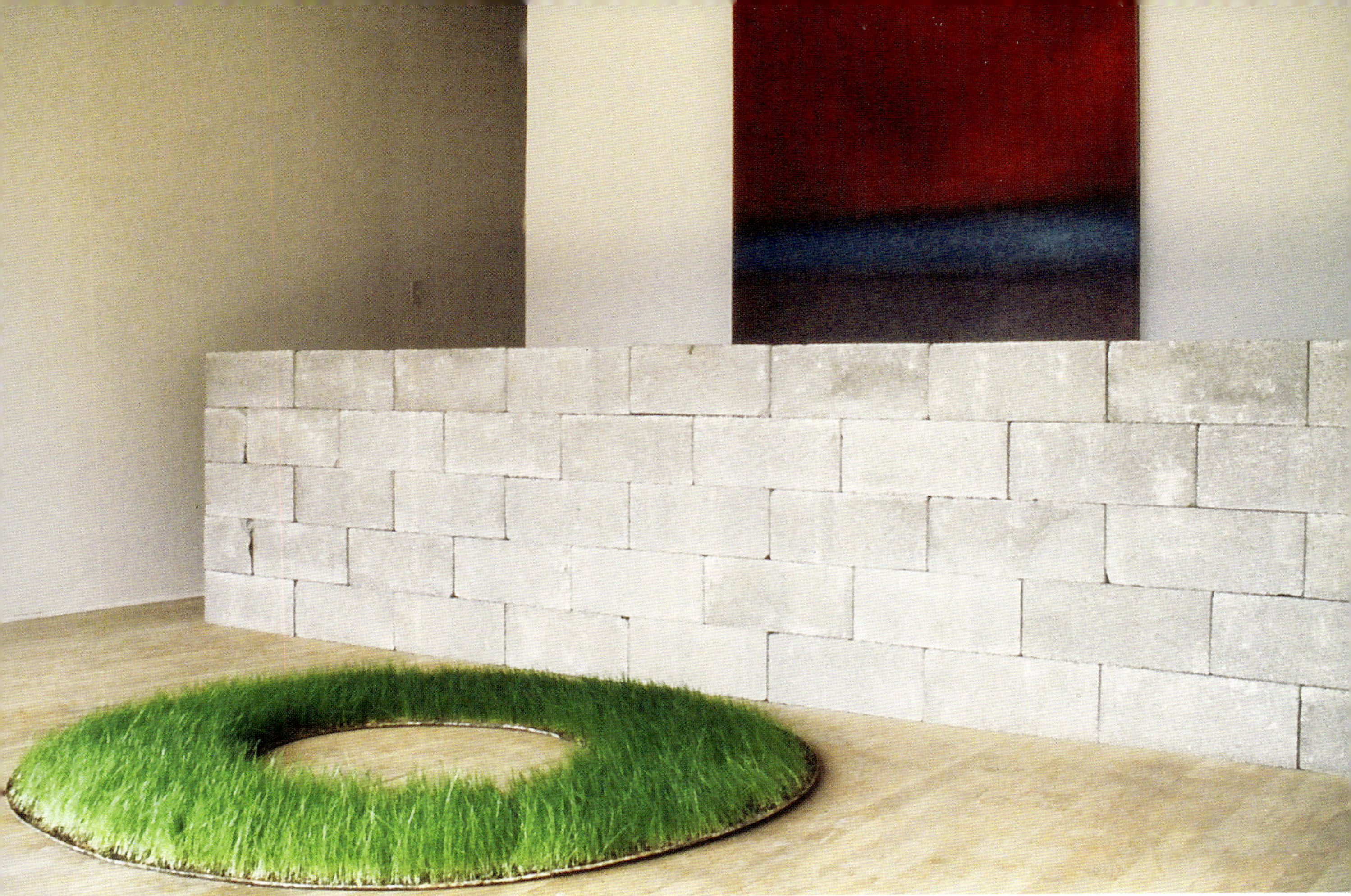

Hidden Entrances, 1994, Annika Sundvik Gallery, New York, installation view

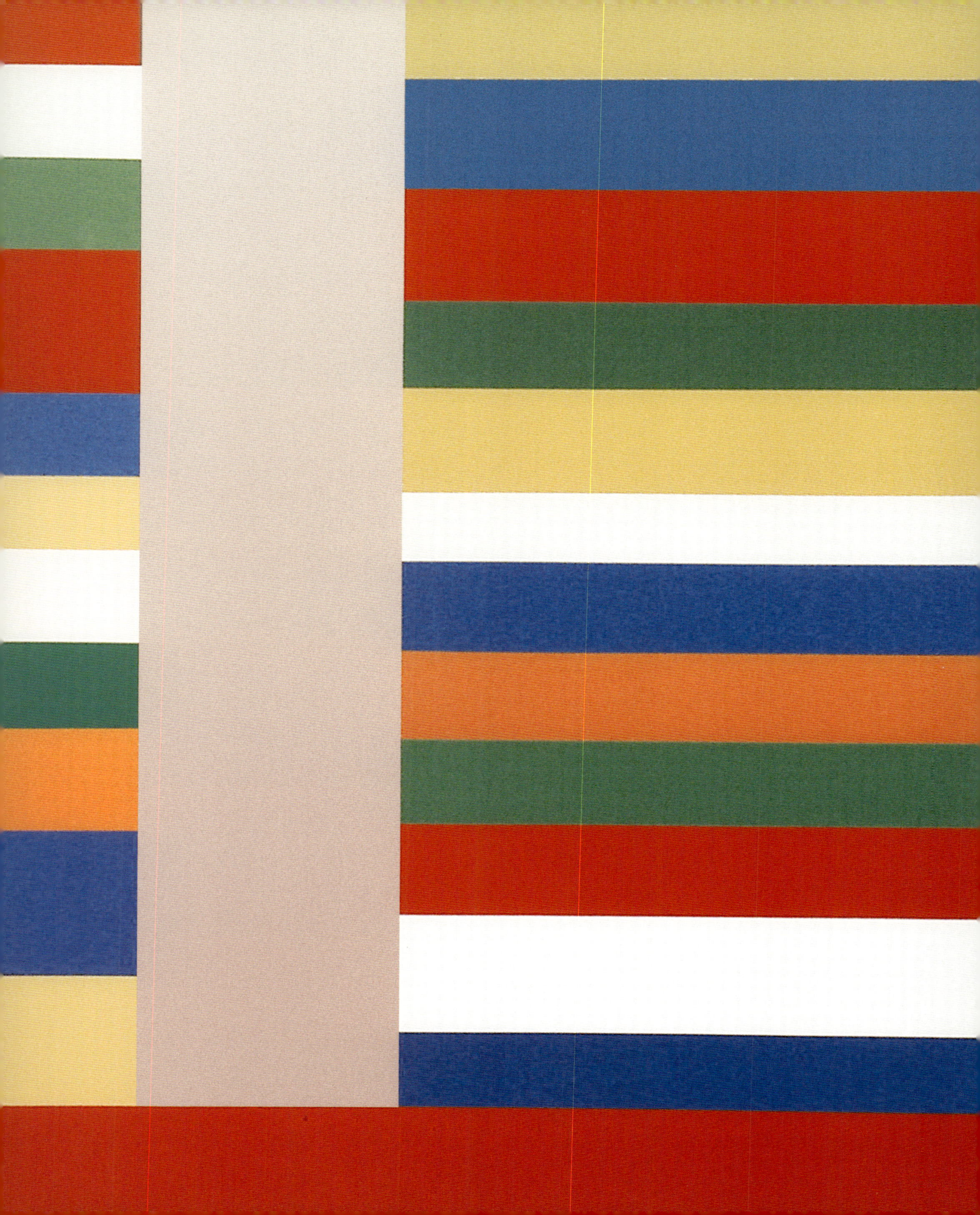

PLATES

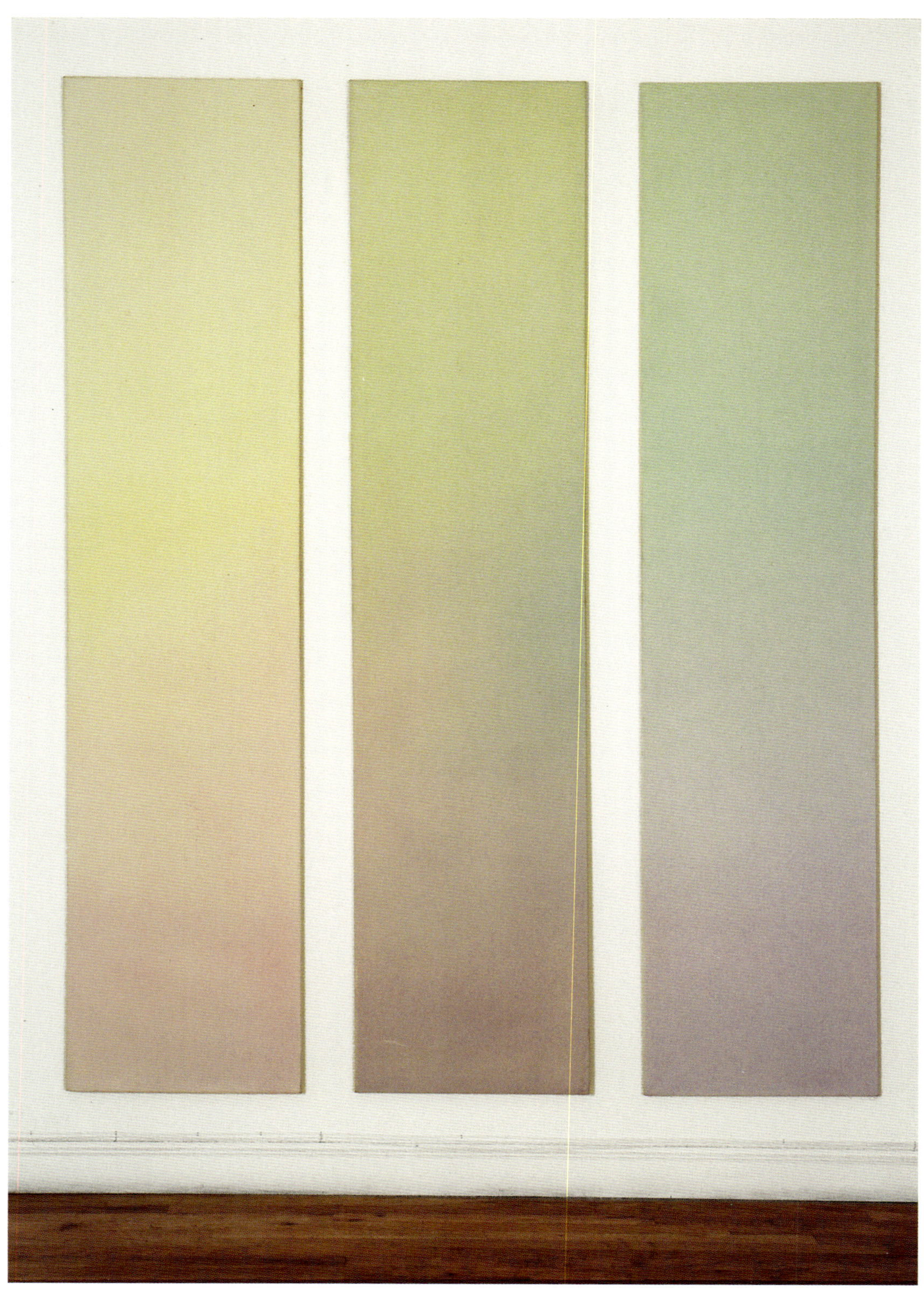

Tryptich, 1978
Pigment, acrylic, and canvas
94 x 70 inches overall
Exhibited 1986, Daniel Newburg Gallery, New York

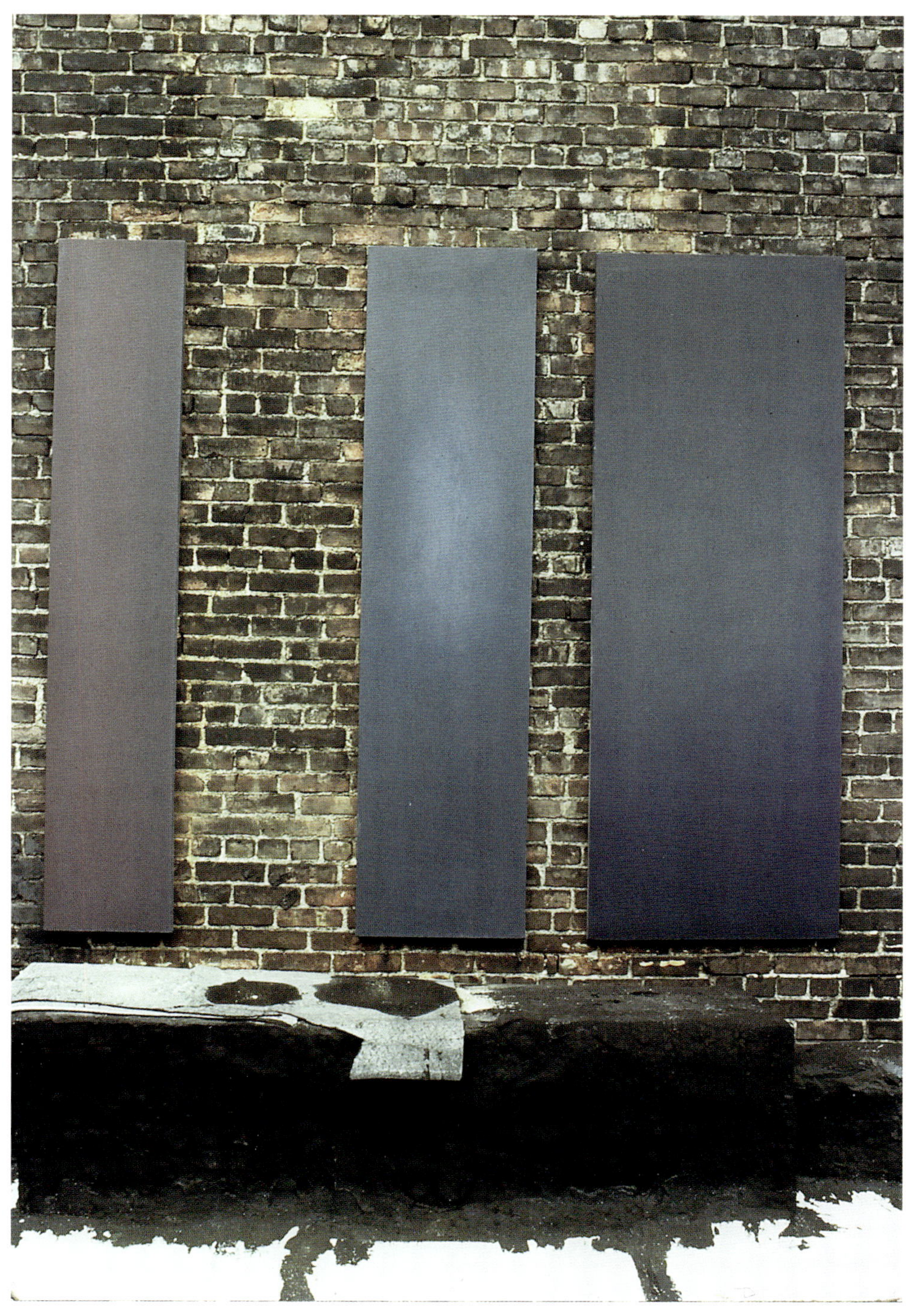

Inside/Outside (Prison), 1979
Acrylic on canvas
6 x 5 feet overall

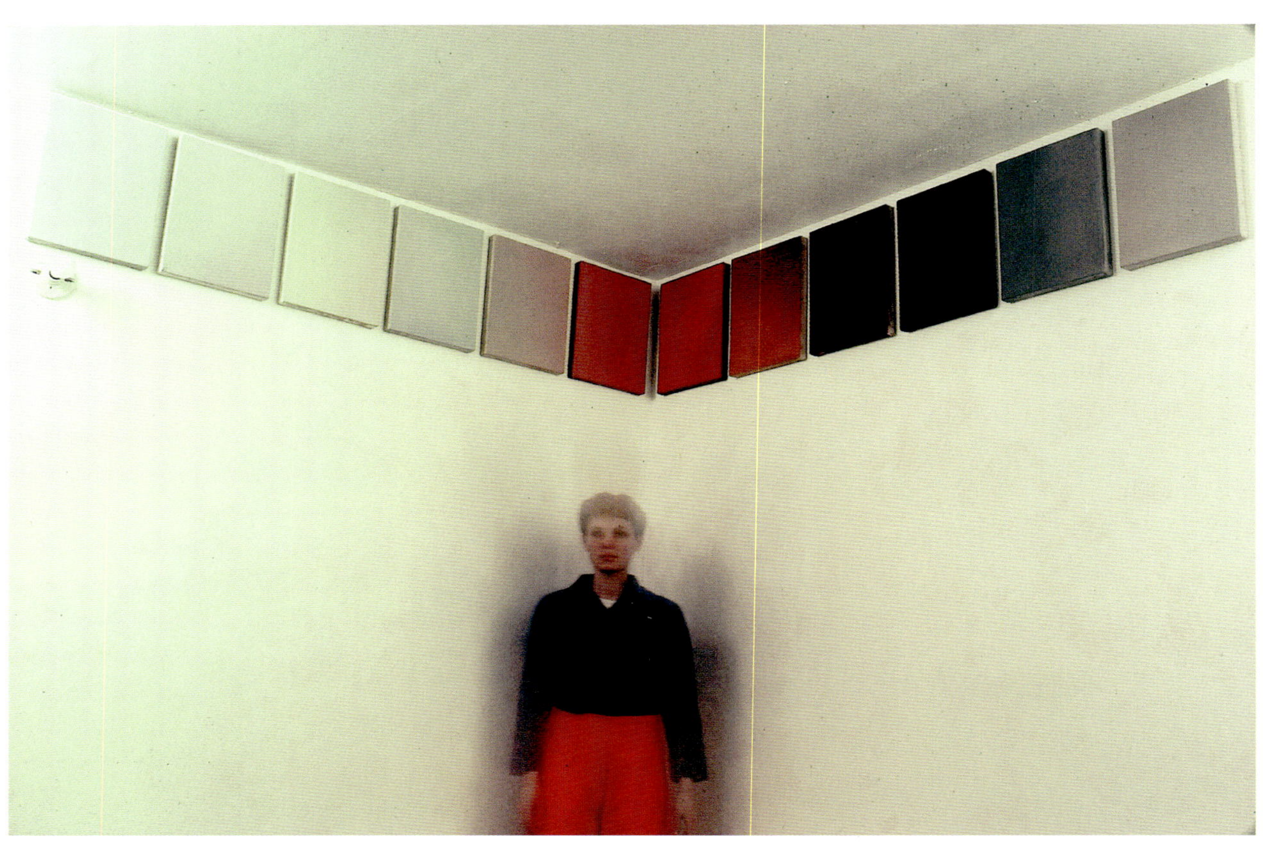

Untitled, 1980
Acrylic on canvas
12 panels, 16 x 12 inches each

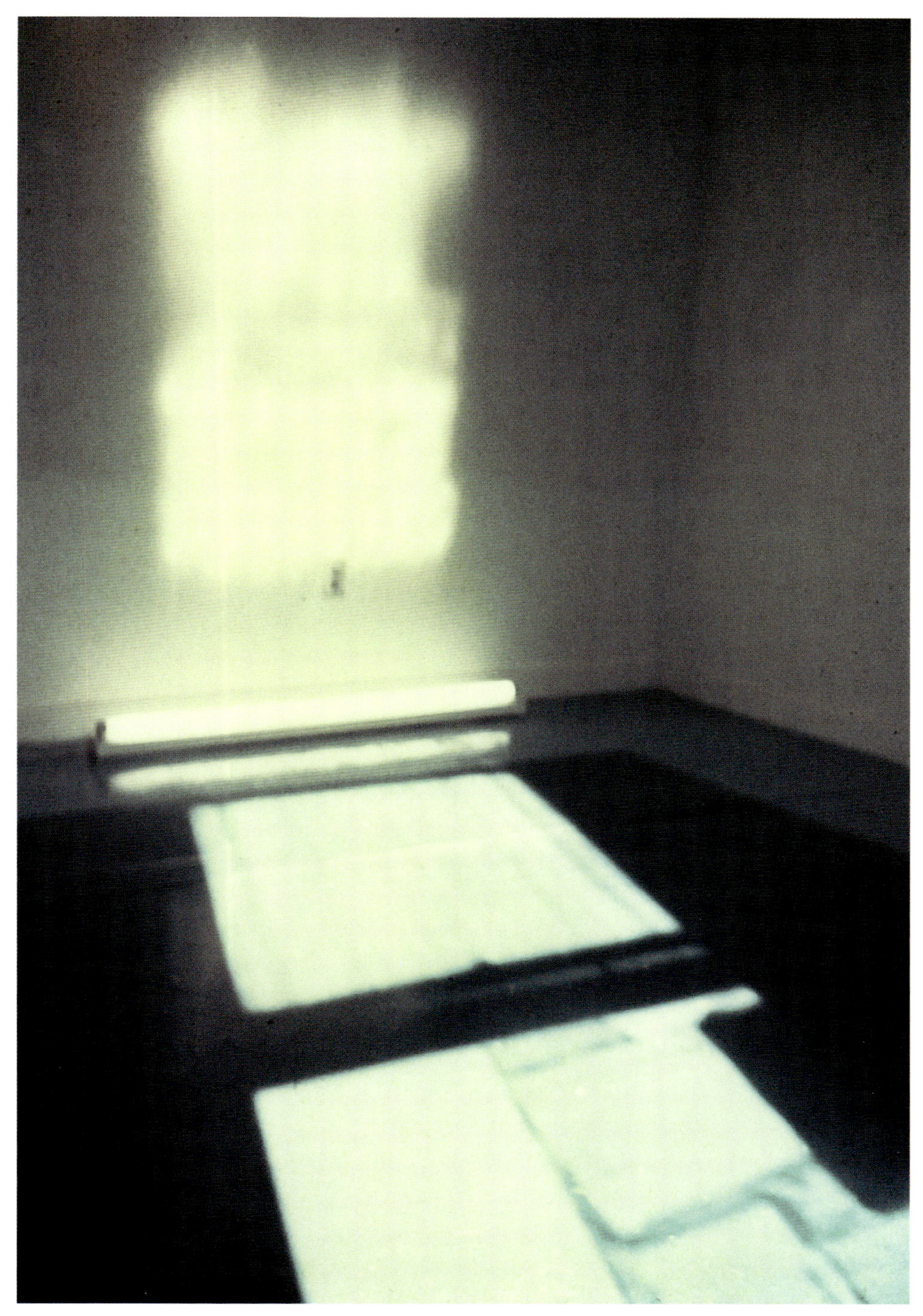

2B, 1980
Installation, front wall
Artist's studio

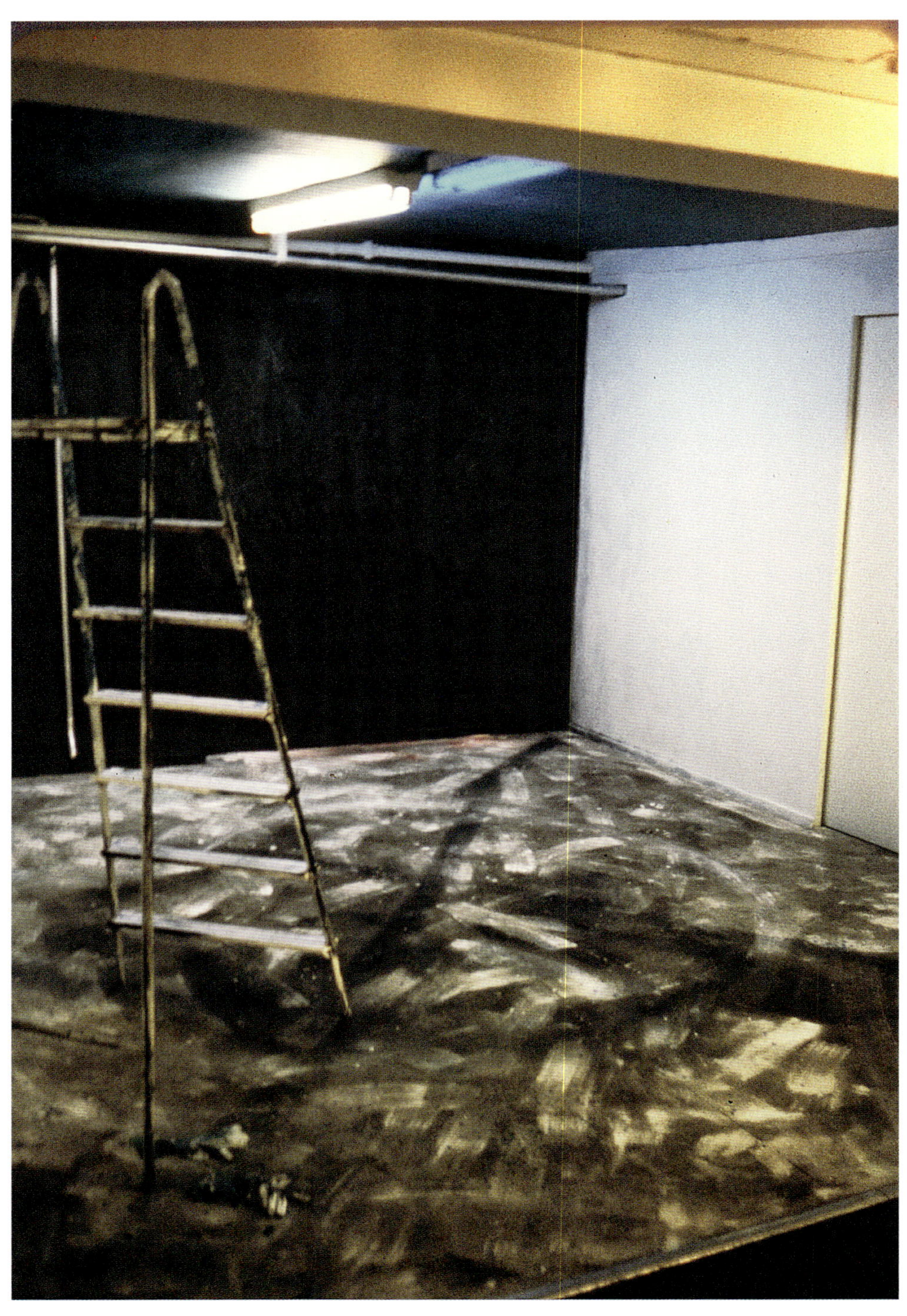

Night & Day, Night & Day, Night & Day, 1980
Felix Handschin Galerie, Basel, Switzerland

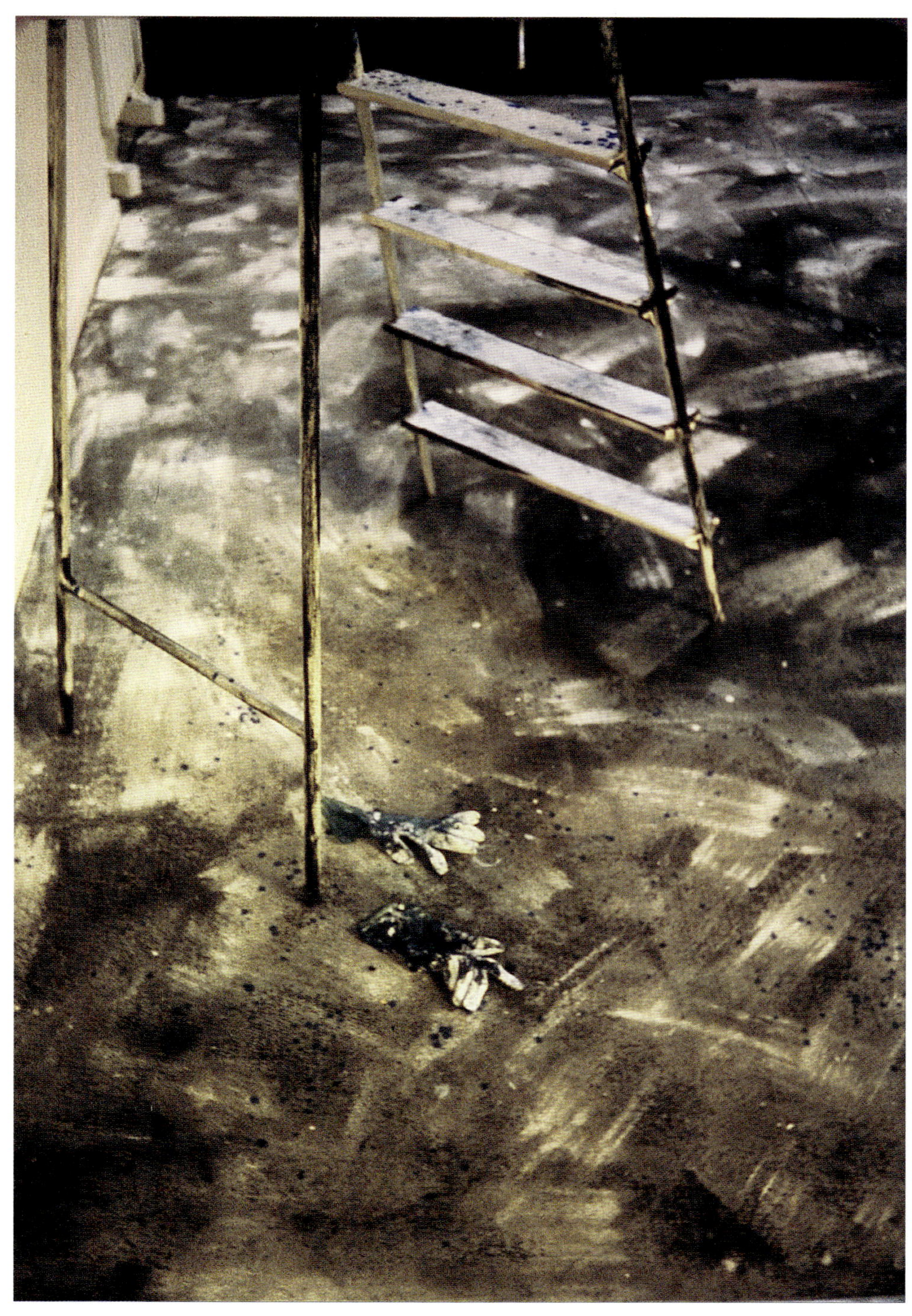

Night & Day, Night & Day, Night & Day, 1980
Felix Handschin Galerie, Basel, Switzerland
Floor detail

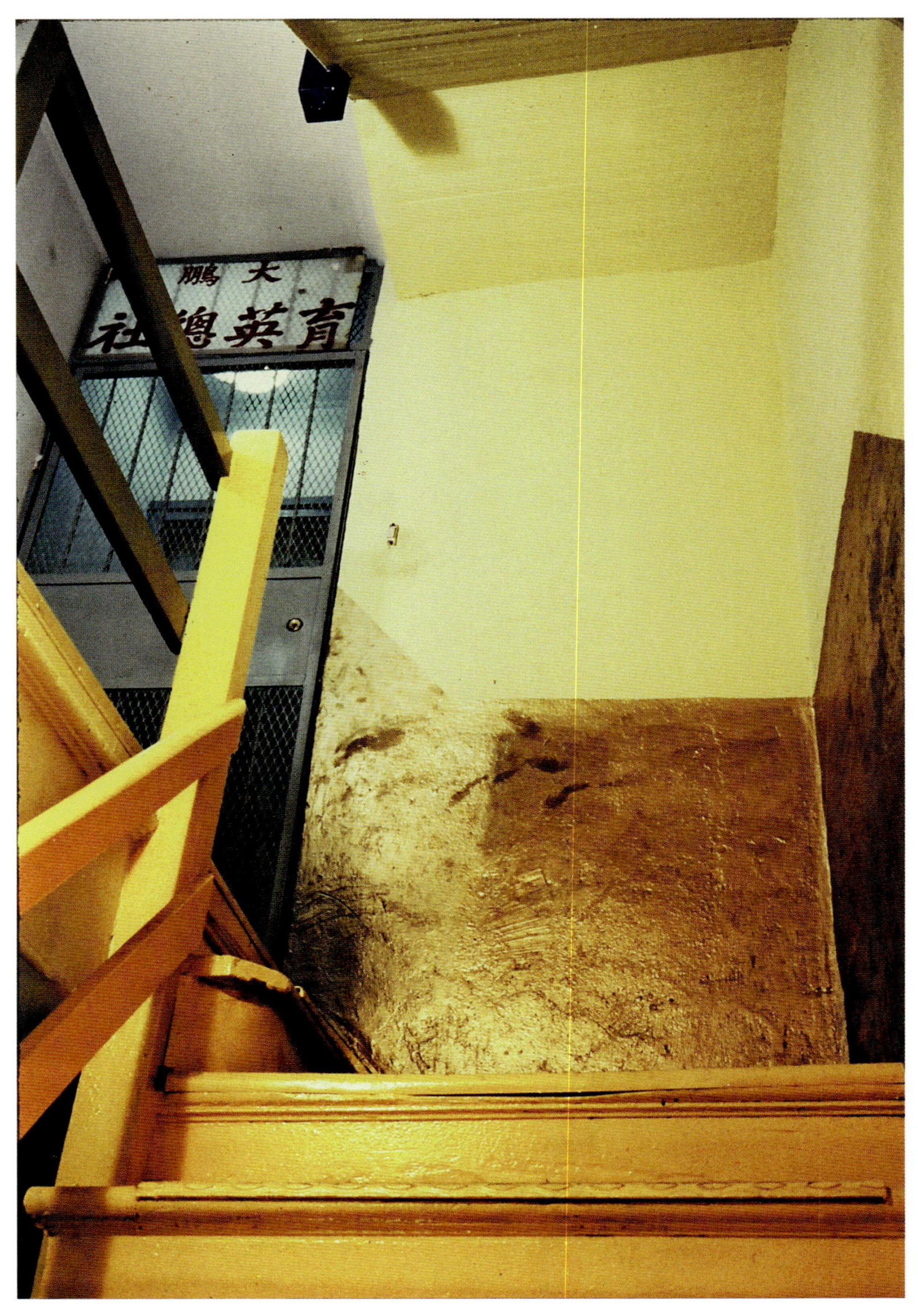

Stairwell, 1984
Installation, oil and acrylic paints
3rd Floor, Catherine Street, New York

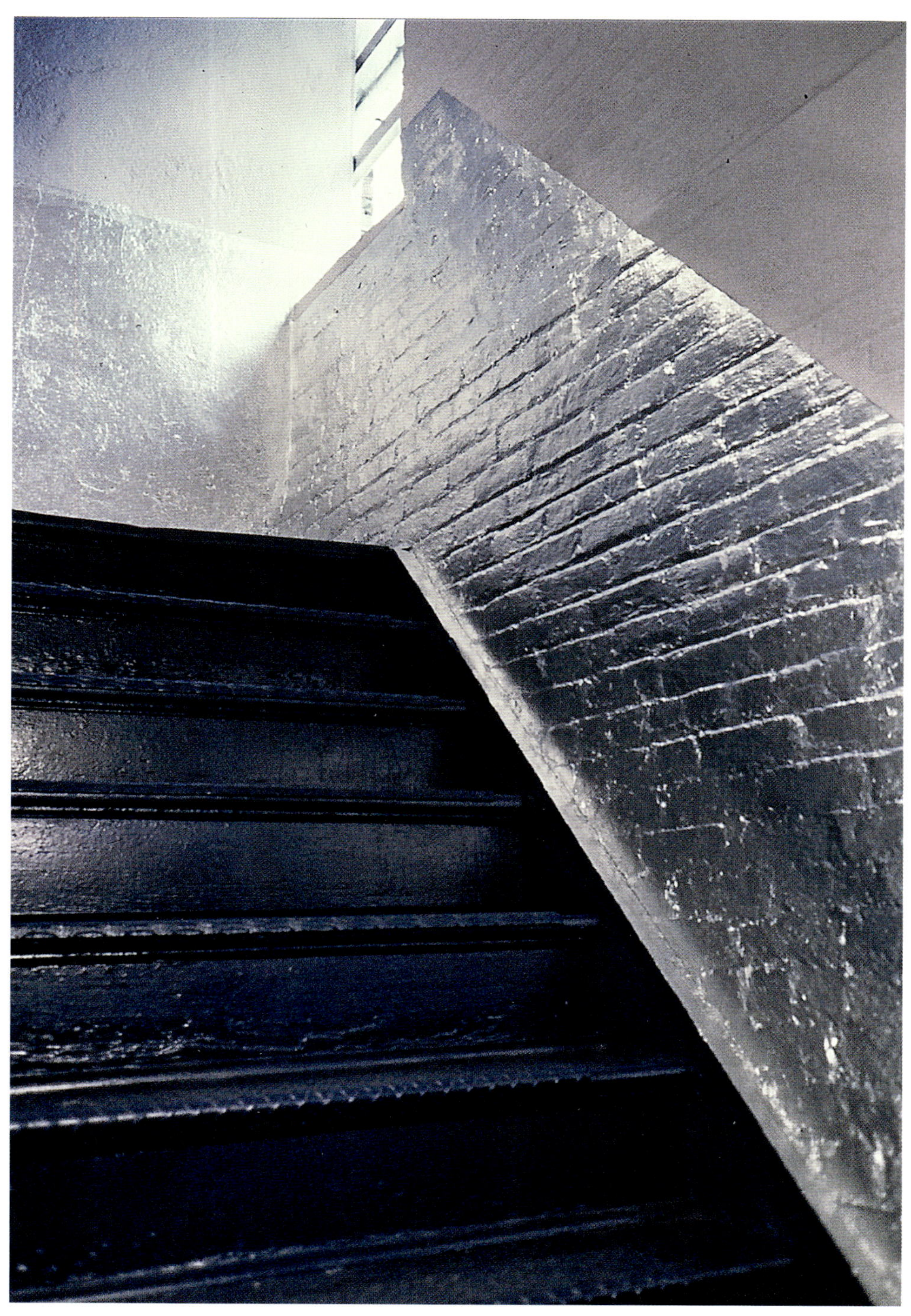

Stairwell, 1984
Installation, oil and acrylic paints
5th Floor, Catherine Street, New York

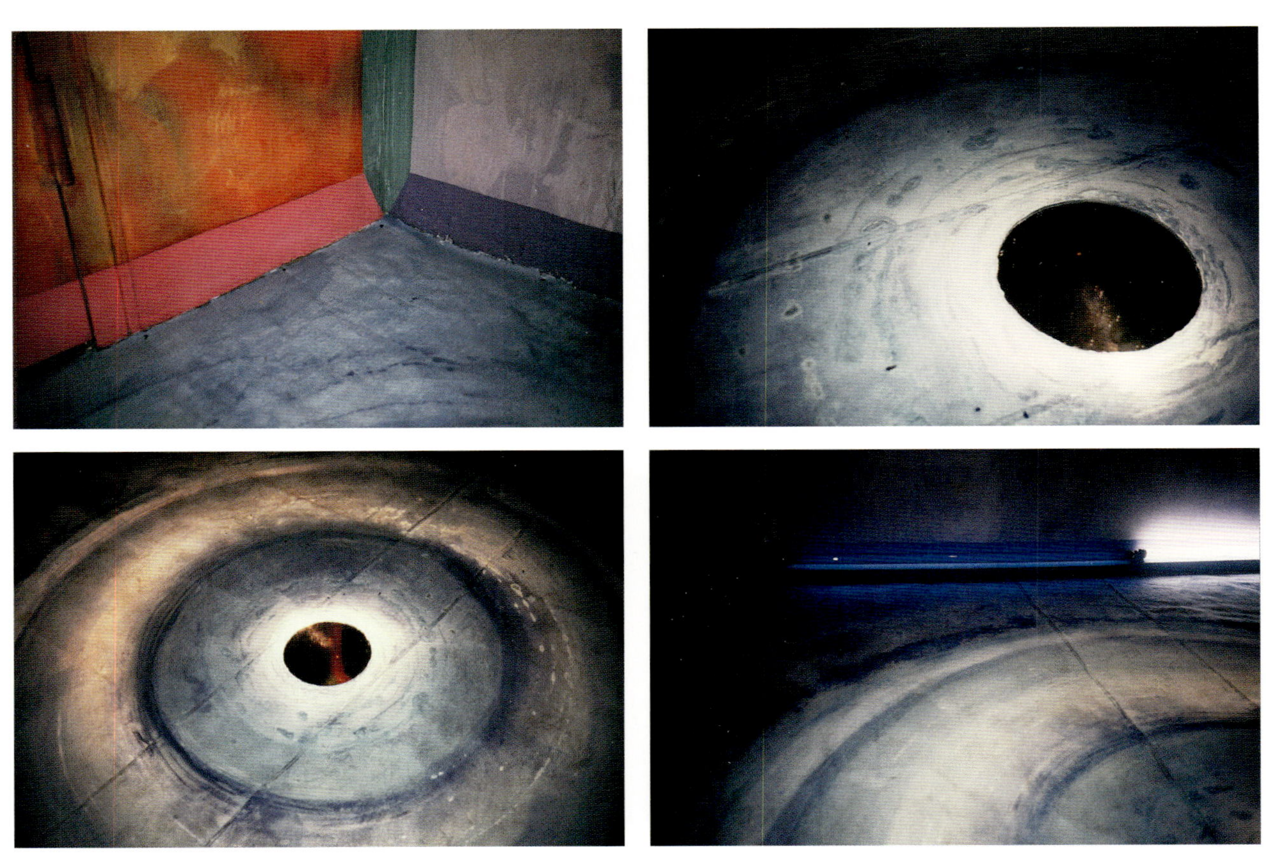

Cube, 1985–1986
Floor detail
Artist's studio

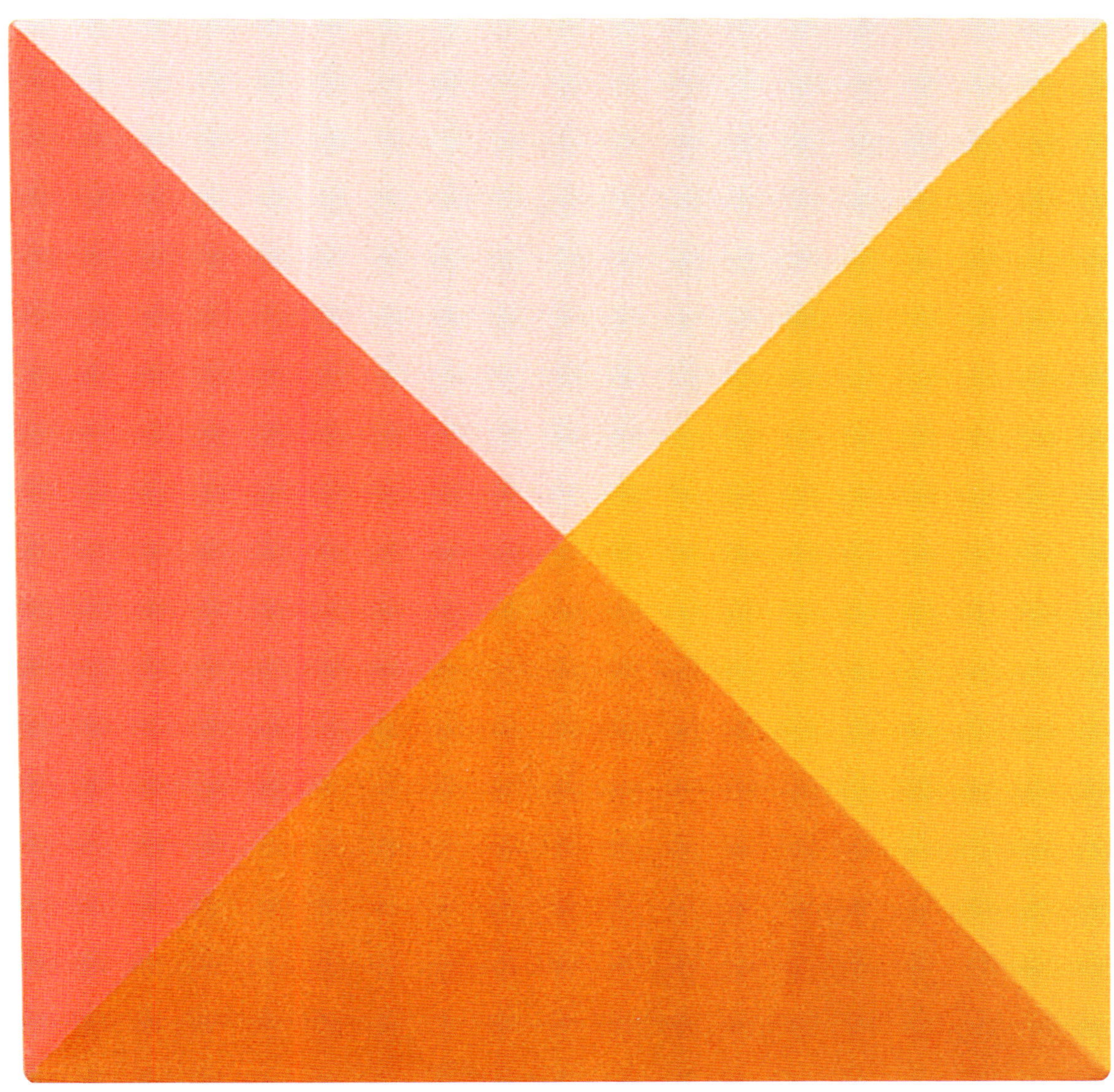

Sunradio, 1986
Oil on linen
18 x 18 inches

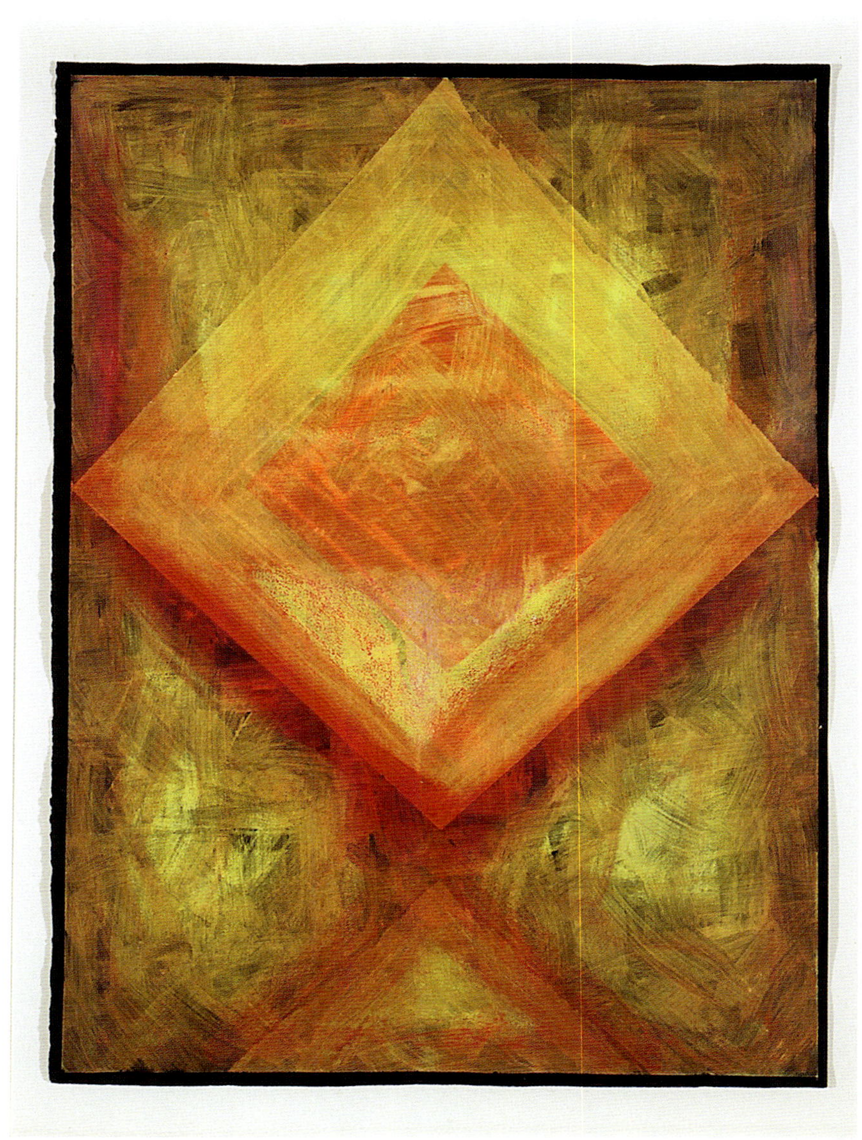

Untitled, 1986
Mixed media on paper
29 x 22 inches

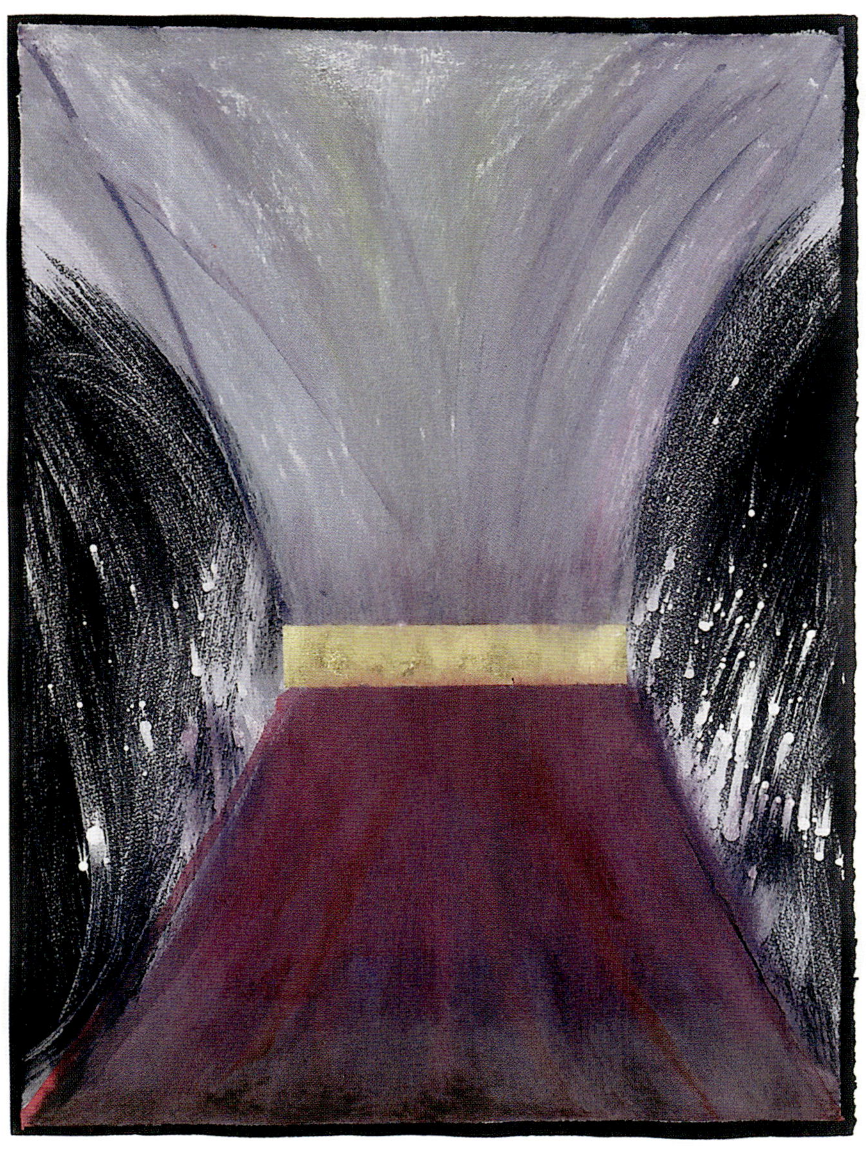

Untitled, 1986
Mixed media on paper
29 x 22 inches

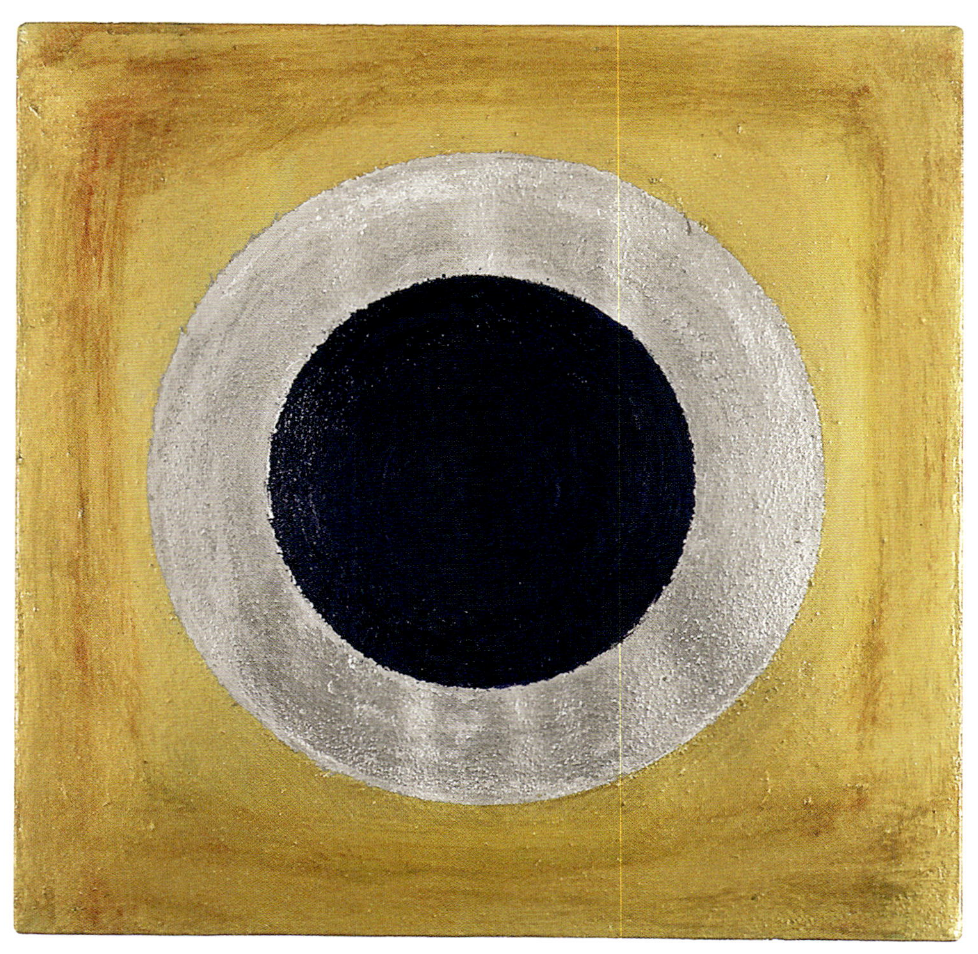

Rota, 1986
Oil on canvas
12 x 12 inches

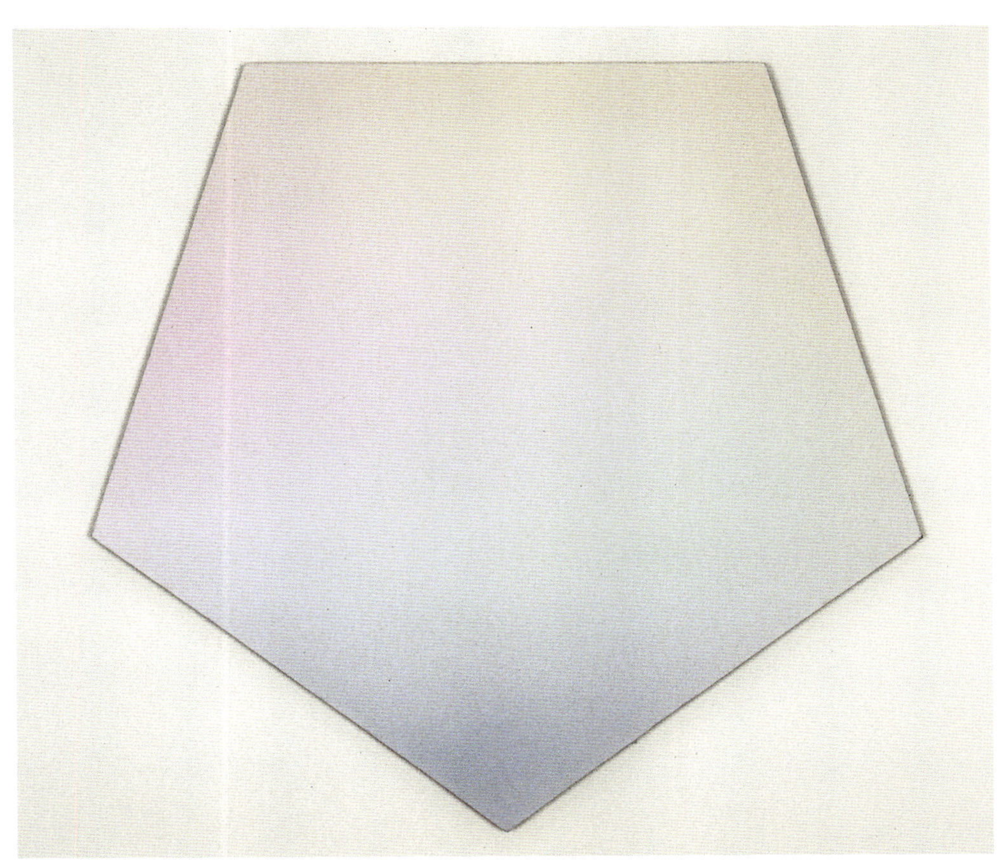

Eurus, 1986
Acrylic on canvas
54 x 56 inches

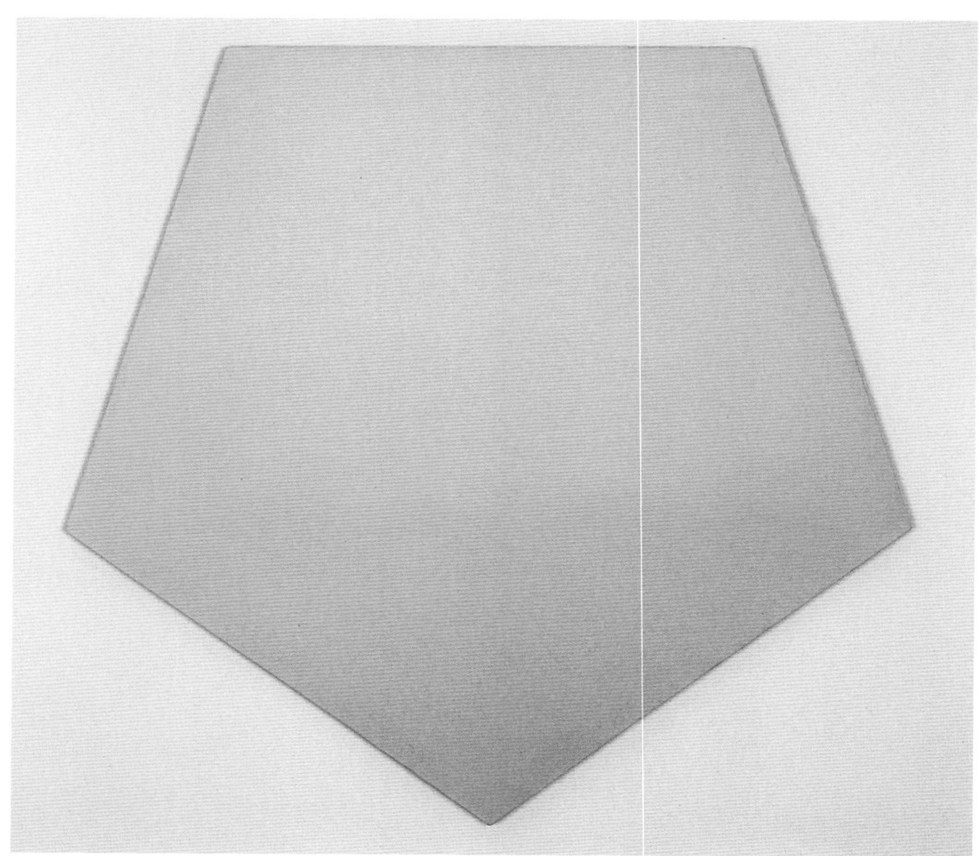

Zephyr, 1986
Acrylic on canvas
54 x 56 inches

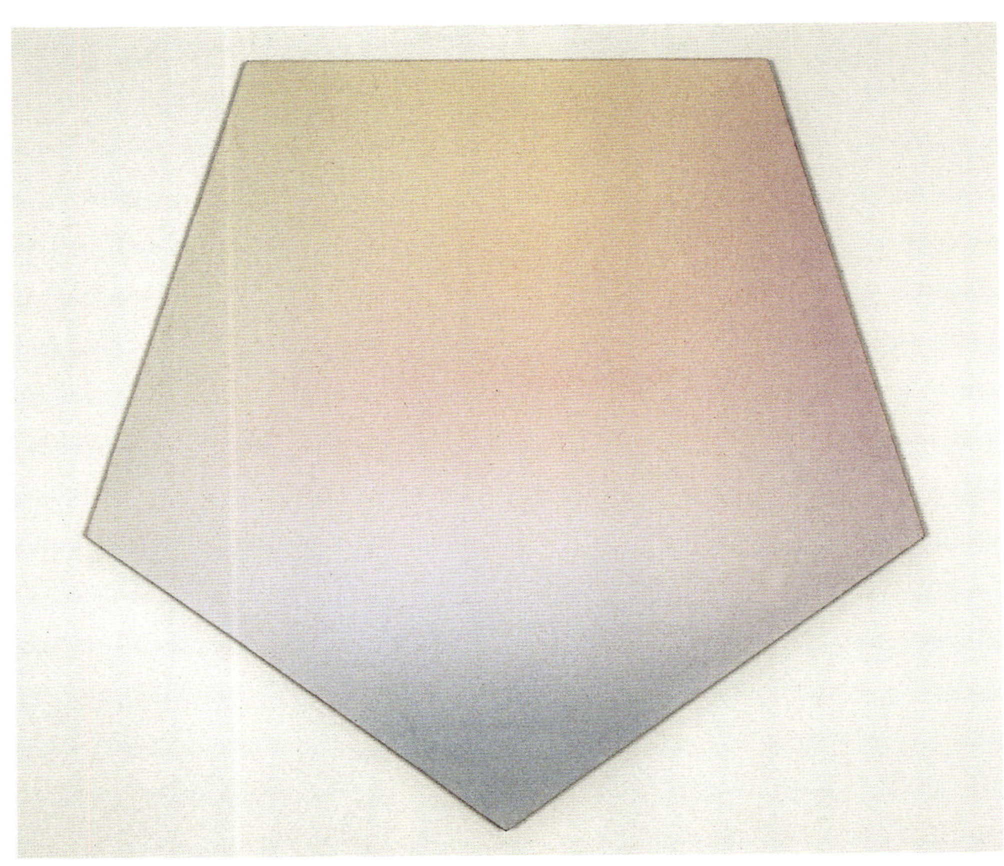

Notus, 1986
Acrylic on canvas
54 x 56 inches

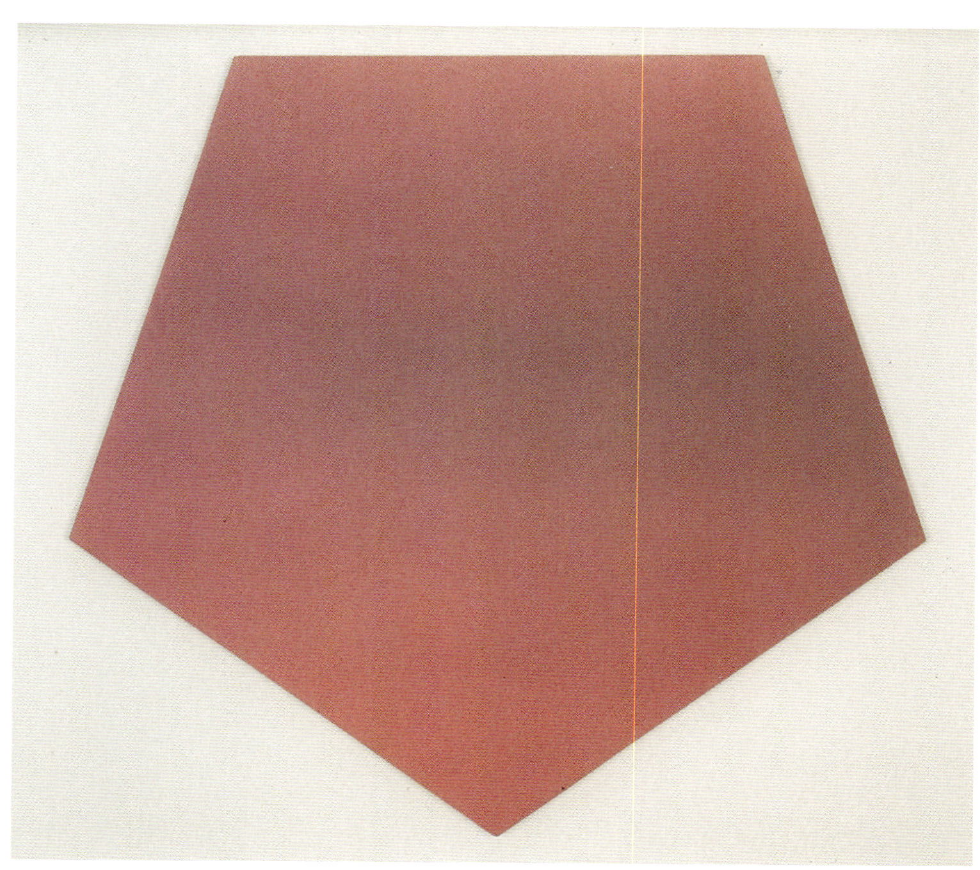

Borus, 1986
Acrylic on canvas
54 x 56 inches

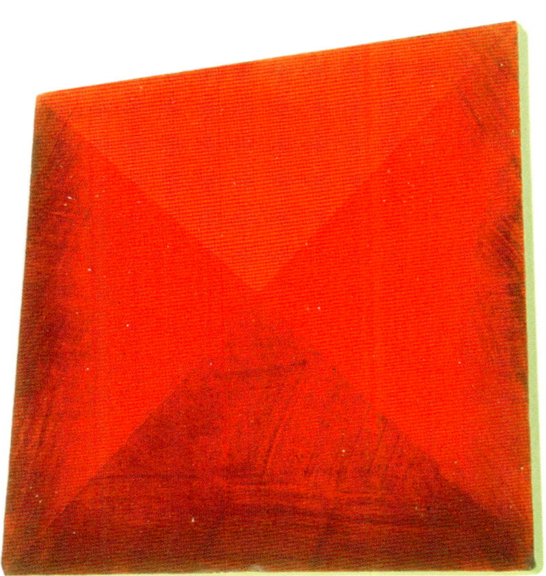
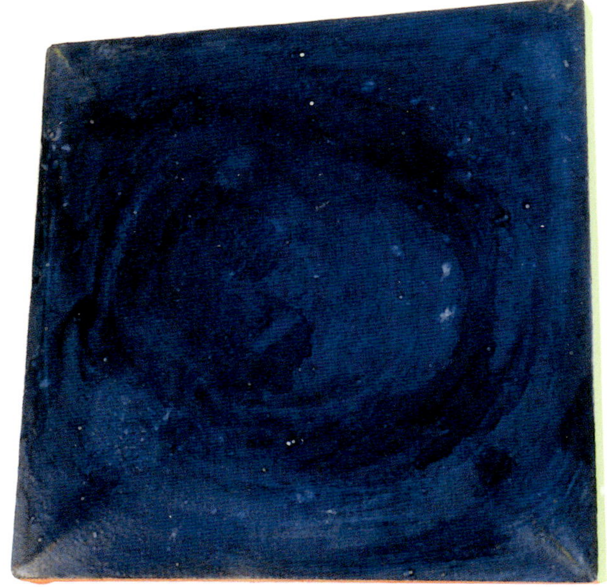

Untitled, 1987
Oil on canvas
9 x 9 inches each

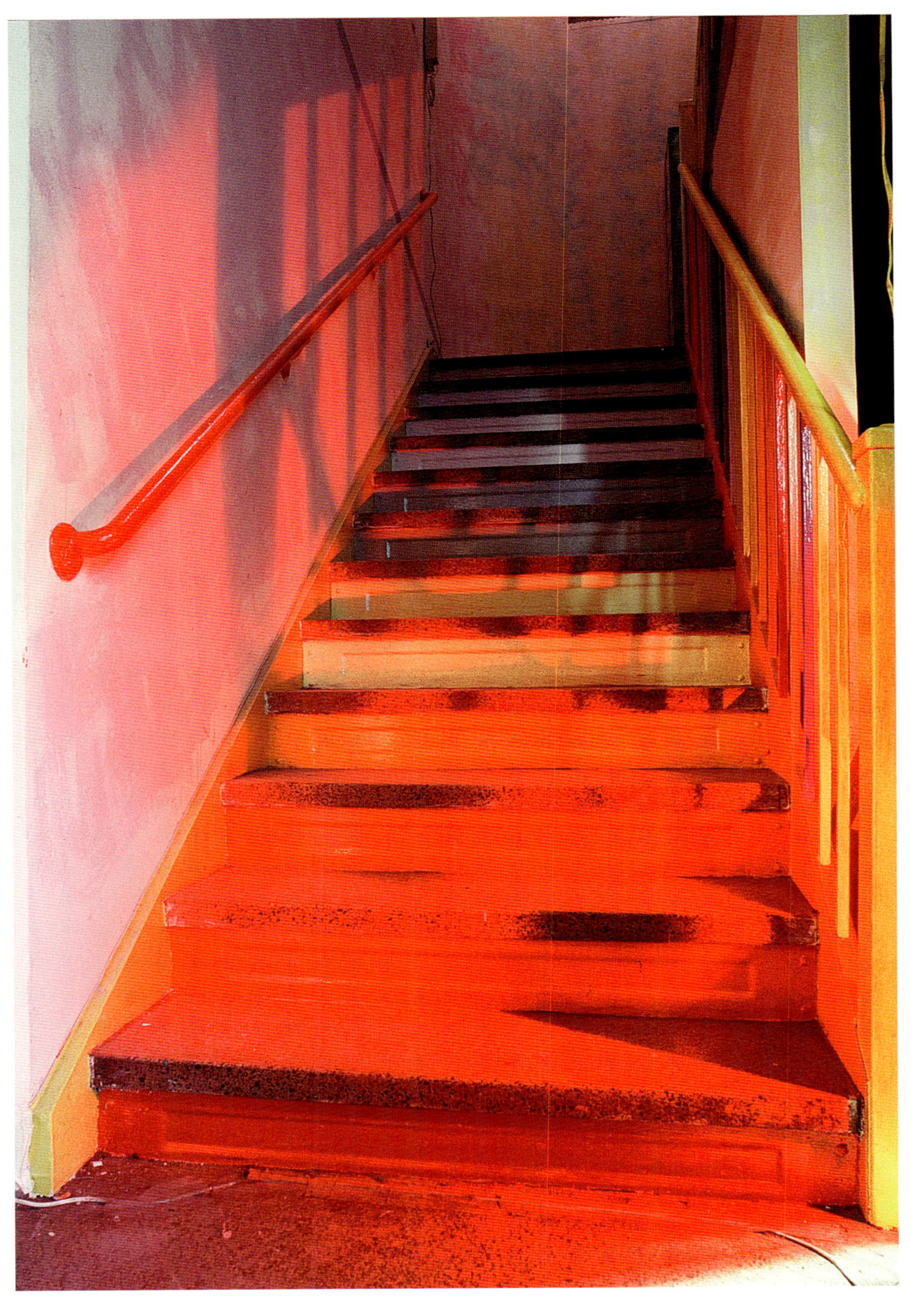

Stairwell, 1987
White Columns, New York

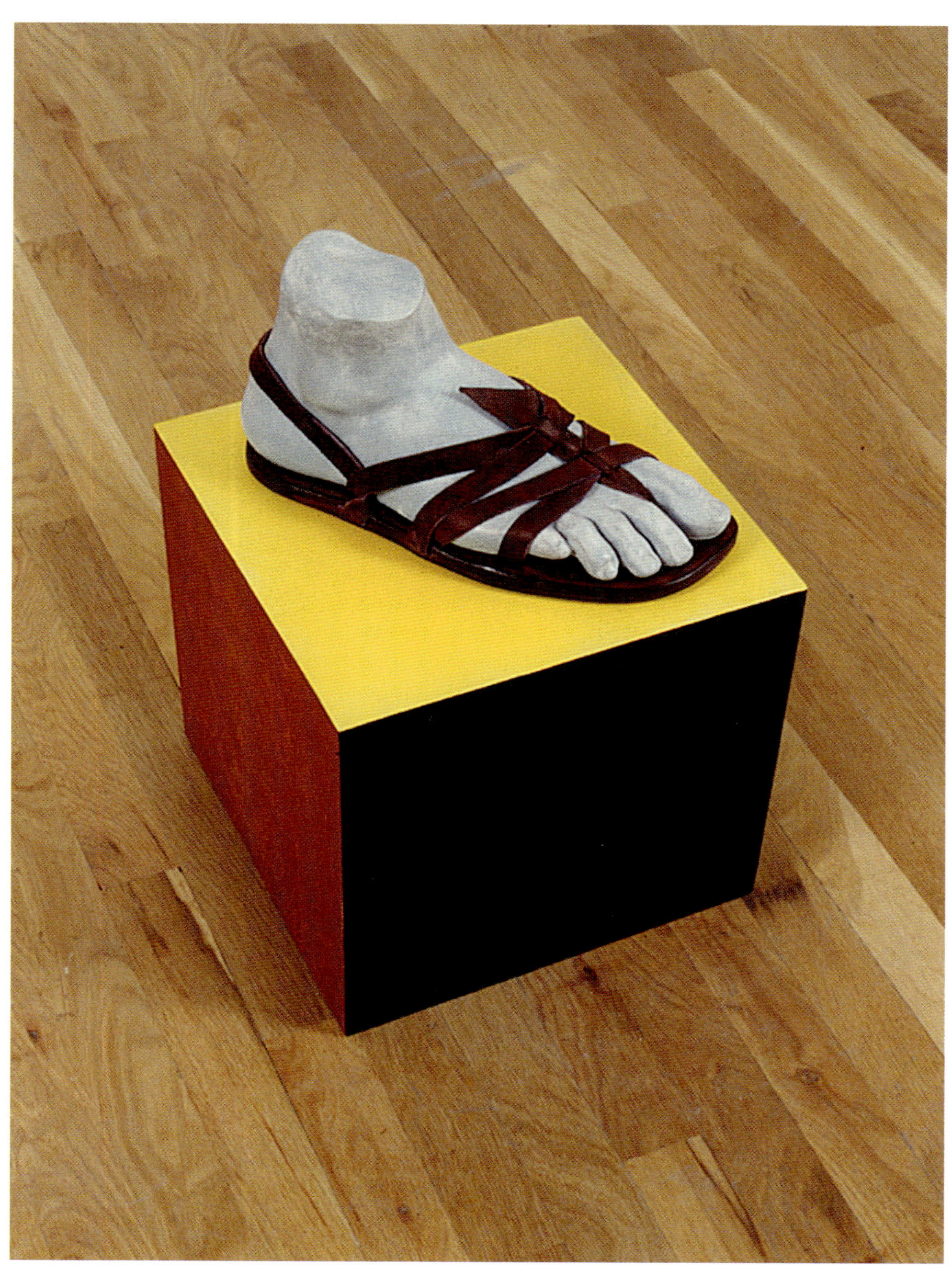

Prezo, 1987
Acrylic, board, plaster, and leather
12 x 12 x 12 inches

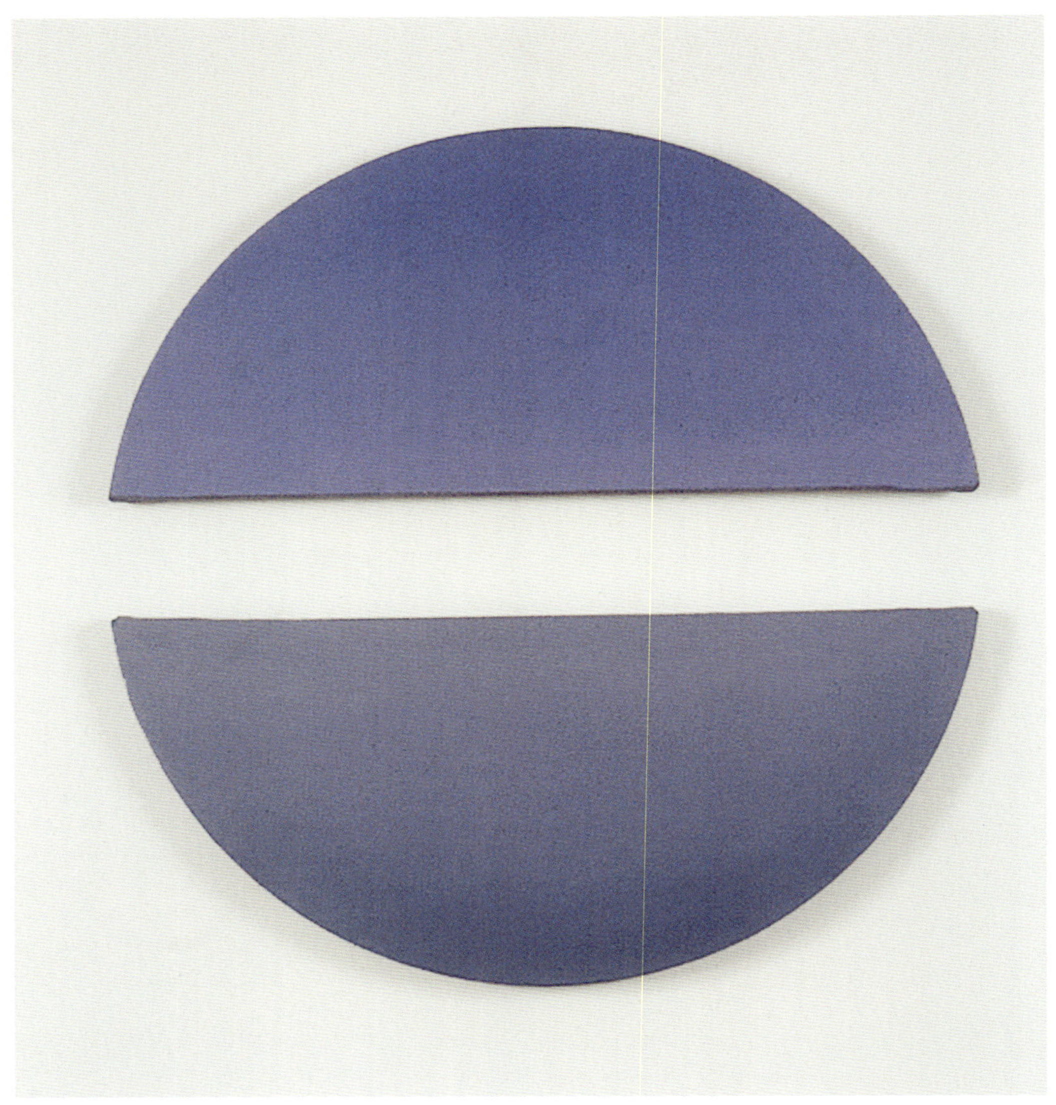

Libera, 1987
Oil on canvas
15 7/8 inches diameter

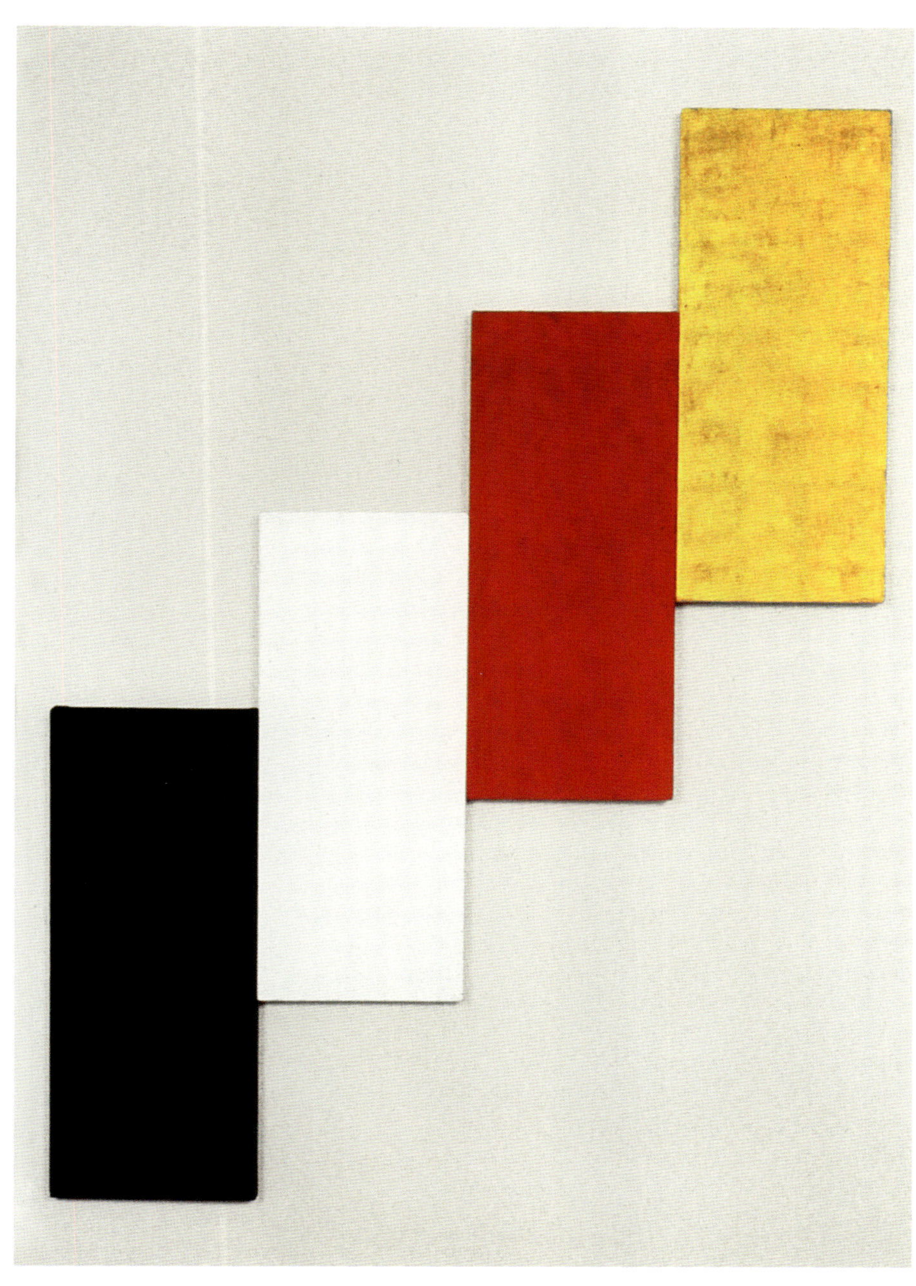

Classic, 1987
Oil on canvas
49 x 36 inches

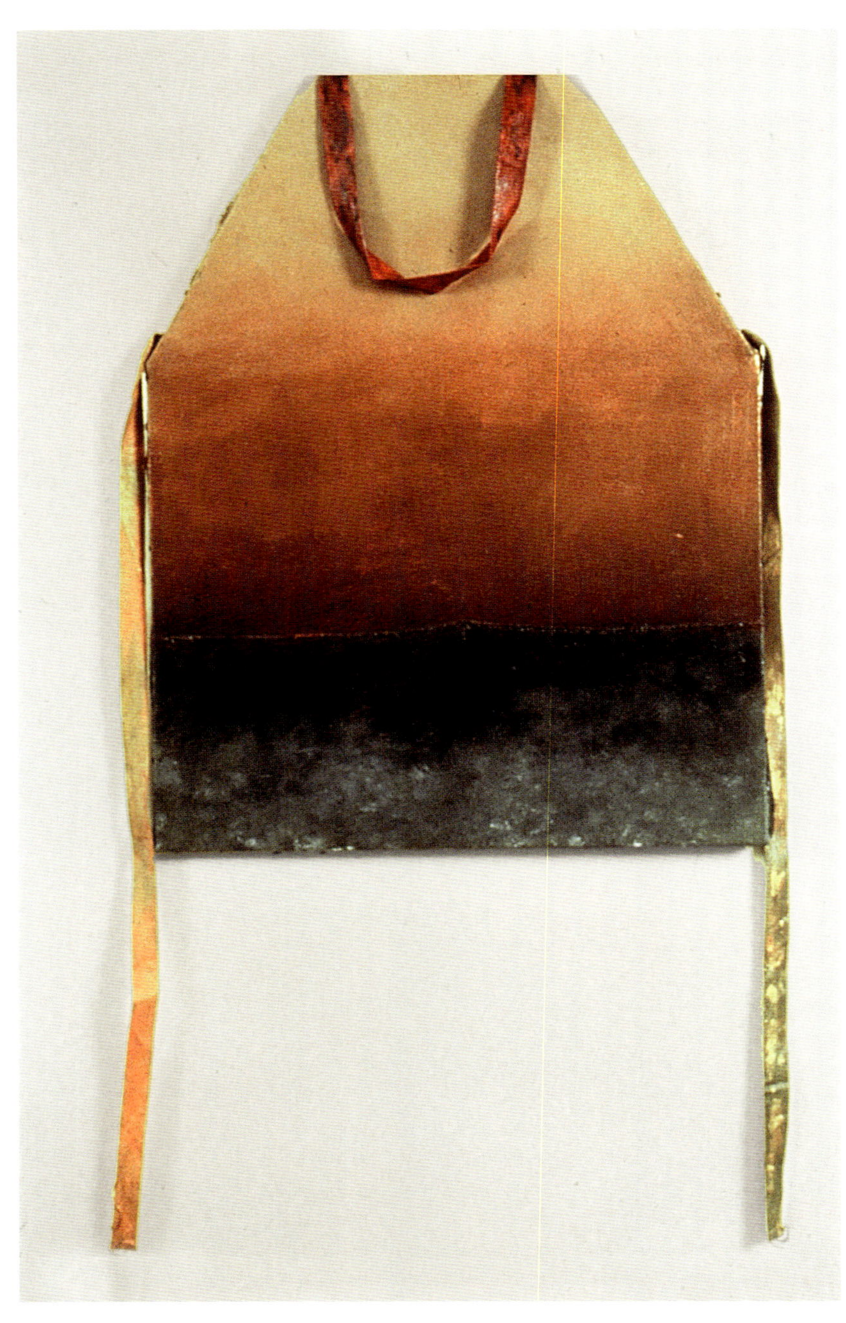

Brilo, 1987
Oil on canvas
23 1/2 x 18 inches

Sago, 1987
Oil on canvas
46 x 11 7/8 inches

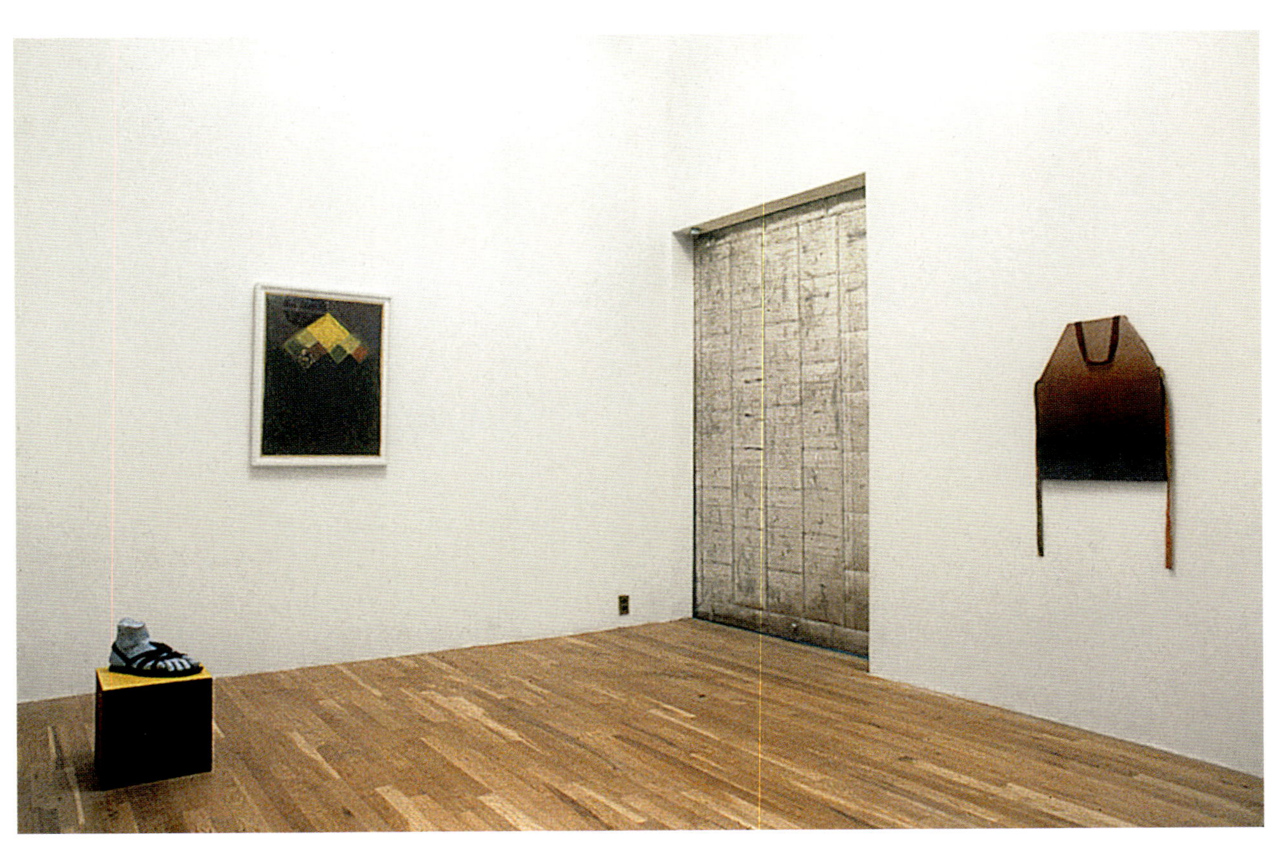

Installation view, 1988
Daniel Newburg Gallery, New York

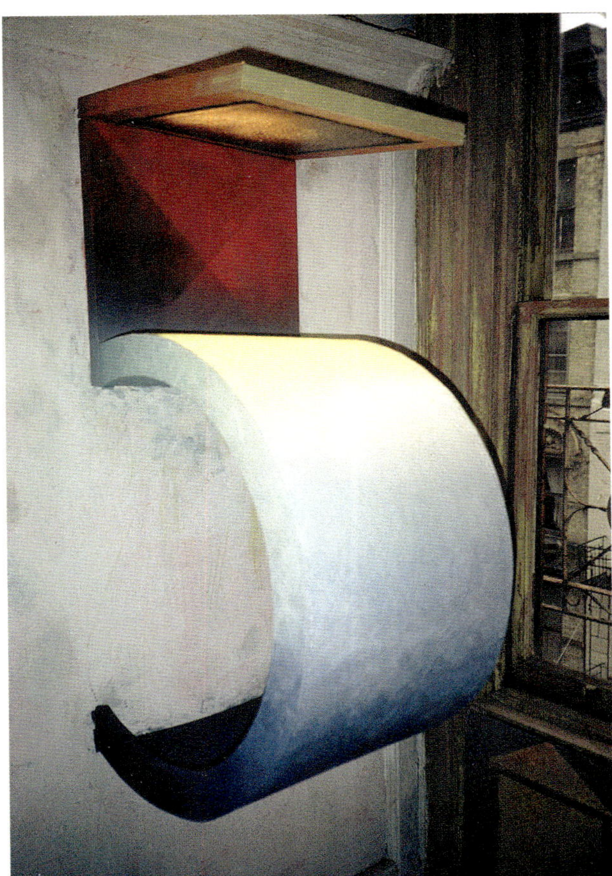

Five, 1988
Oil on canvas, wood, and aluminum
44 x 17 x 21 inches

Five is shaped like the number from which it takes its name, and made of a curved part, a canvas, and a window. Staring into it from the front presents one with a convergence between three kinds of surface, three possibilities for light: in front of one's face, a diagonally divided square painted with reds; above it, serving as the horizontal bit of the figure five, the window, made of yellowish frosted glass, which inflects light with the properties of both concentration and dispersal as it projects it downward; below that, the top of the five's curve, a fairly thick surface in that here the paint is applied over a china clay ground, a tactility both absorbent and reflective, a curved surface and therefore never parallel to one's field of vision except at a single, entirely hypothetical, point, and elusiveness which is a property of what is also the most thing like part of the work. And, in that it is white turning to blue where it meets the wall, that is, as it gets further away from the viewer, a surface which is there but always engaged in slipping away, white reflecting light, changing to blue and in that inventing distance (reconvening the properties of the sky). A nonhomogenous pictorial surface, a space made out of the primary colors where white—absolute light, or light as the principle of disembodiment—intervenes in the series yellow-red-blue (expansion-hovering-recession) as the work comes closest to the viewer. Being understood as a space, it is therefore at no time exclusively a surface, but can instead only be understood as a movement through appearances, founded in three kinds of luminosity, the translucency of glass, the interior glow of oil paint, the reflective white surface which turns into distance, each of which depends on a concept of completeness—the figure five, a sign standing for an amount—and therefore of being as opposed to construction in some way, but which constitutes that idea of being entirely in terms of its deconstruction, of deferral. Everything here is present as something which cannot possibly be entirely present, definitively outside the interests of historical meaning, which is moral, categorical, obsessed with context (e.g., meaning in Richter or Beuys), but also irreducible to any idea of either expression or its corollary, *thingness.*

An excerpt from *Beyond Piety: Critical Essays on the Visual Arts, 1986–1993* by Jeremy Gilbert-Rolfe

Reversal, 1988
Pigment and acrylic on canvas
45 x 30 inches

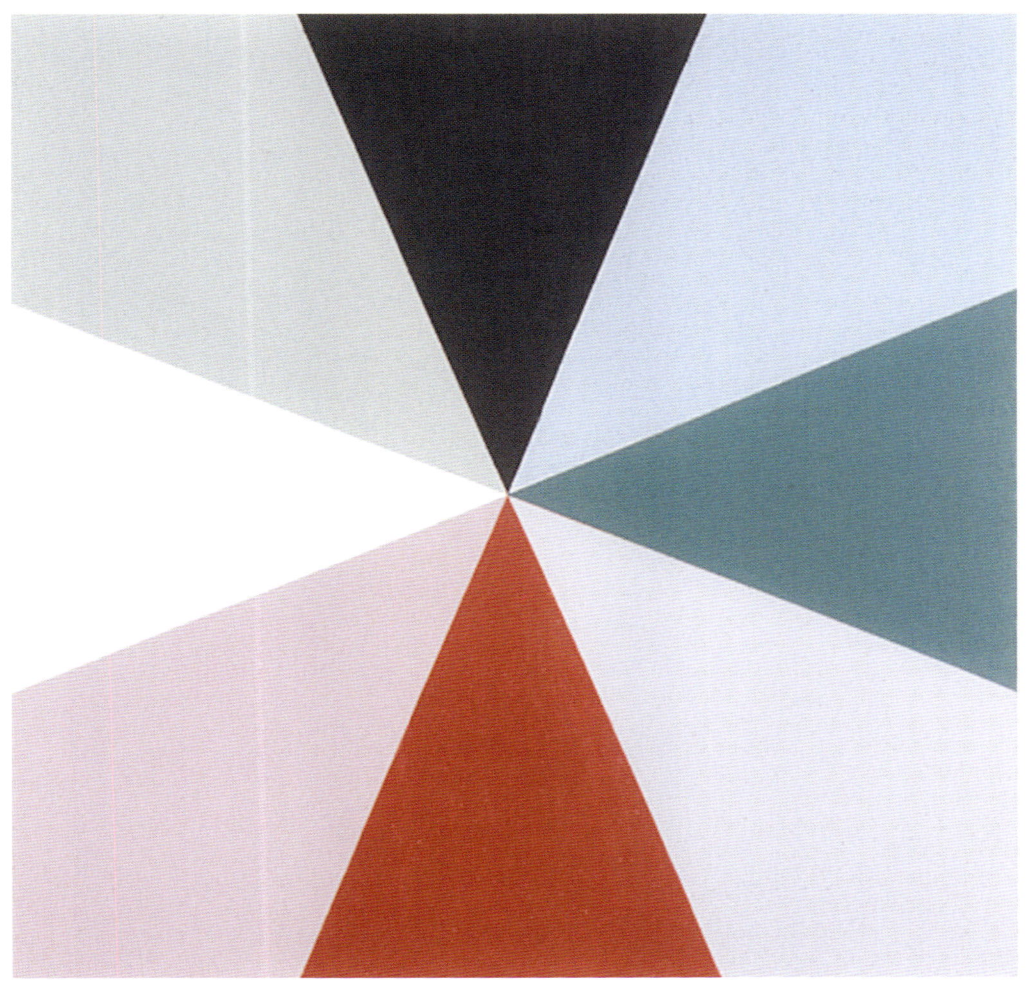

Center, 1989
Pigment in dispersion on canvas
17 x 17 inches

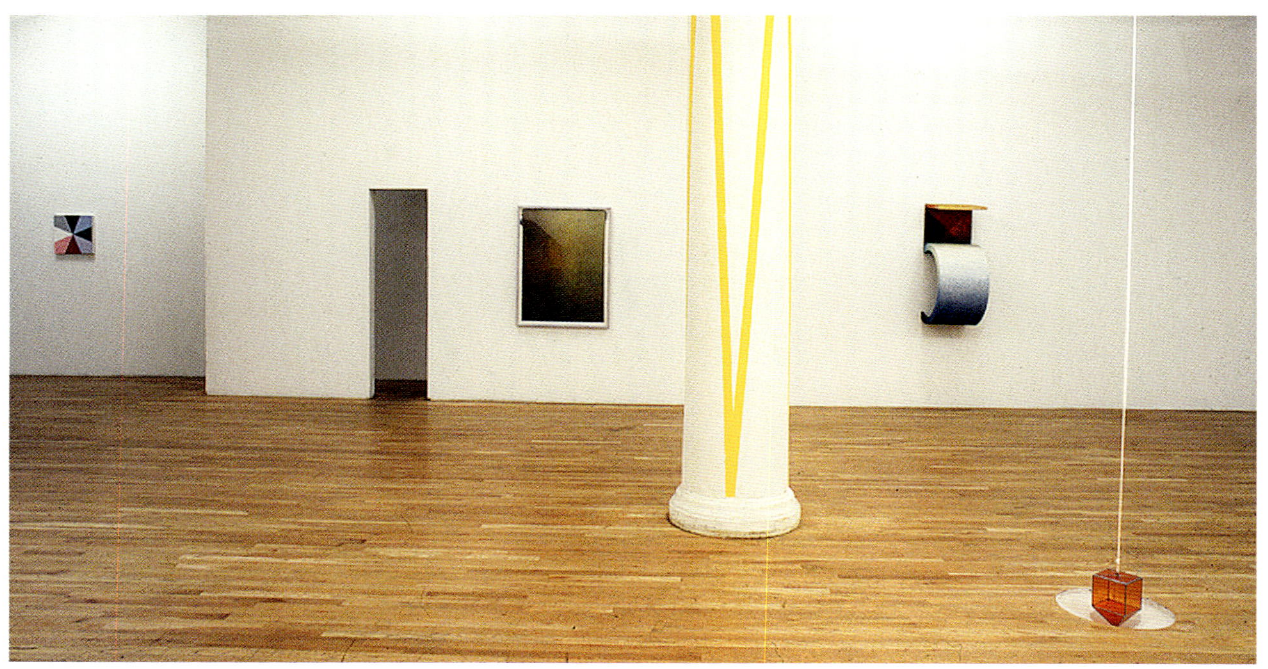

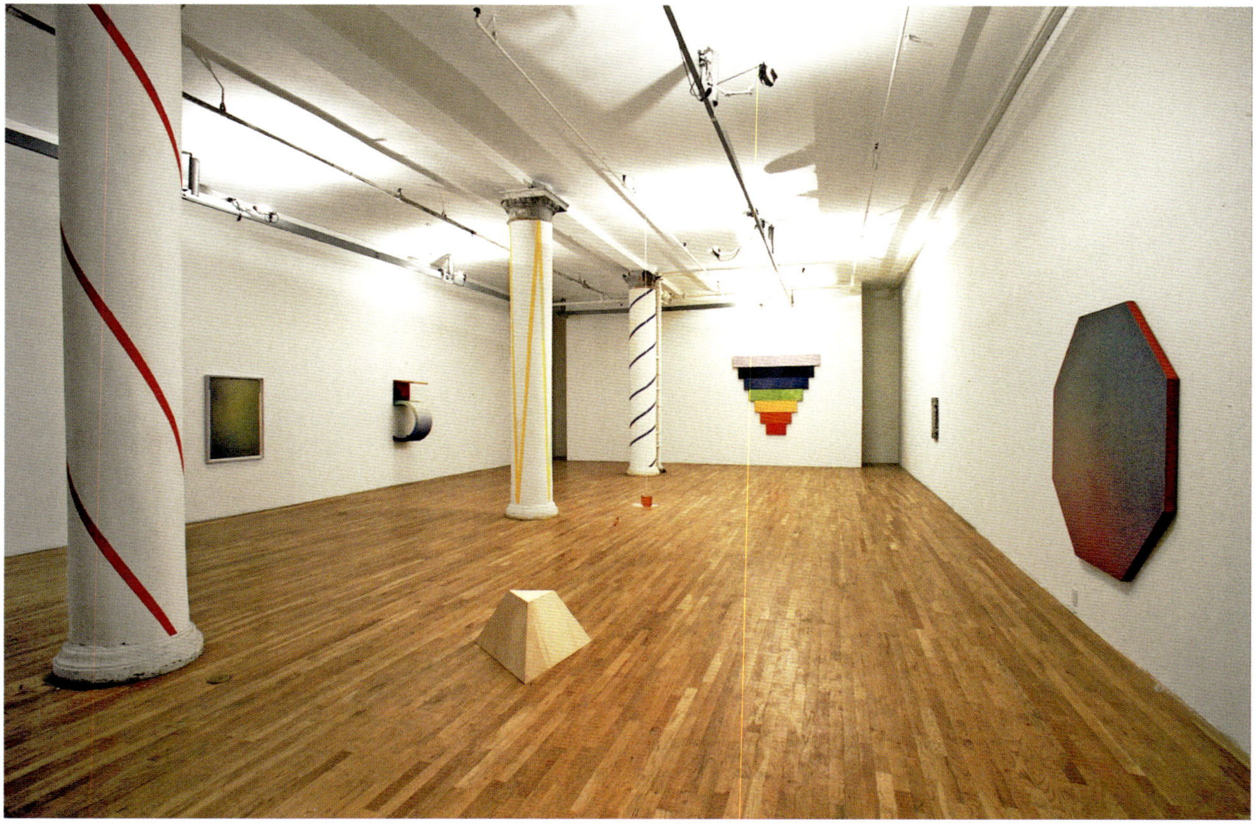

Installation views, 1989
Daniel Newburg Gallery, New York

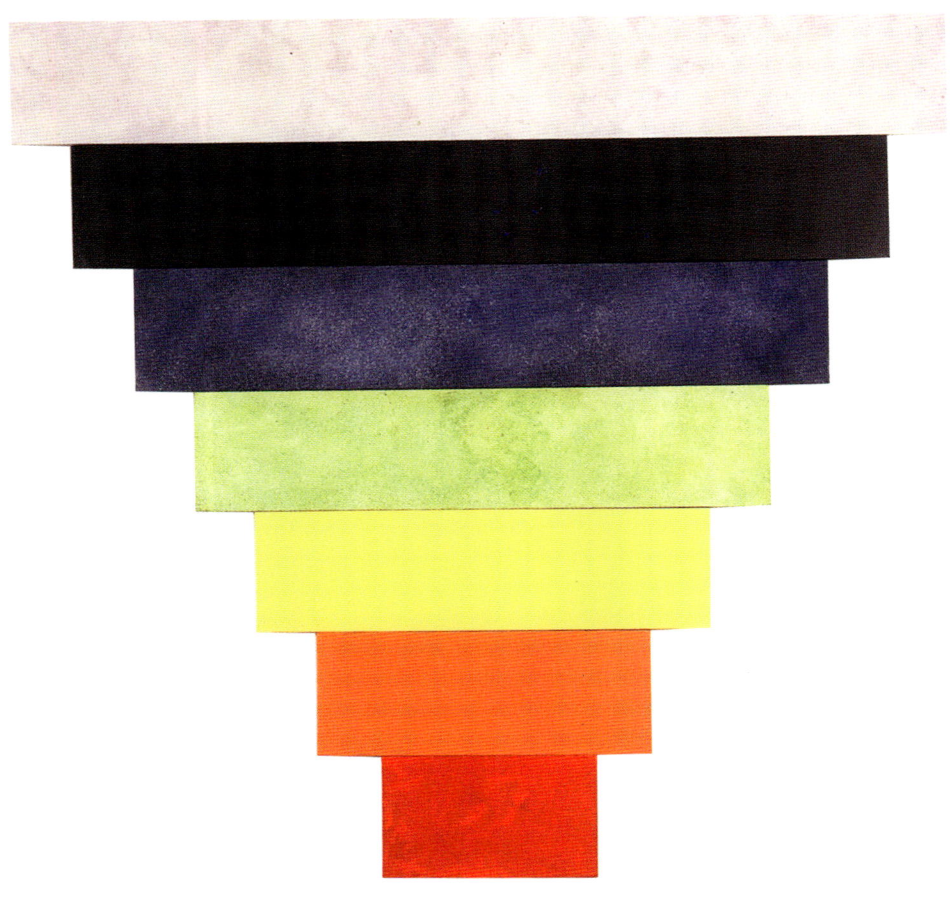

Bridge, 1989
Pigment and acrylic on canvas
78 x 74 1/2 inches

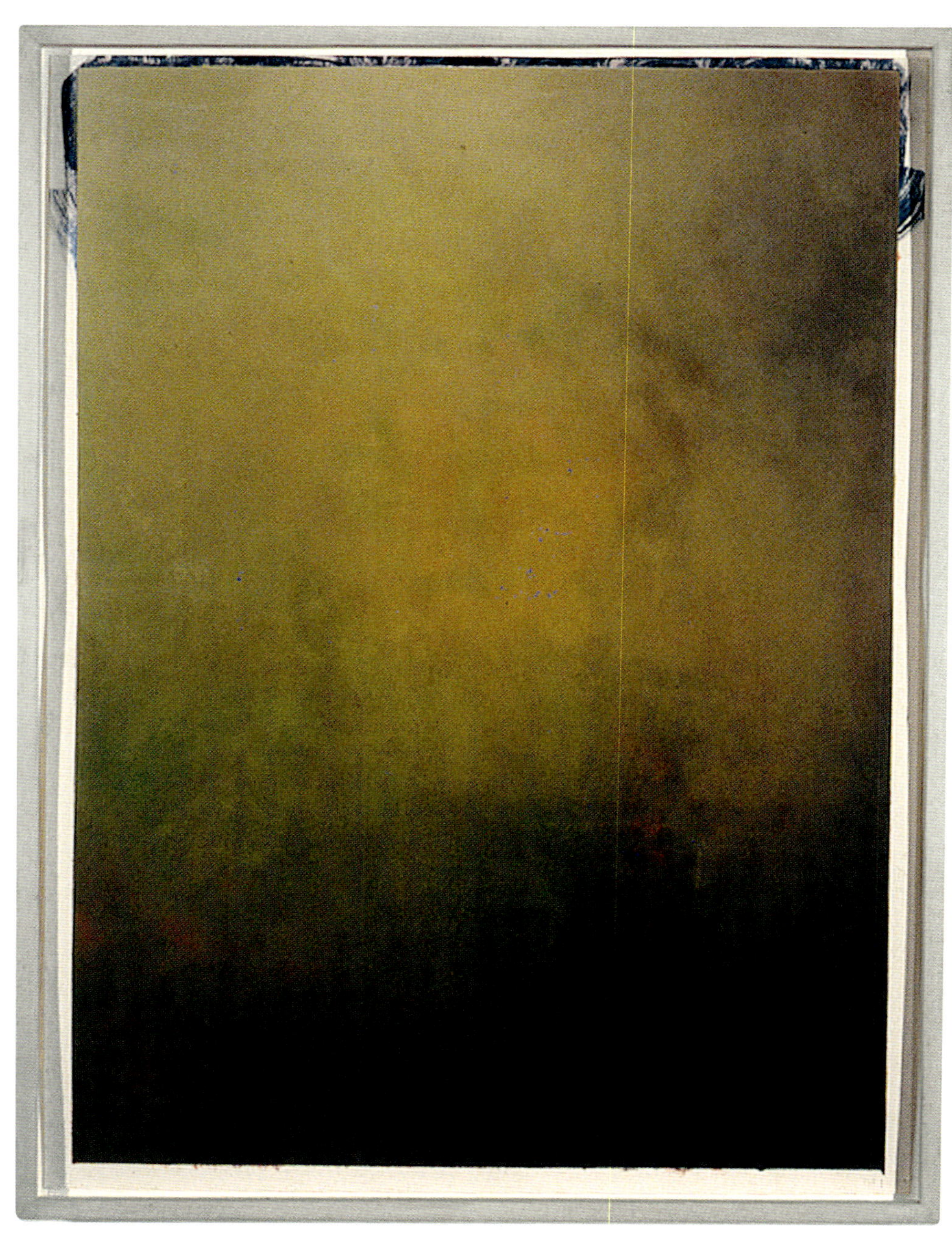

Rainbow, 1989
Oil on paper
45 x 33 3/4 inches

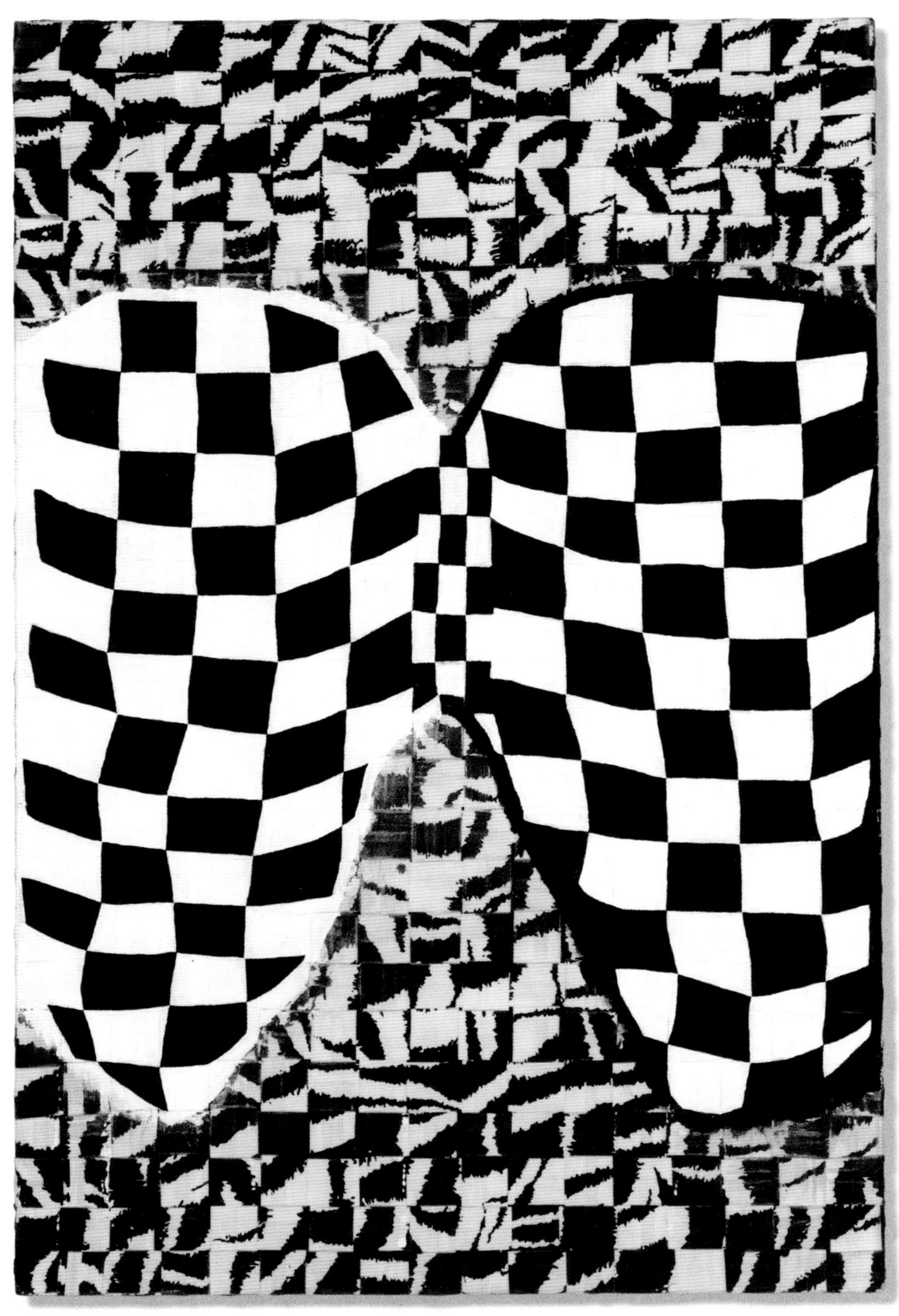

Zebra, 1989
Acrylic and printed fabric
26 1/4 x 17 1/4 inches

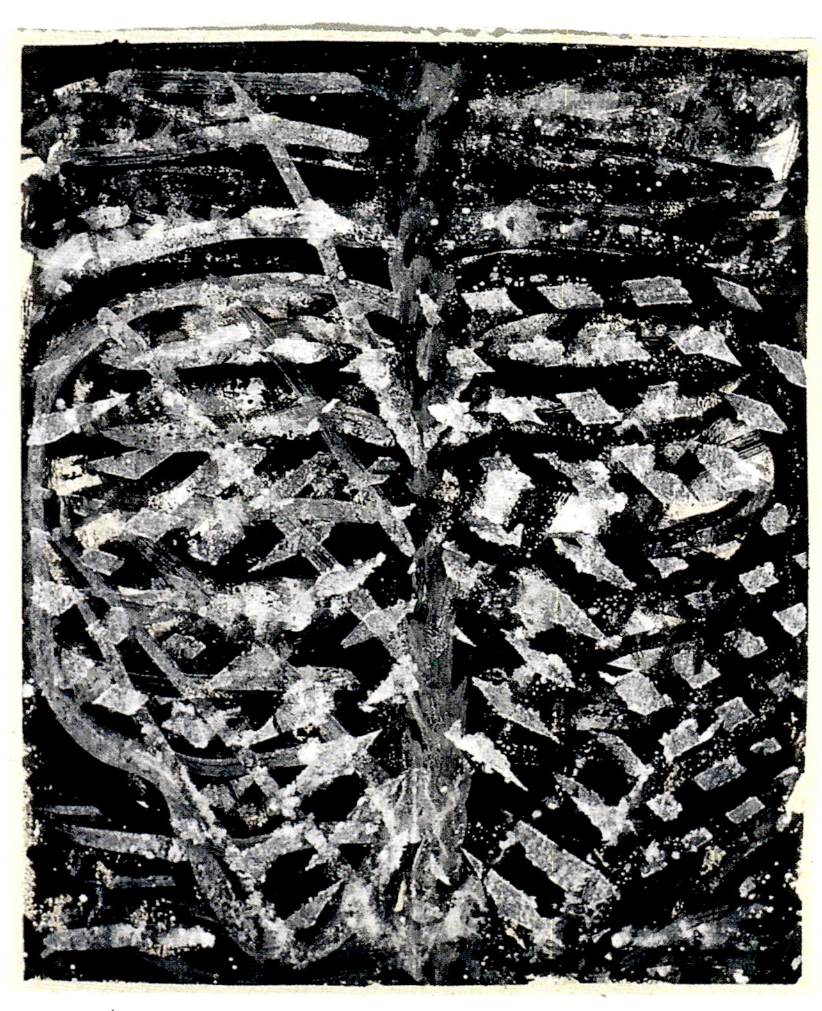

Untitled, 1989
Pigment, oil, and acrylic on paper
26 x 21 inches

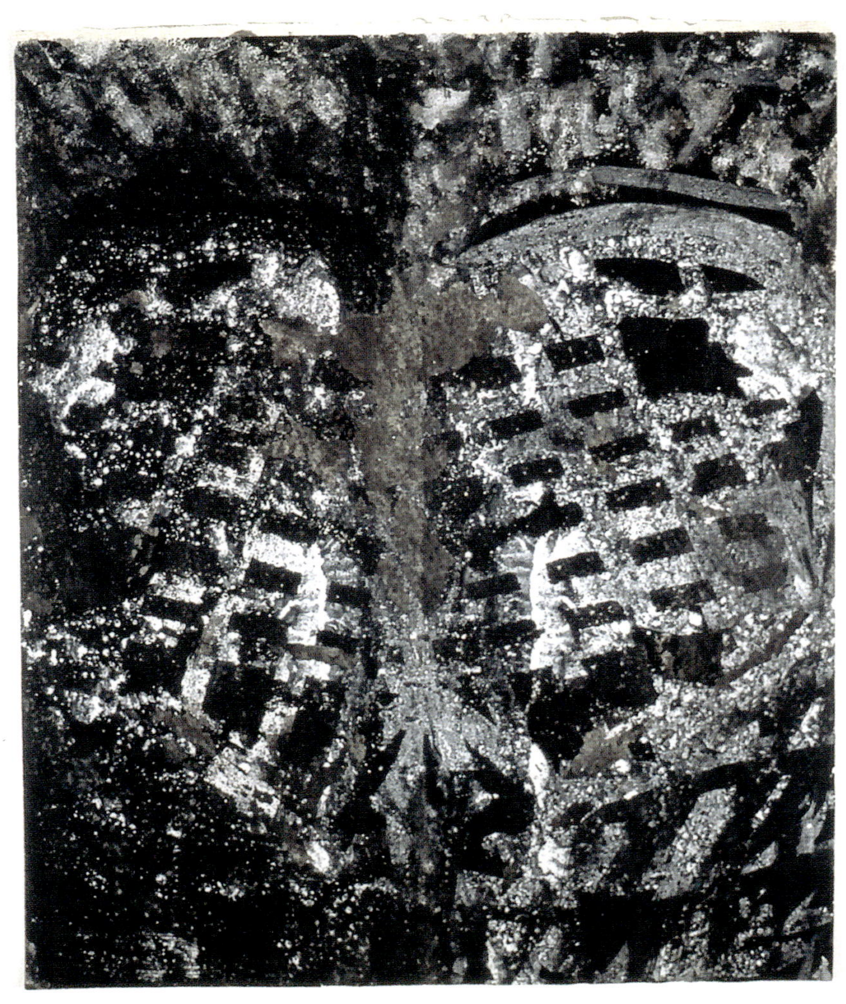

Untitled, 1989
Pigment, oil, and acrylic on paper
24 3/8 x 20 inches

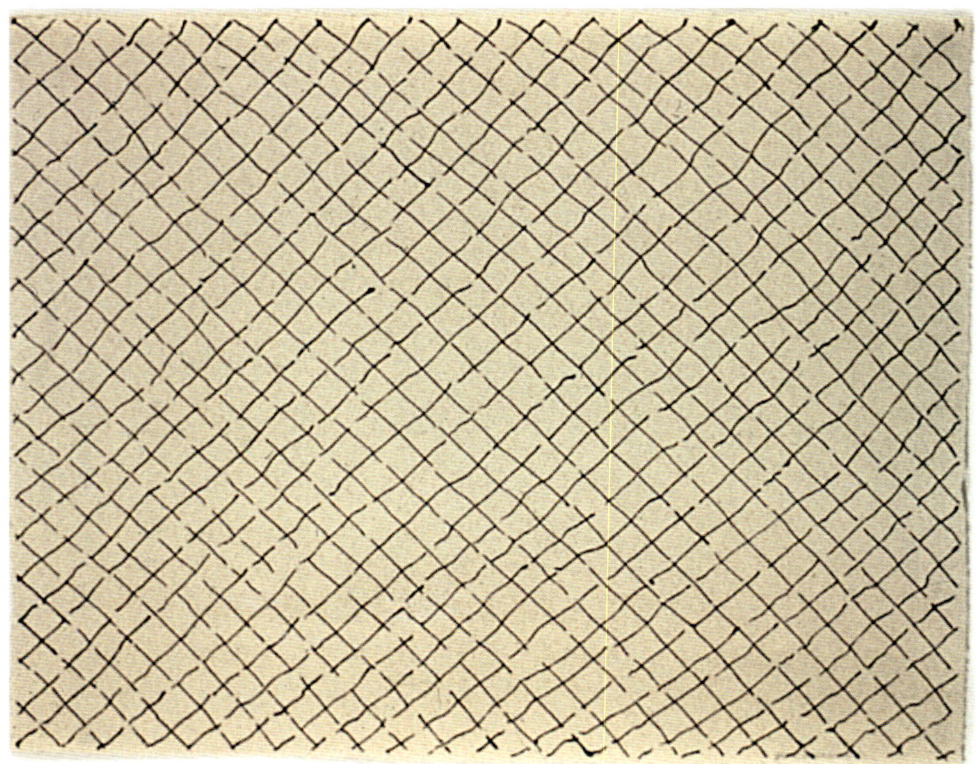

Net, 1989
Ink, chalk, acrylic on canvas
20 5/8 x 25 1/2 inches

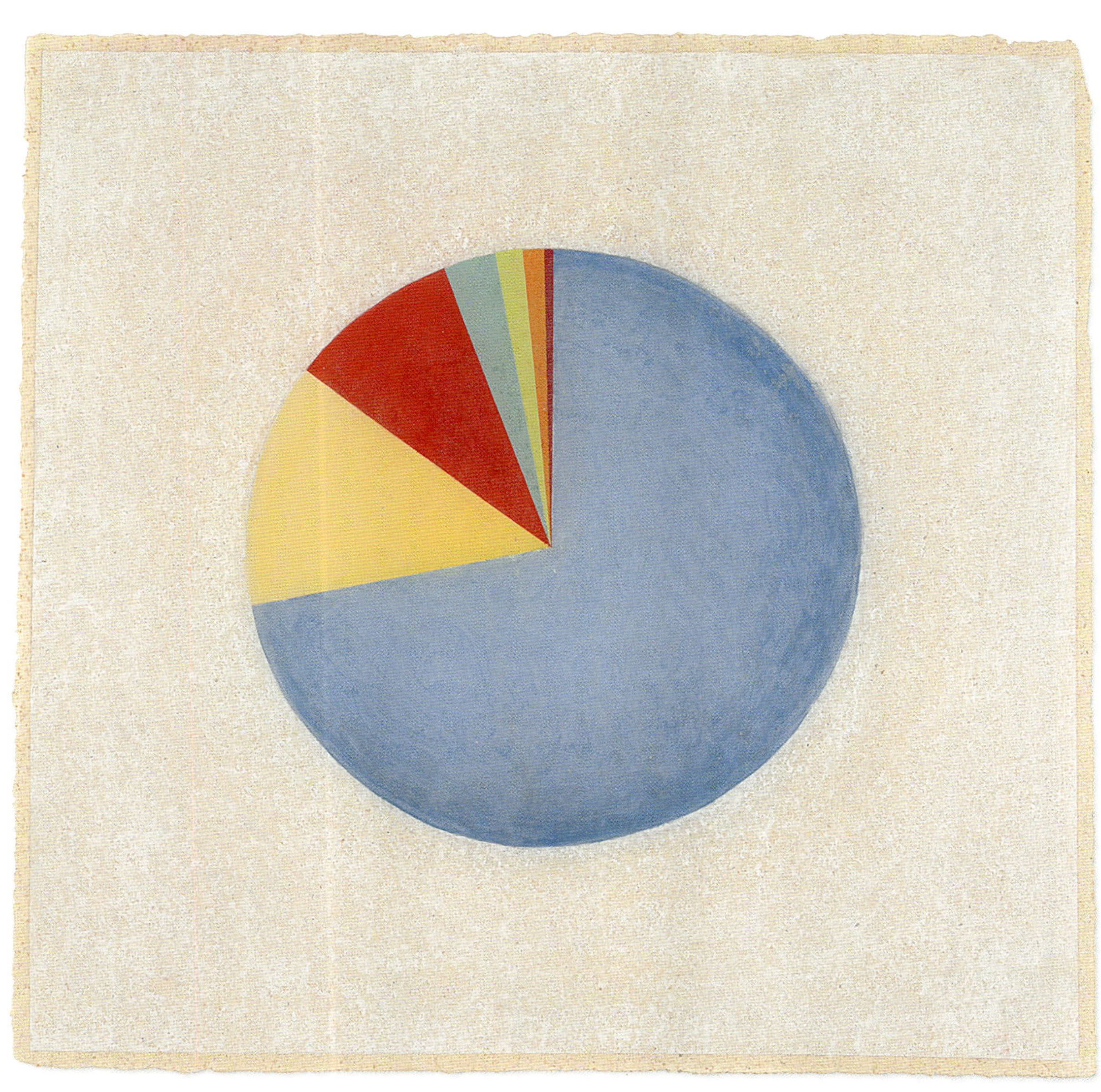

Man Hour, 1989
Pigment, chalk, acrylic on paper
17 1/2 x 17 1/2 inches

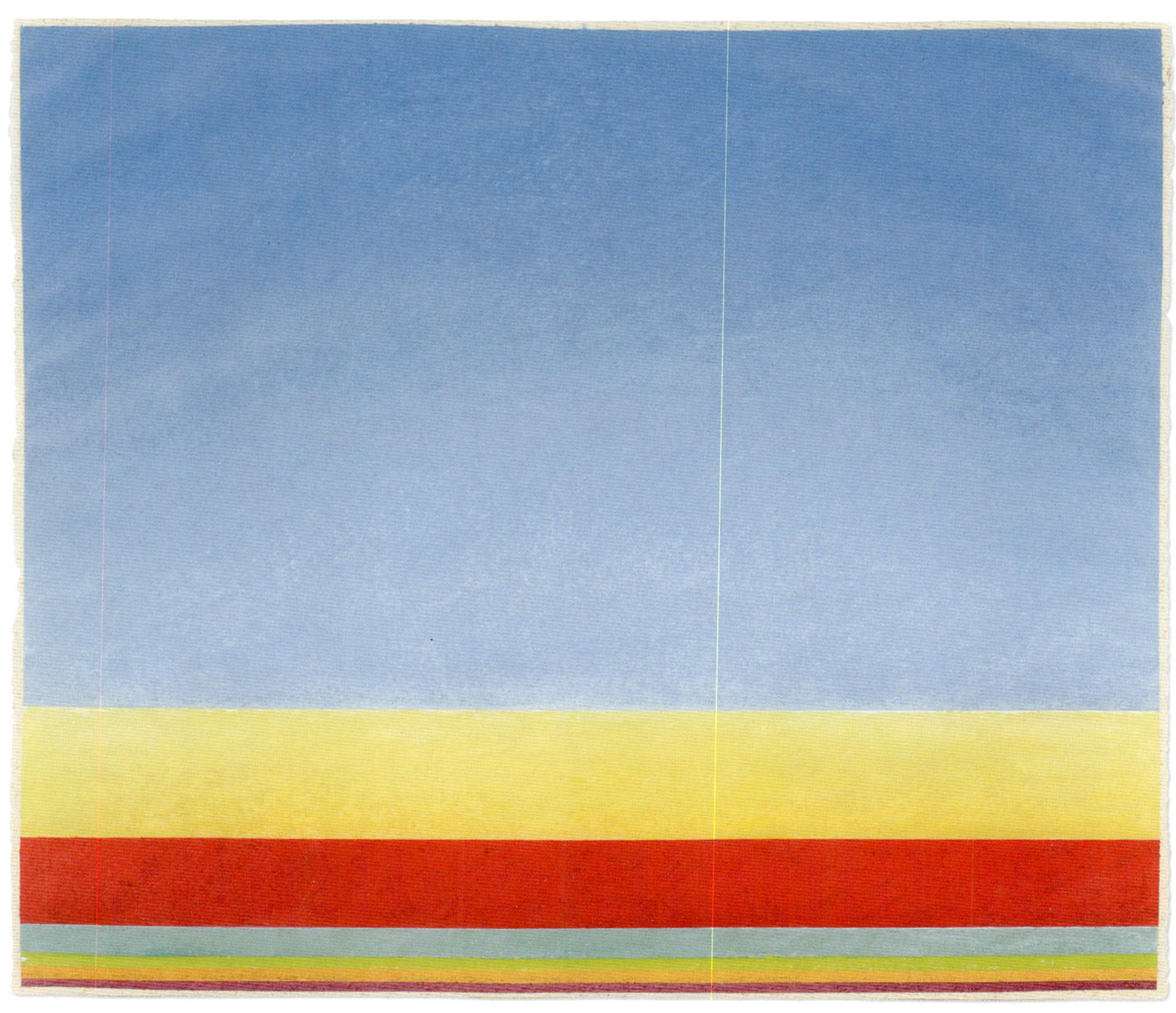

Manscape, 1989
Acrylic on canvas
20 1/2 x 23 1/2 inches

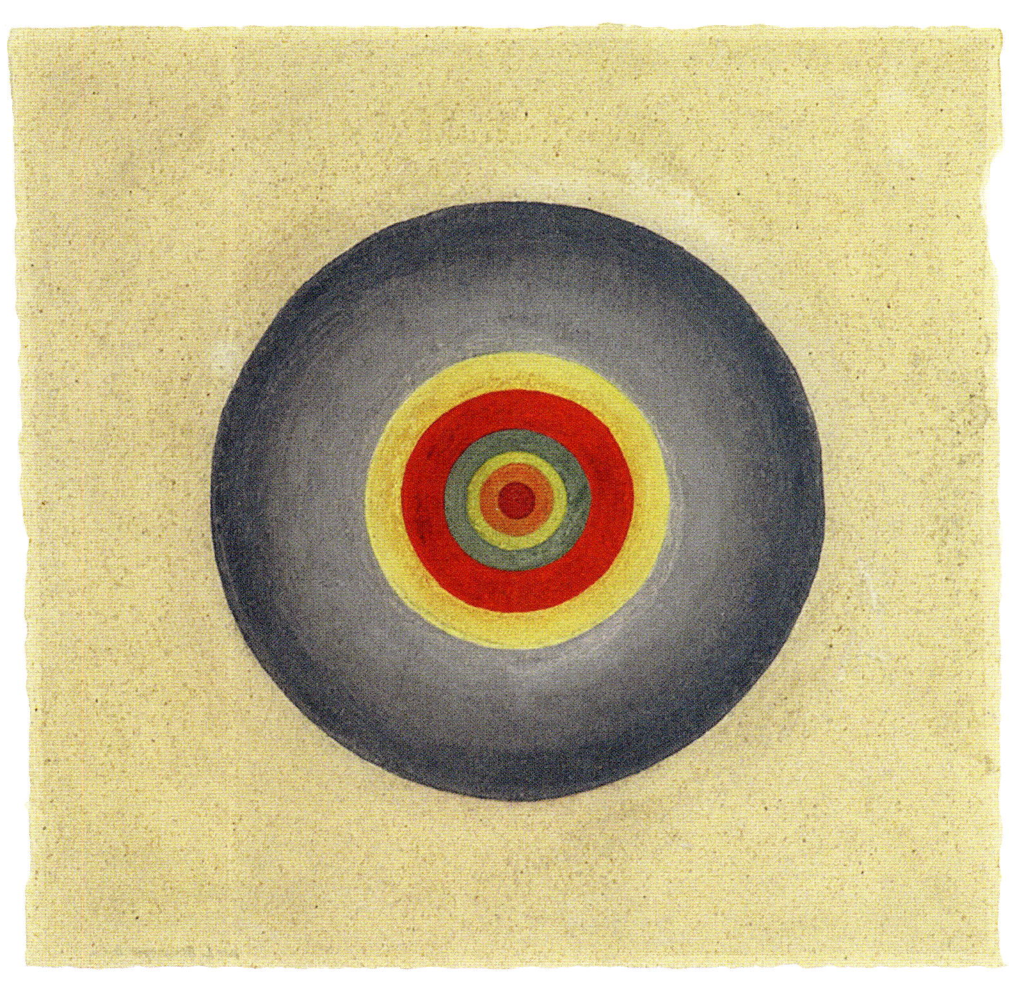

Mandala, 1989
Pigment, chalk, acrylic on paper
15 3/4 x 15 3/4 inches

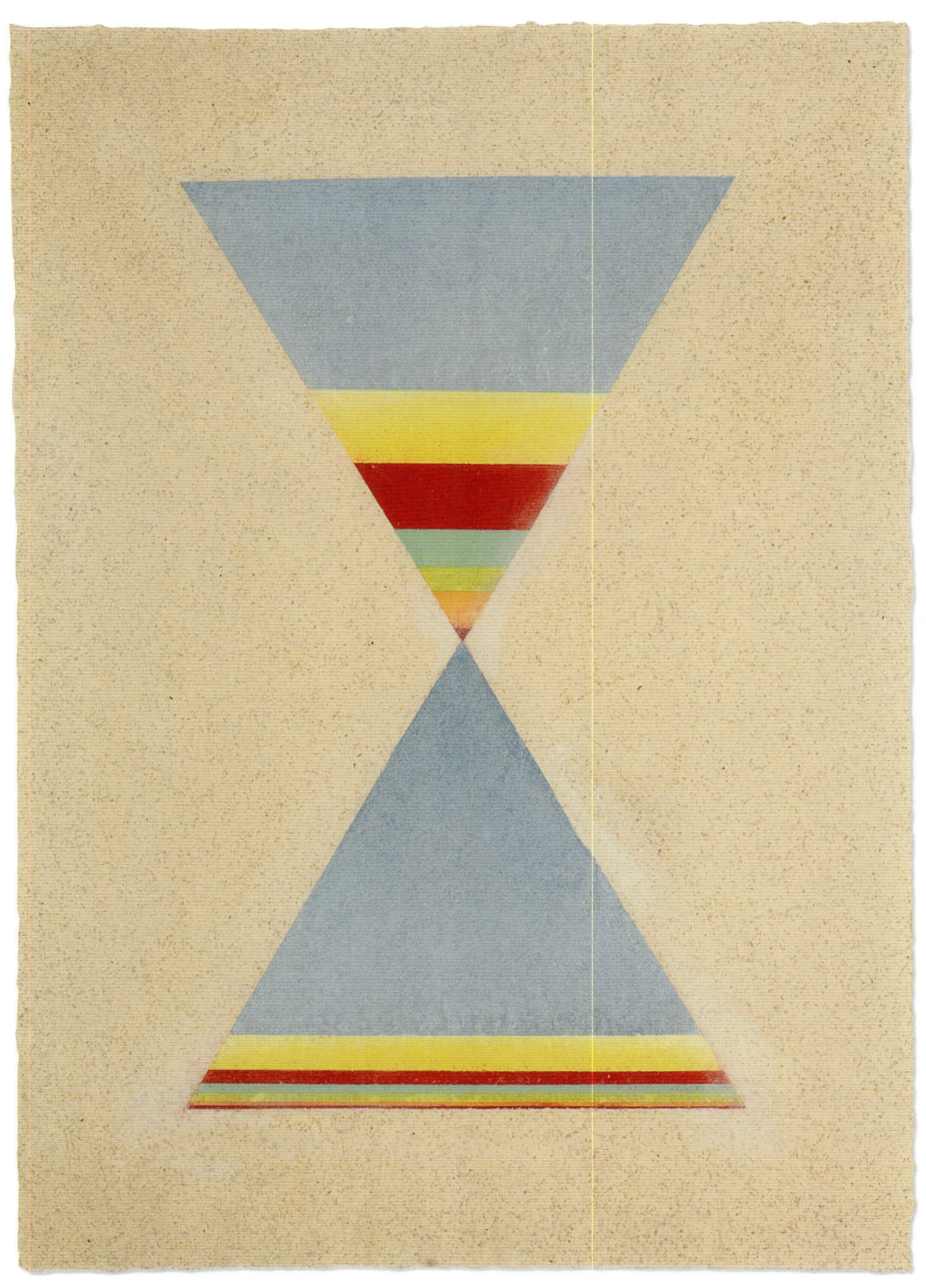

Man Hour, 1989
Pigment, chalk, and acrylic on paper
23 x 15 1/2 inches

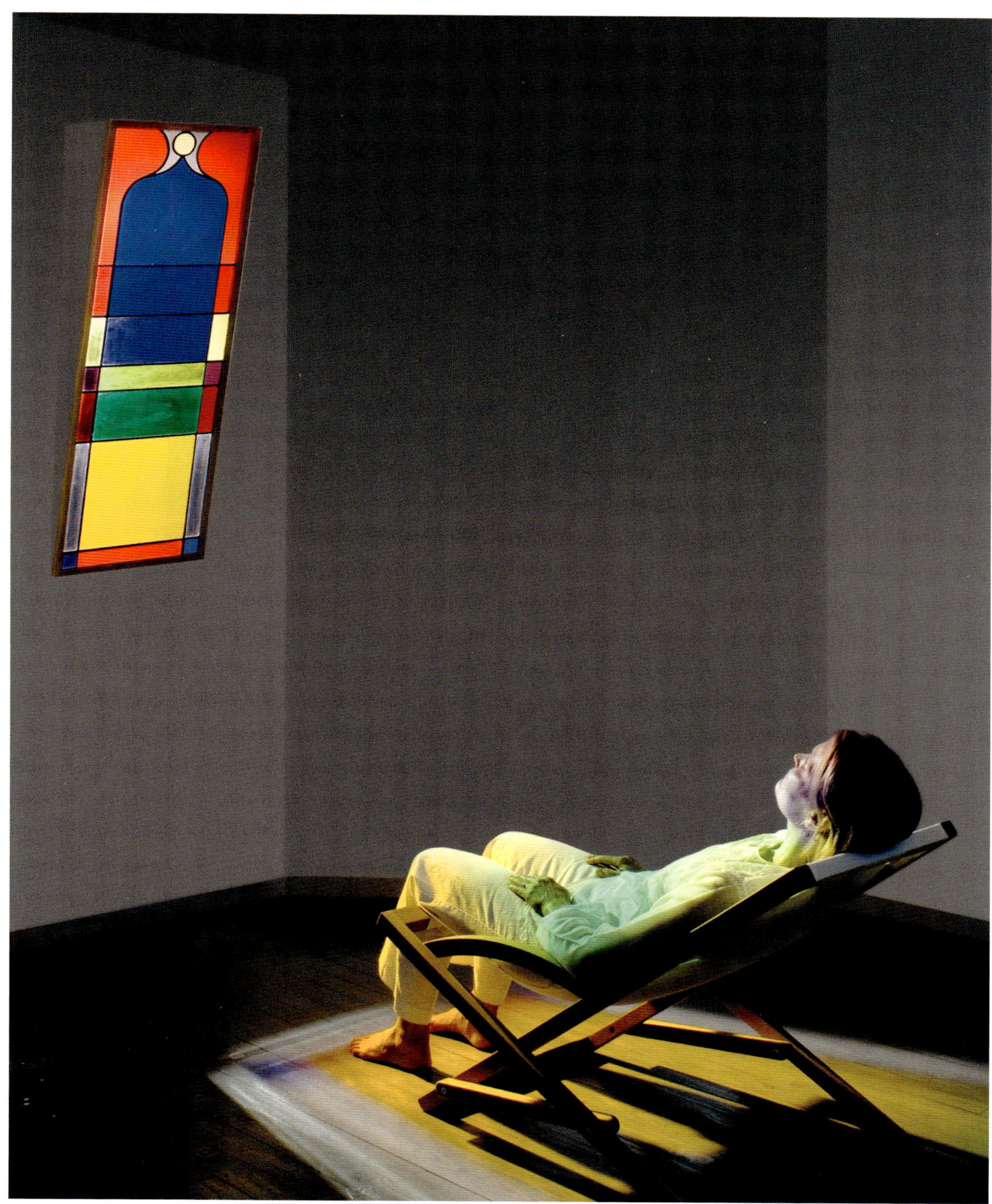

Dr. Babbitt's Chromolume, 1989
Stained glass, cables, and chair
54 1/2 x 19 1/2 inches

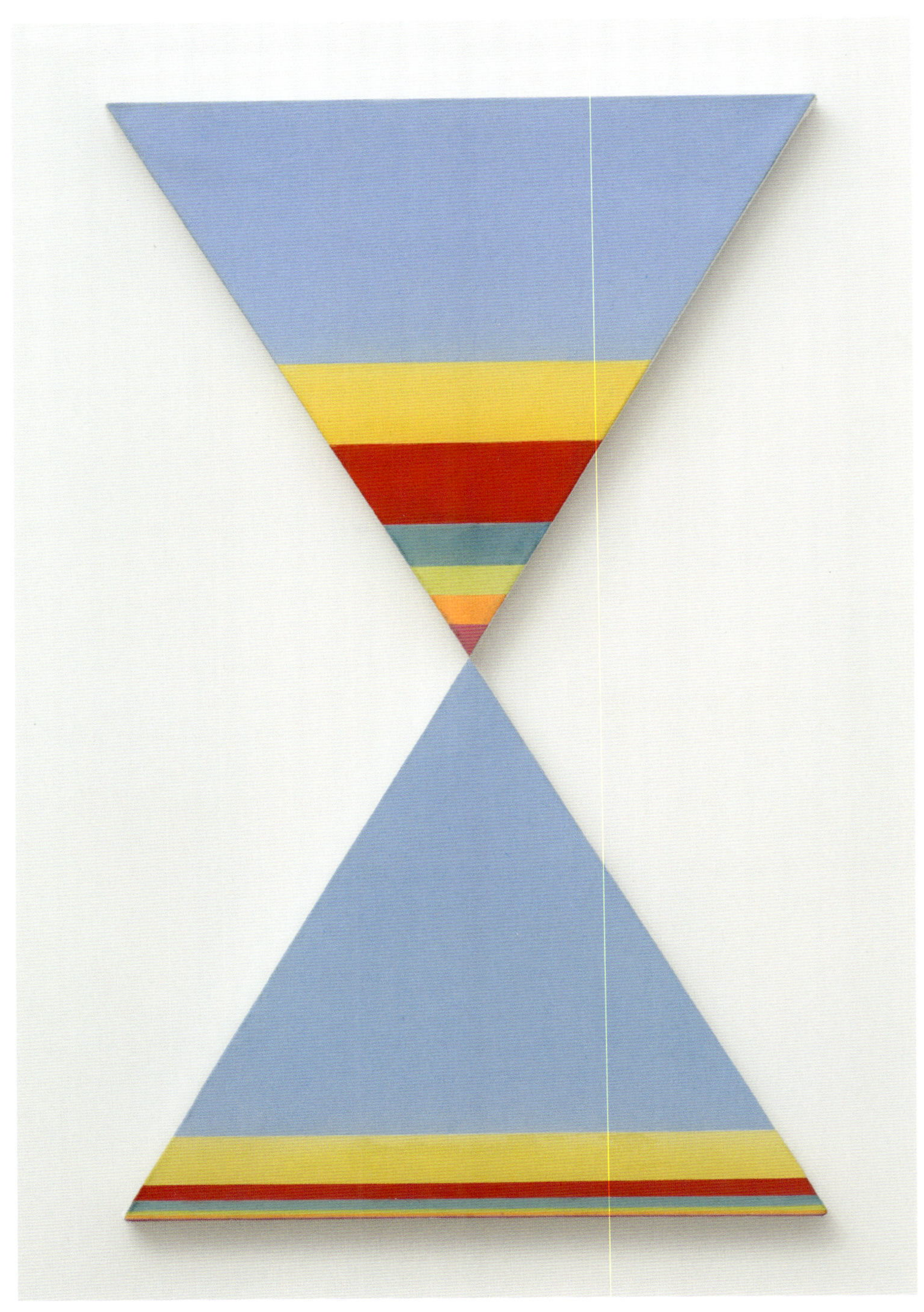

Man Hour, 1990
Acrylic on canvas
42 x 24 inches

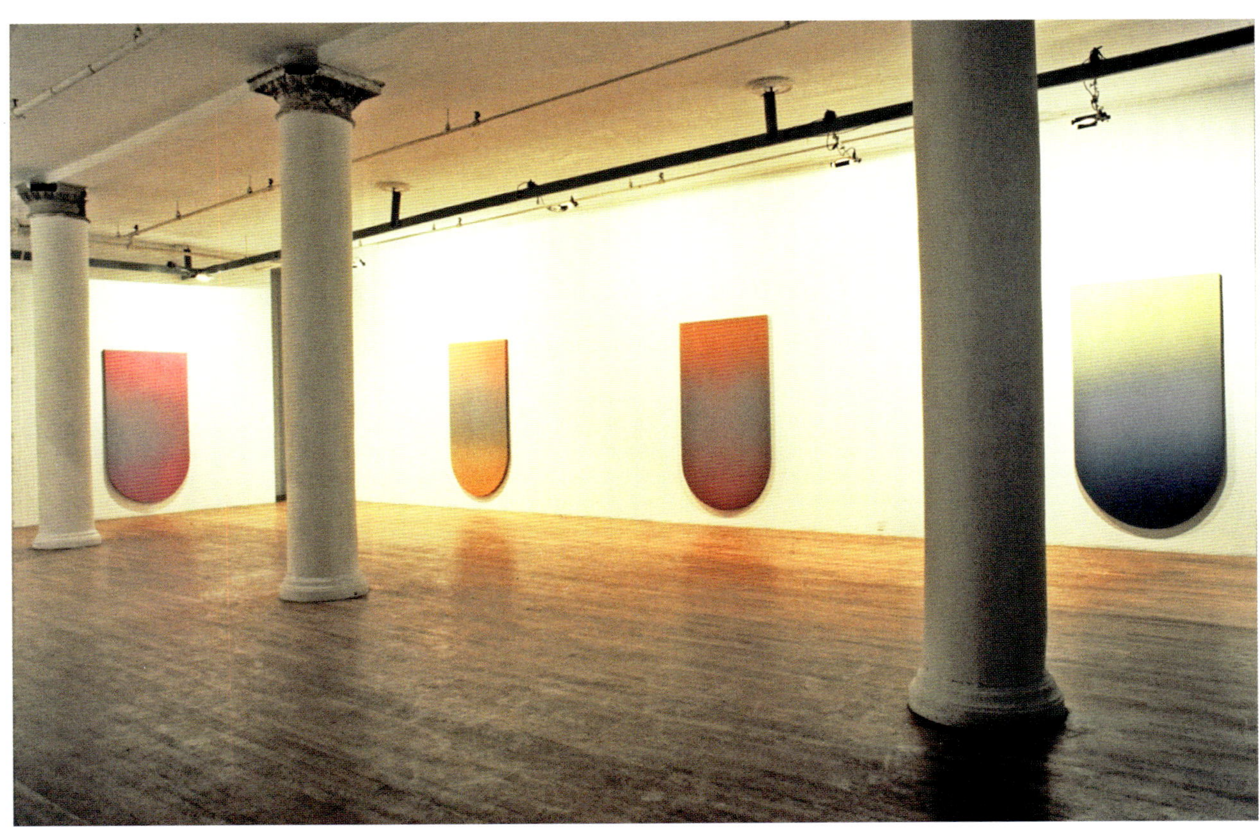

Installation view, 1990
Daniel Newburg Gallery

Red Work, 1990
Acrylic on canvas
95 x 49 inches

High Tower, 1990
Acrylic on canvas
95 x 49 inches

Sure Cure, 1990
Acrylic on canvas
95 x 49 inches

Deo Herculi, 1990
Acrylic on canvas
95 x 49 inches

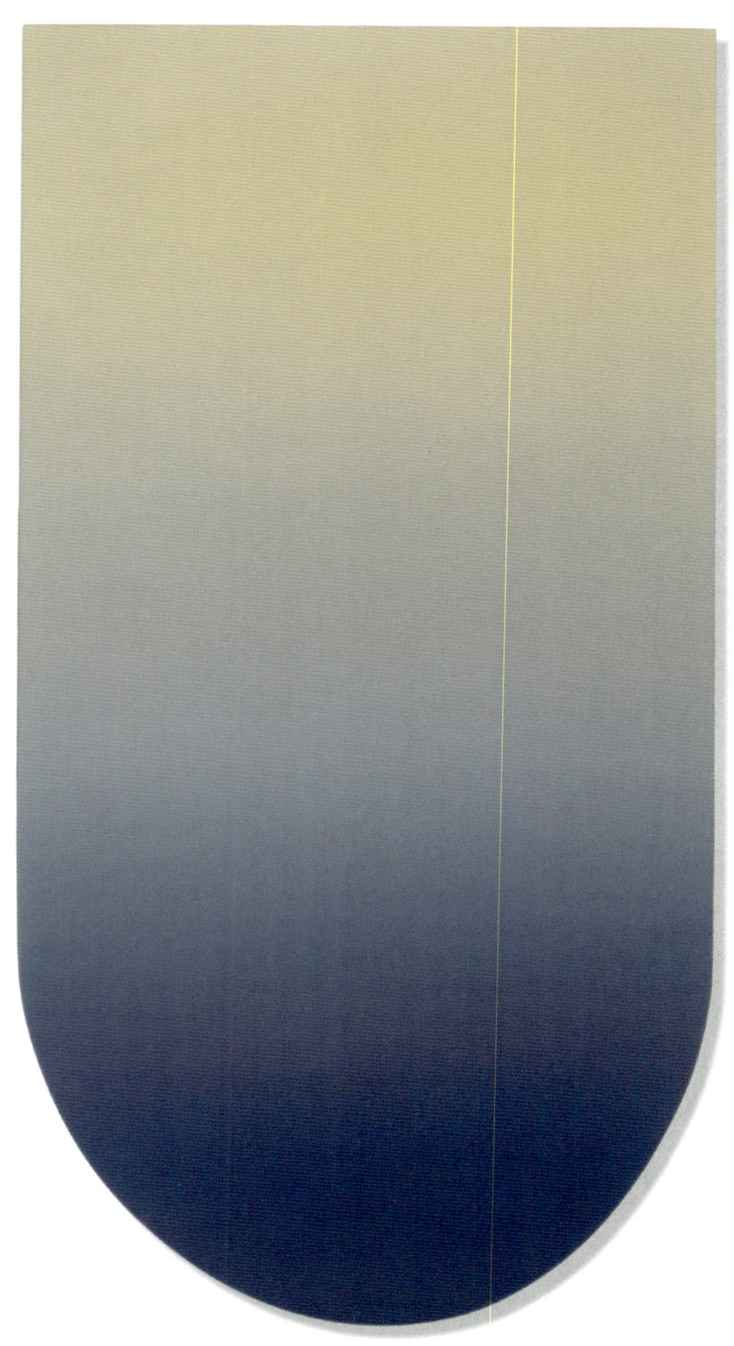

Raphael, 1990
Acrylic on canvas
95 x 49 inches

Fourth of July, 1990
Acrylic on canvas
95 x 49 inches

Phthonos, 1990
Acrylic on canvas
95 x 49 inches

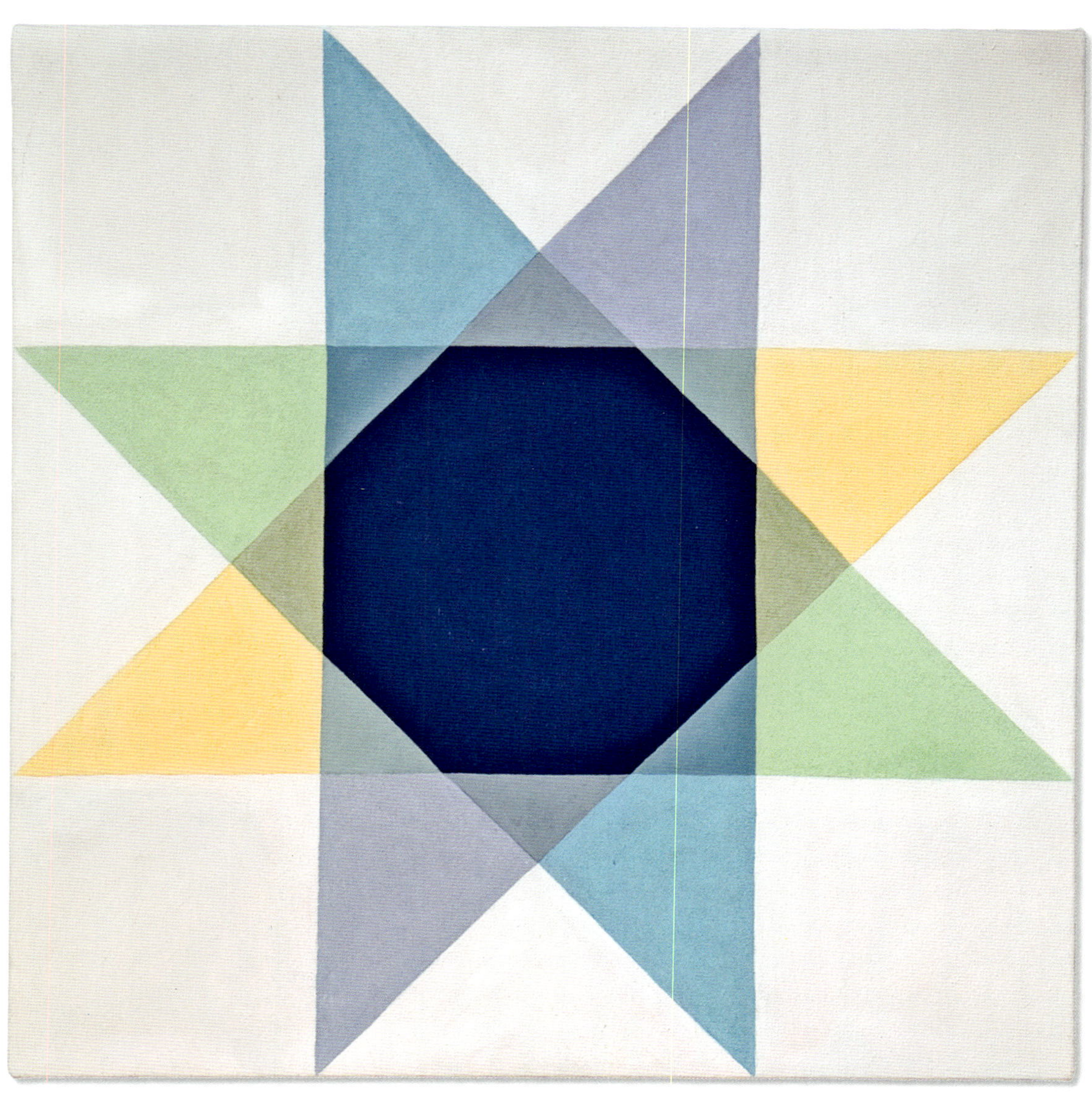

Foundation, 1990
Pigment in dispersion on canvas
17 x 17 inches

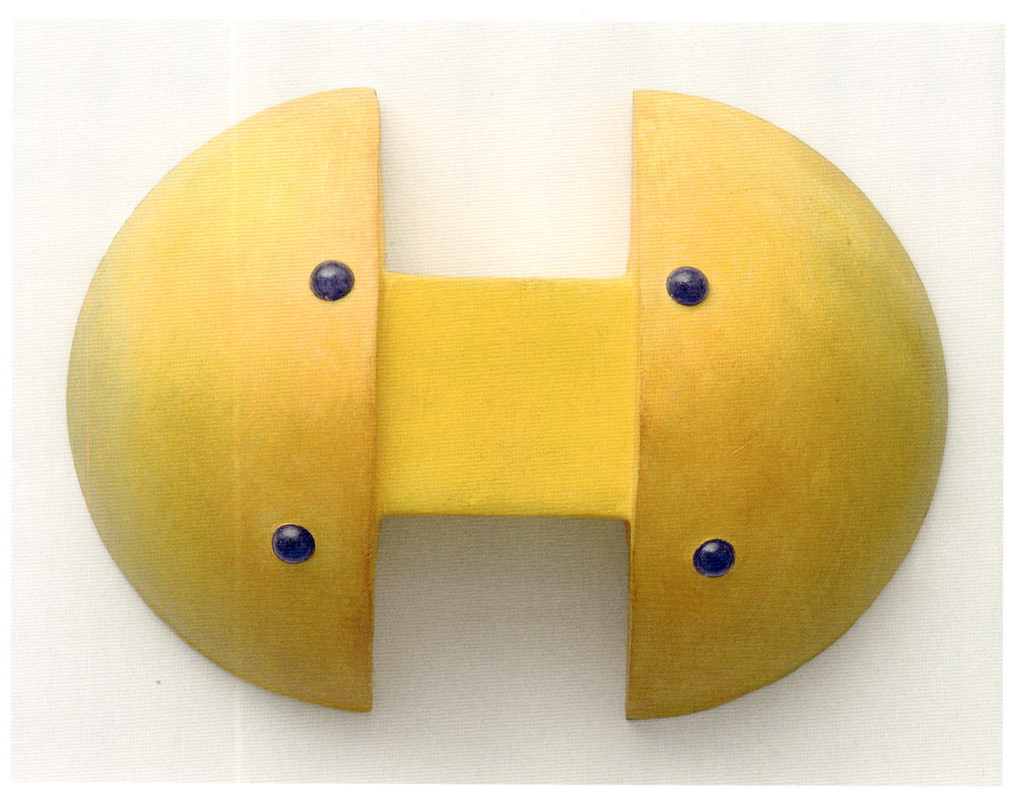

Malek, 1990
Plaster and pigments on acrylic
9 x 11 1/2 x 4 inches

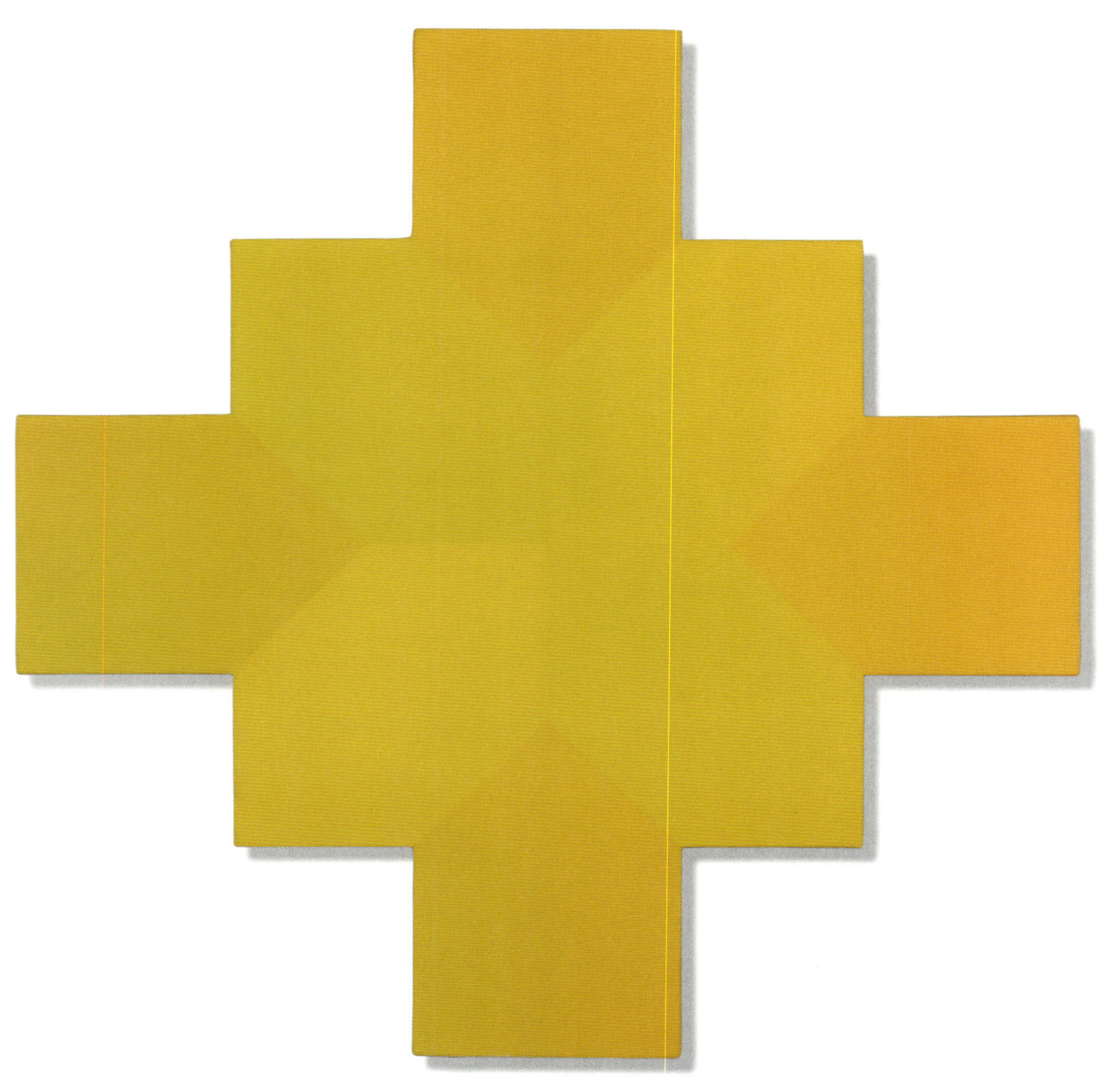

Natura Naturans, 1990
Pigment and acrylic on canvas
54 1/4 x 54 1/4 inches

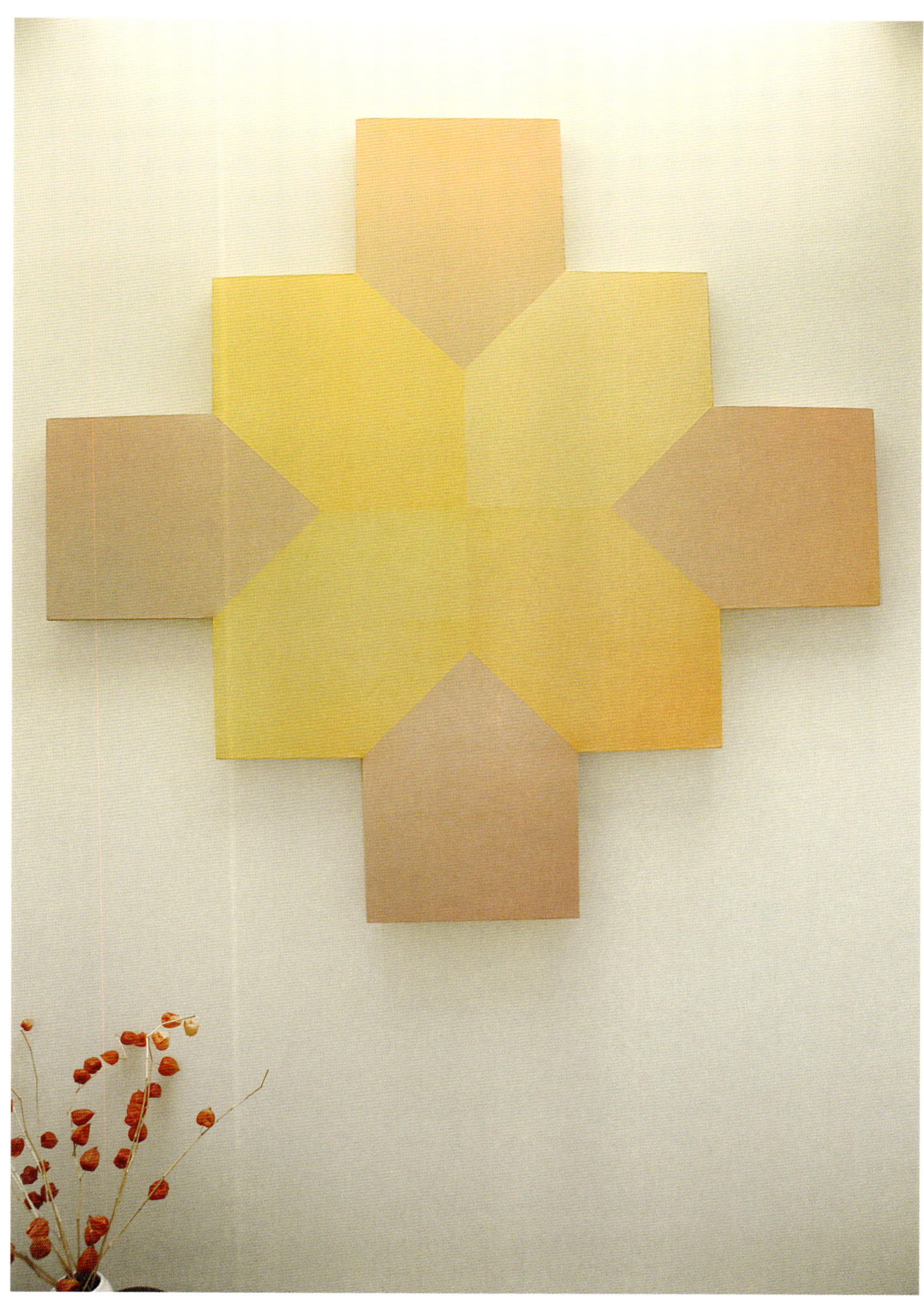

Sensible – Super Sensible, 1990
Acrylic on canvas
72 x 72 inches

Untitled, 1987–1990,
Pigments, acrylic on canvas
24 x 72 inches

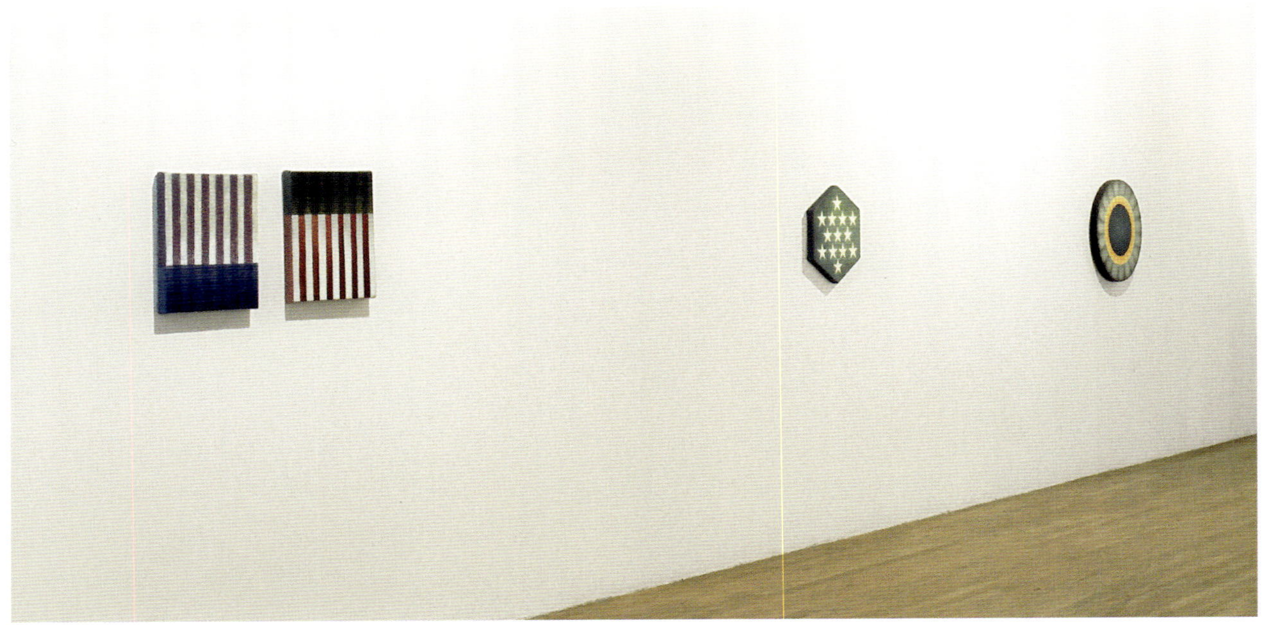

Installation view, 1992
Novus Ordo Seclorum
Daniel Newburg Gallery, New York
From left: *Mohawk Valley, Treetops,
United States of America, Abracadabra*

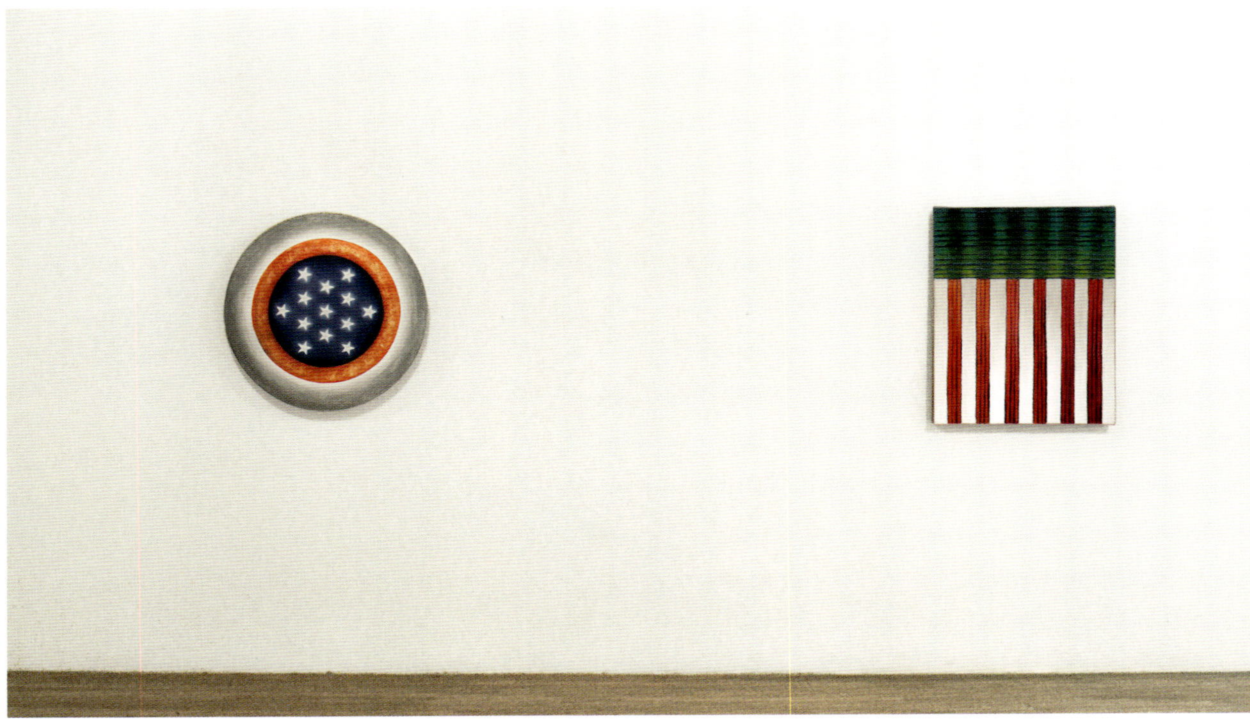

Left*: July the Fourth,* 1992
Right: *Treetops,* 1992

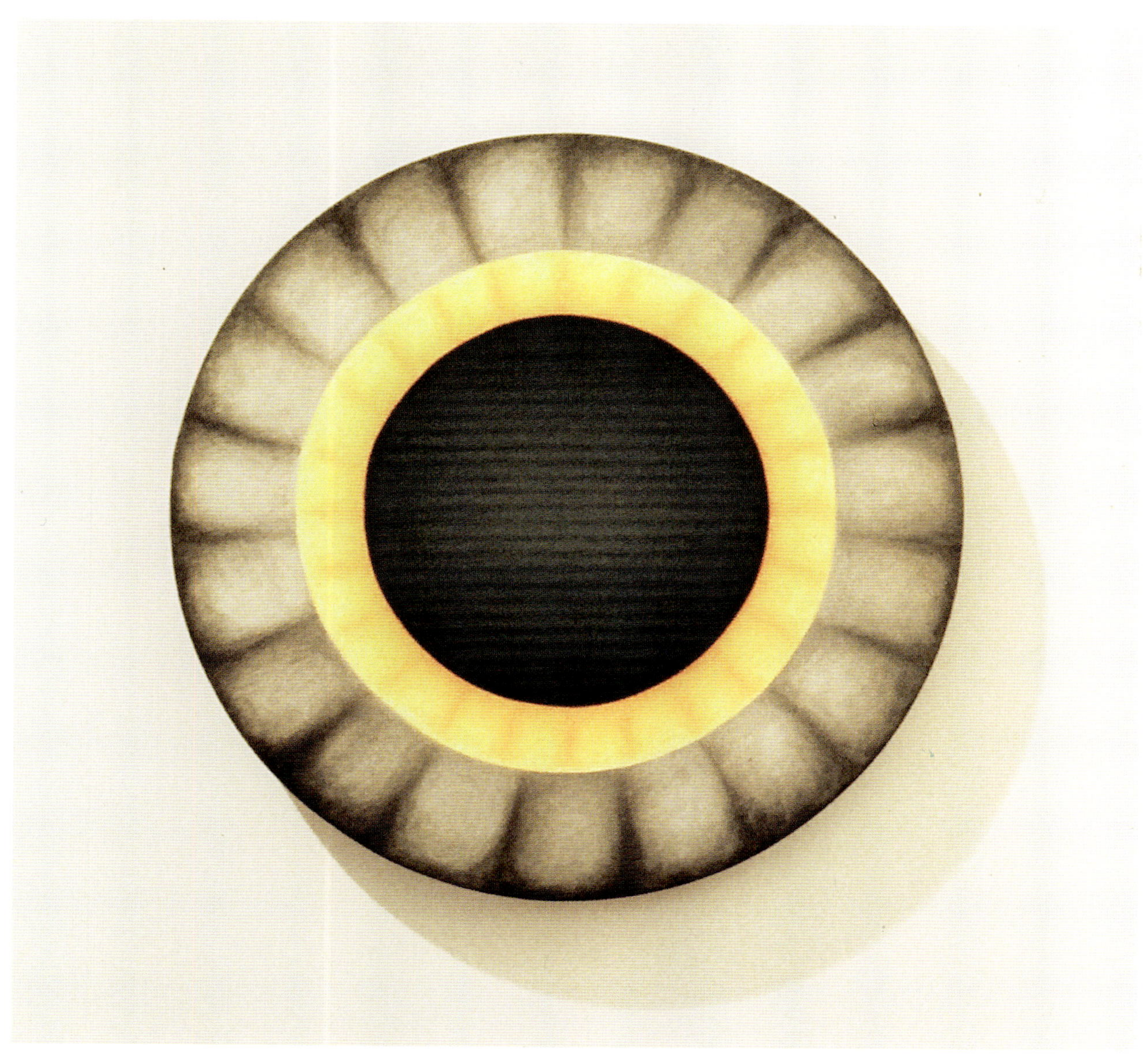

Abracadabra, 1992
Oil on canvas
24 inch diameter

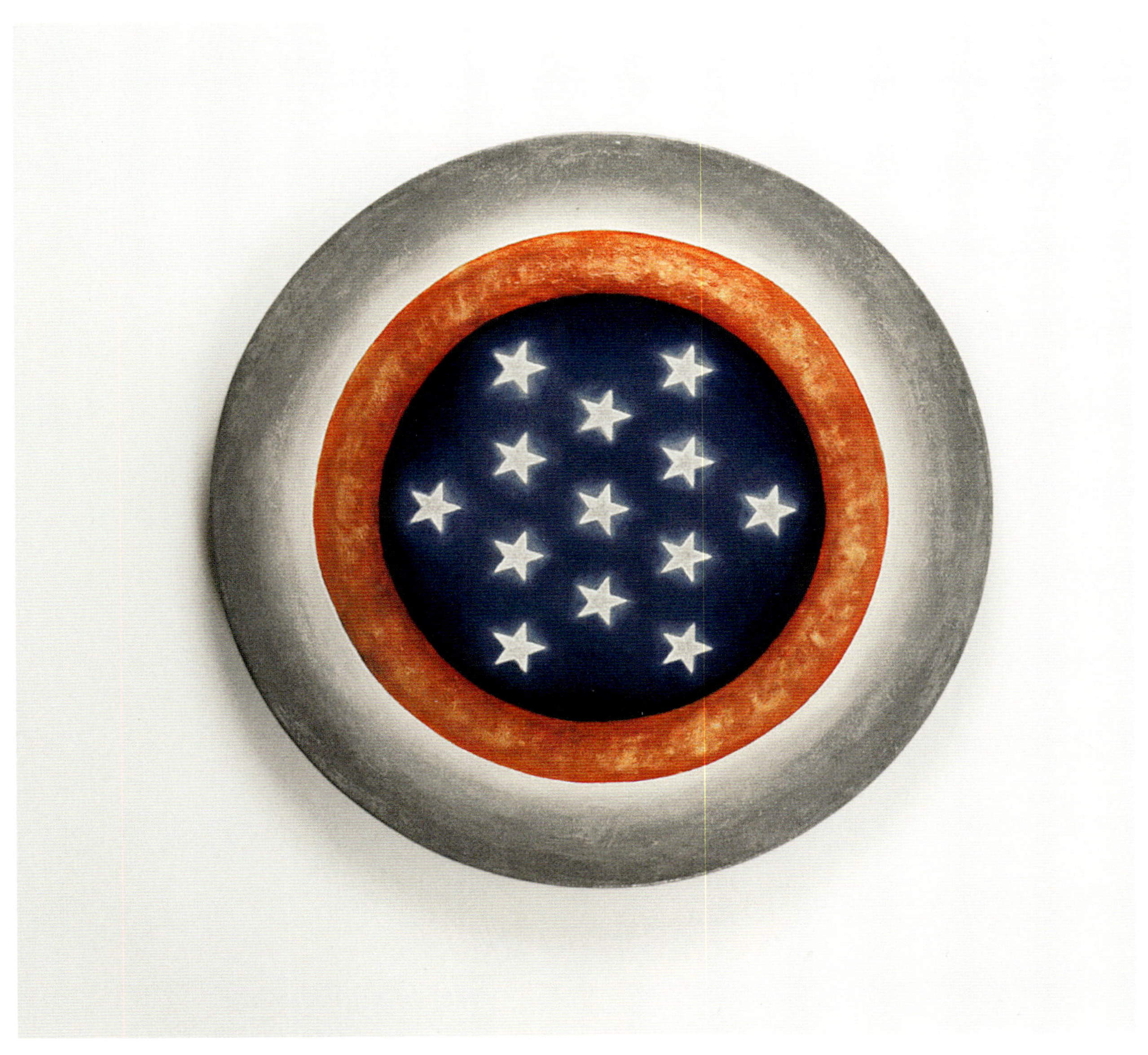

July the Fourth, 1992
Oil on canvas
30 inches diameter

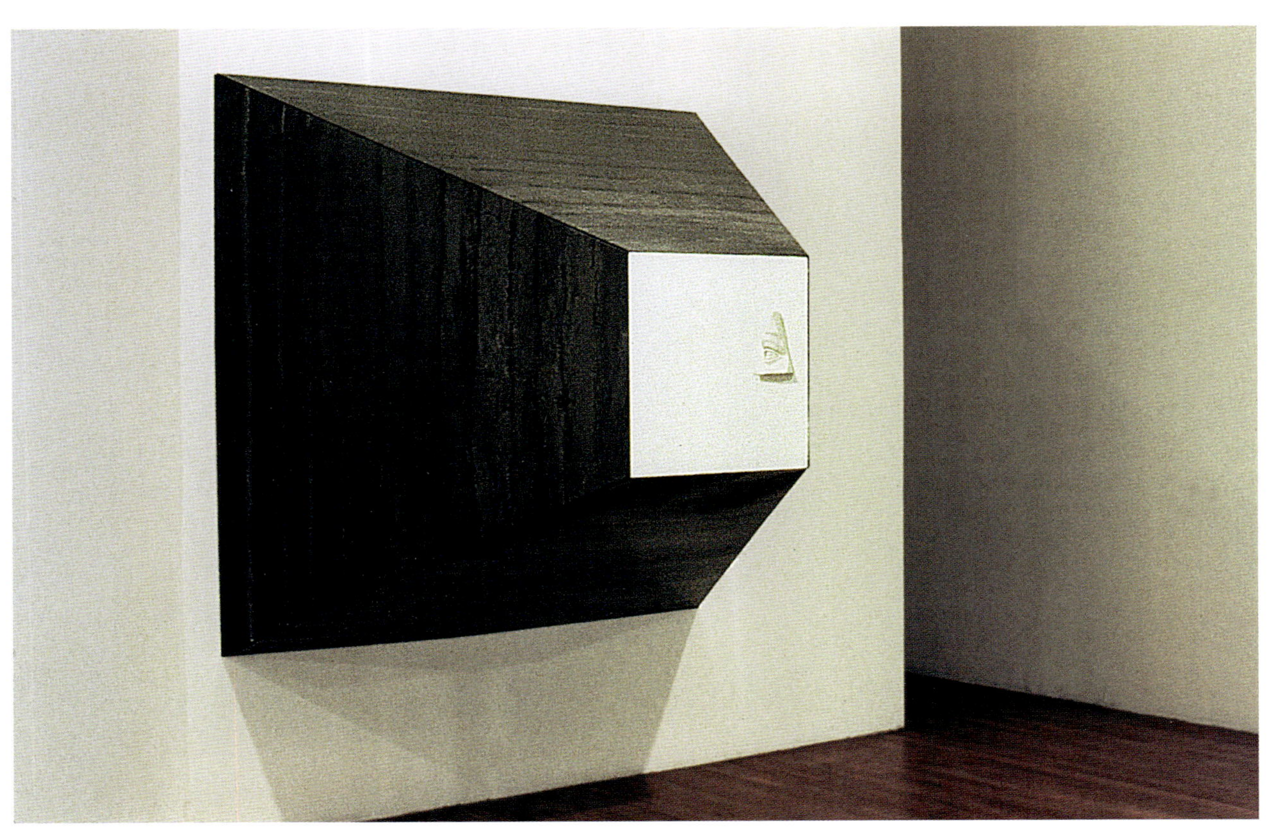

Annuit Coeptis, 1992
Oil paint, steel, mirror
70 x 70 inches

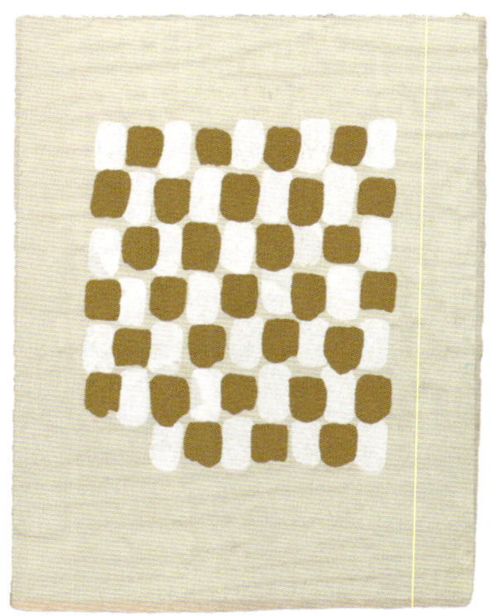

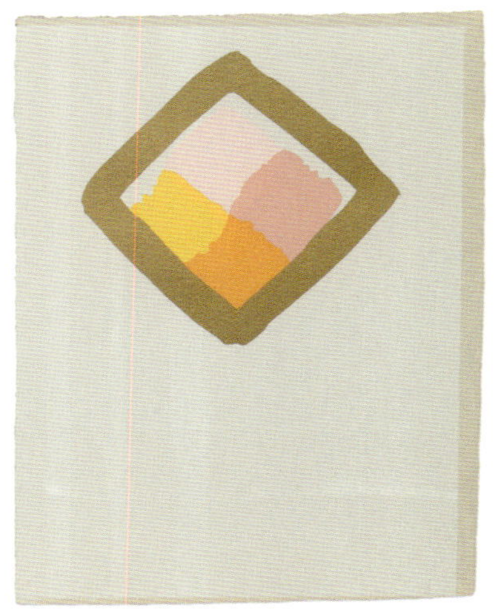
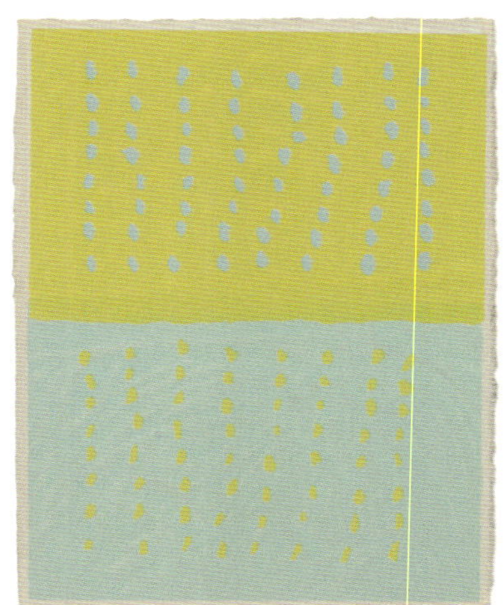
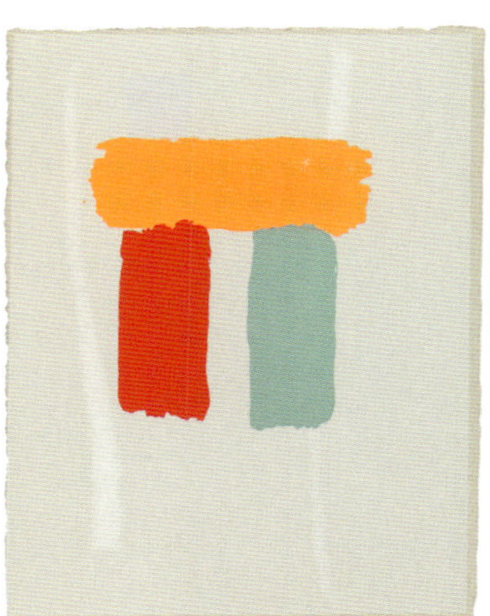

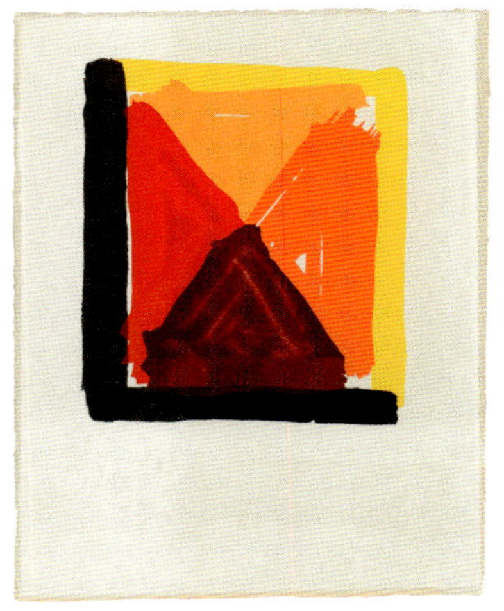
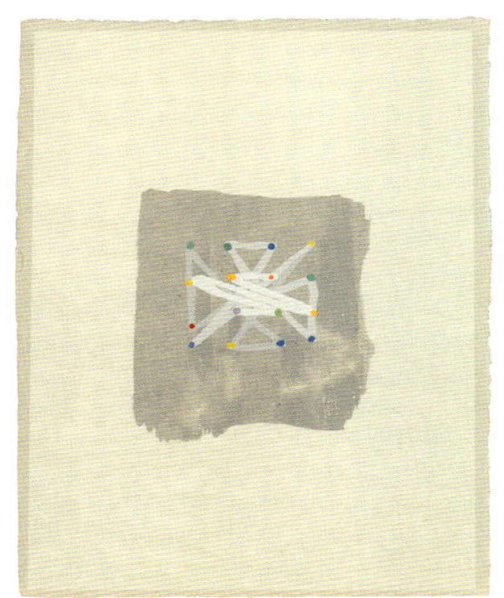
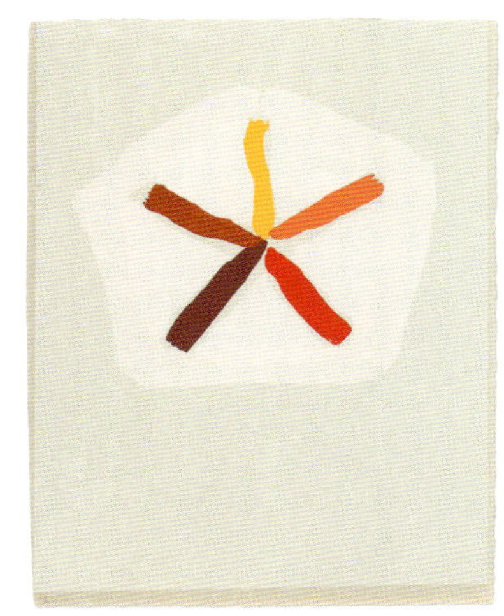

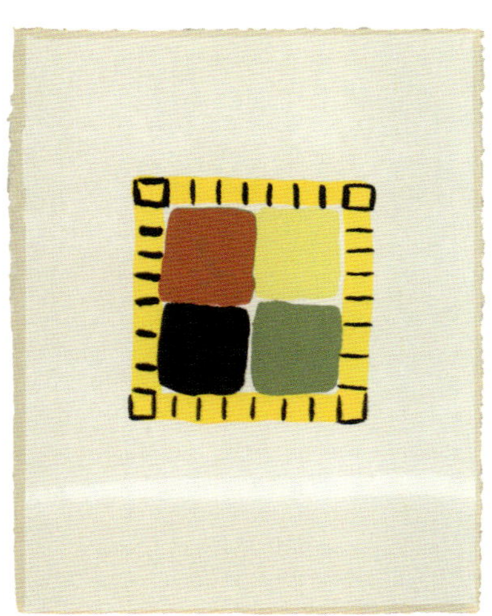

Secret of Youth!, 1992
Silkscreen print portfolio
Edition of 20

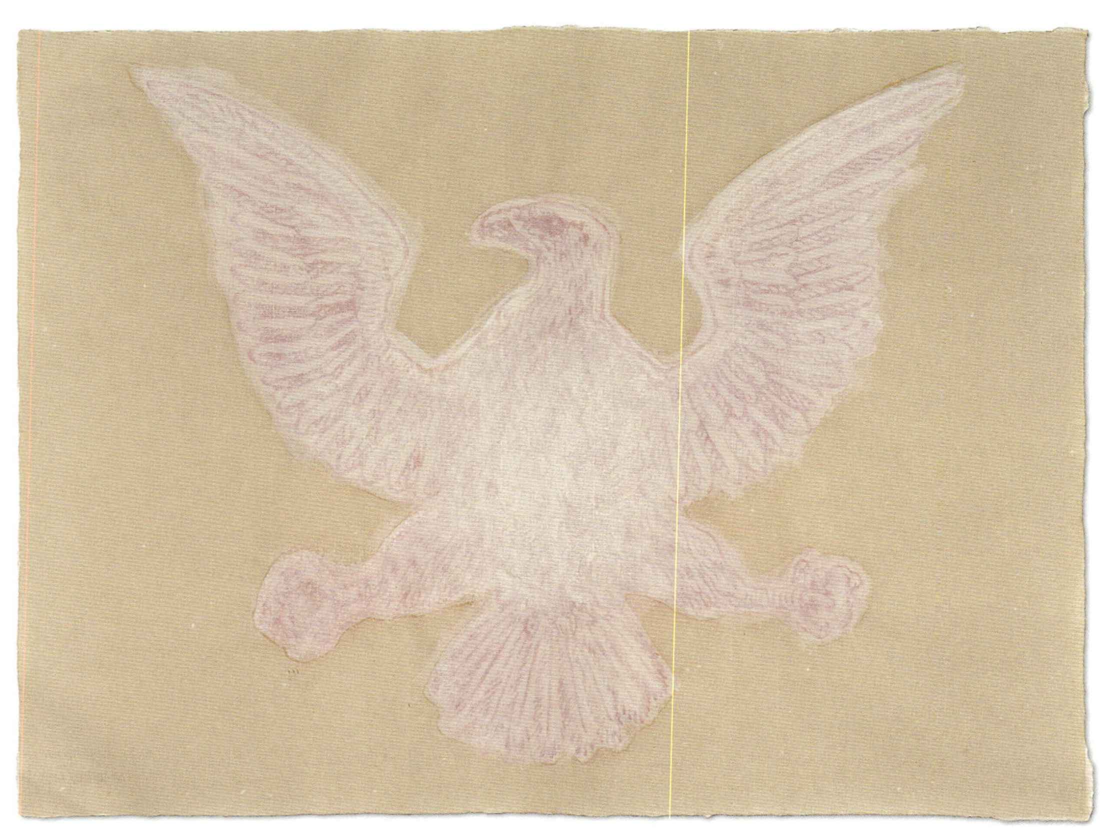

My Desire, 1992
Oil, gesso, Dieu Donne handmade tracing paper
17 x 23 inches

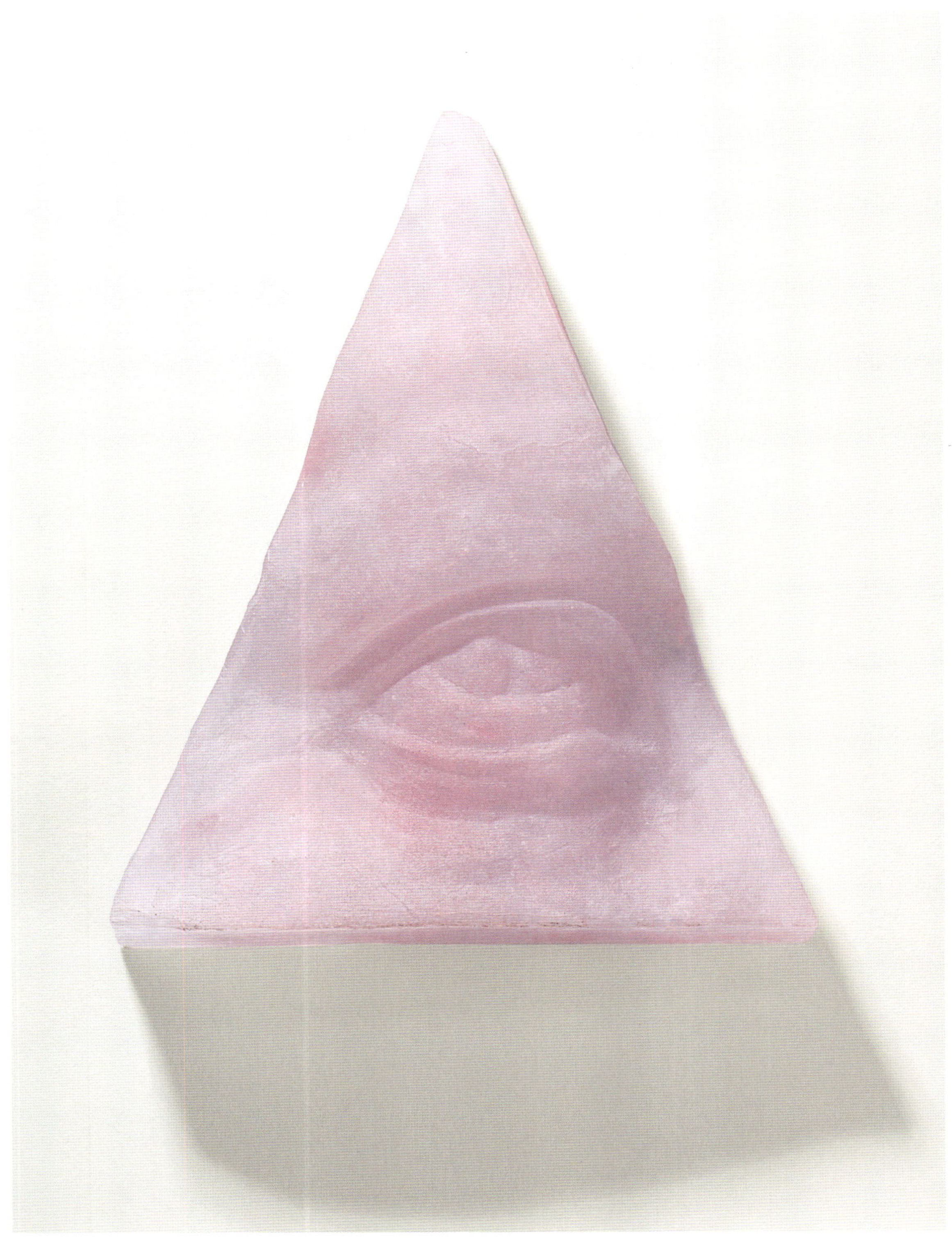

Eye, 1992
Glass
13 x 10 x 2 1/2 inches

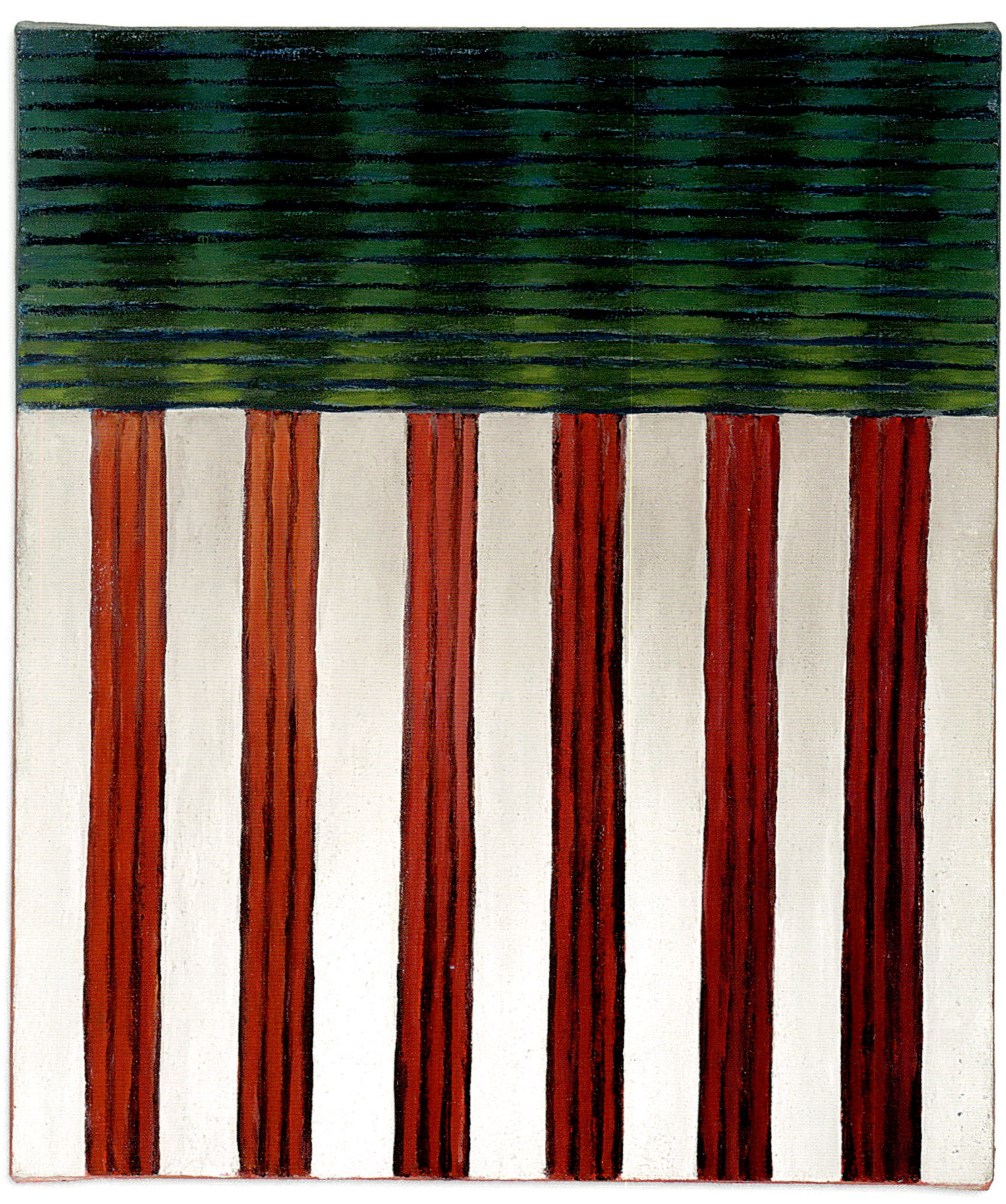

Treetops, 1992
Oil on canvas
34 x 28 inches

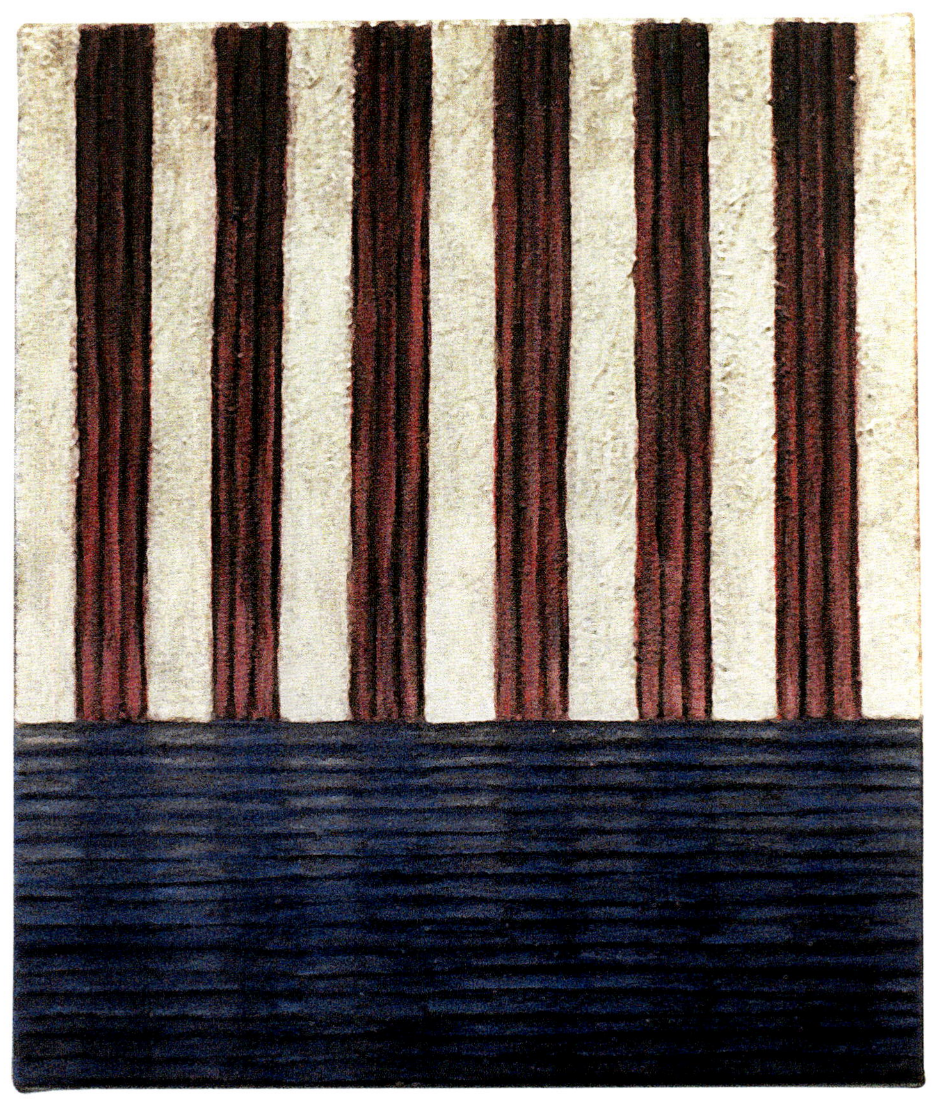

Mohawk Valley, 1992
Oil on canvas
17 x 14 inches

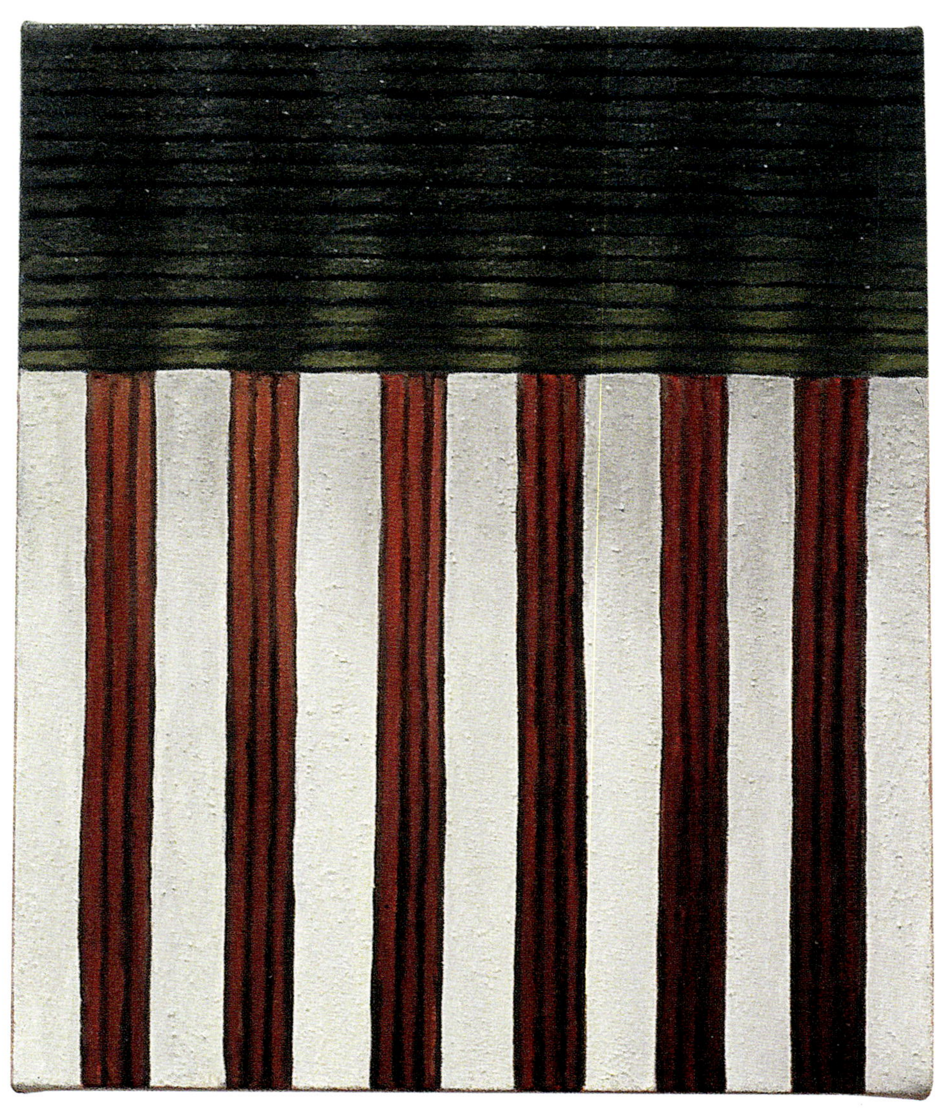

Treetops, 1992
Oil on canvas
17 x 14 inches

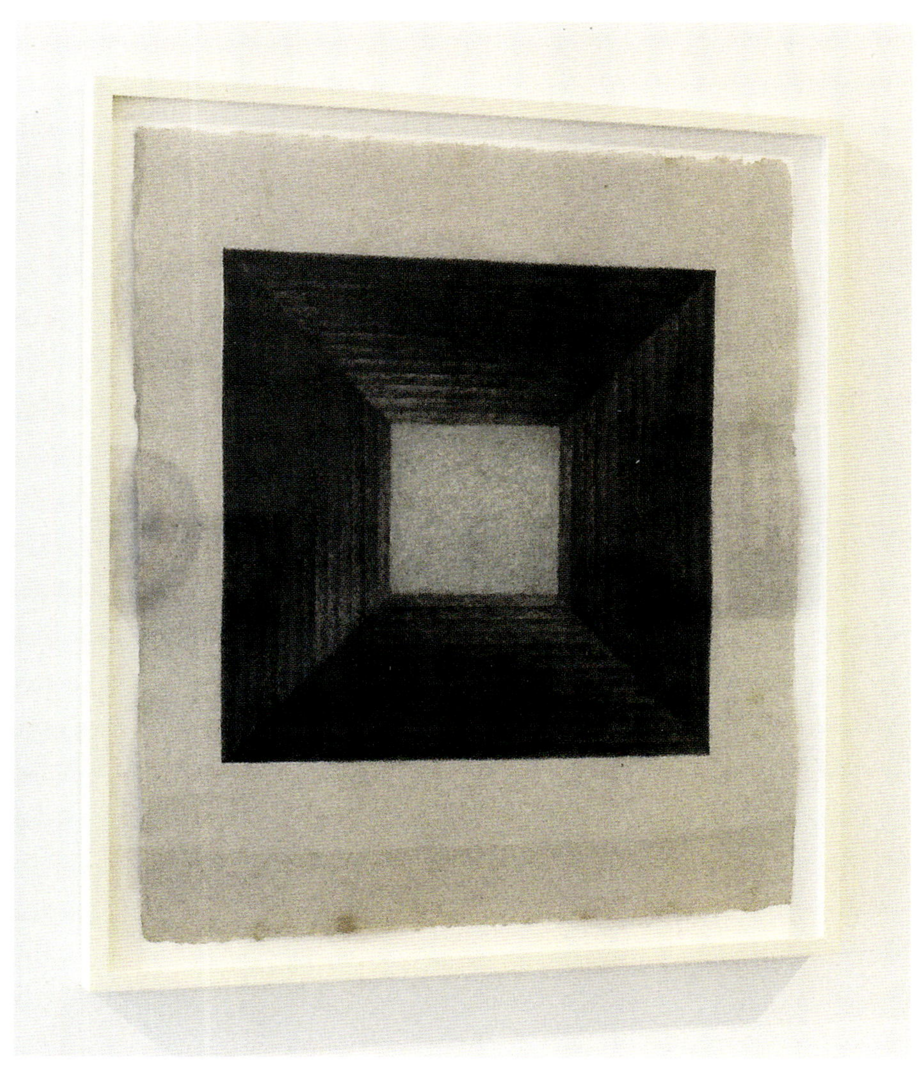

Unfinished Pyramid, 1992
Graphite on paper
27 x 24 inches

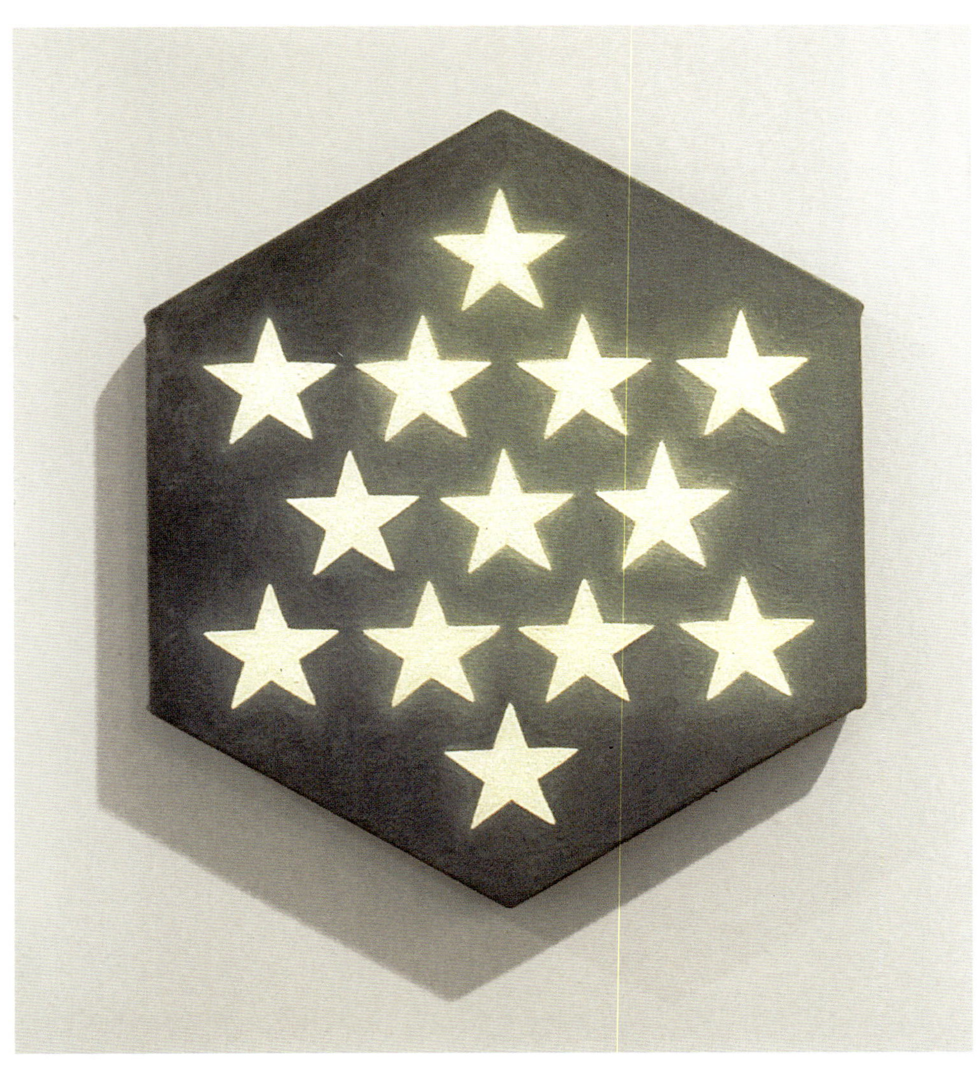

United States of America, 1992
Oil on canvas
16 x 18 inches

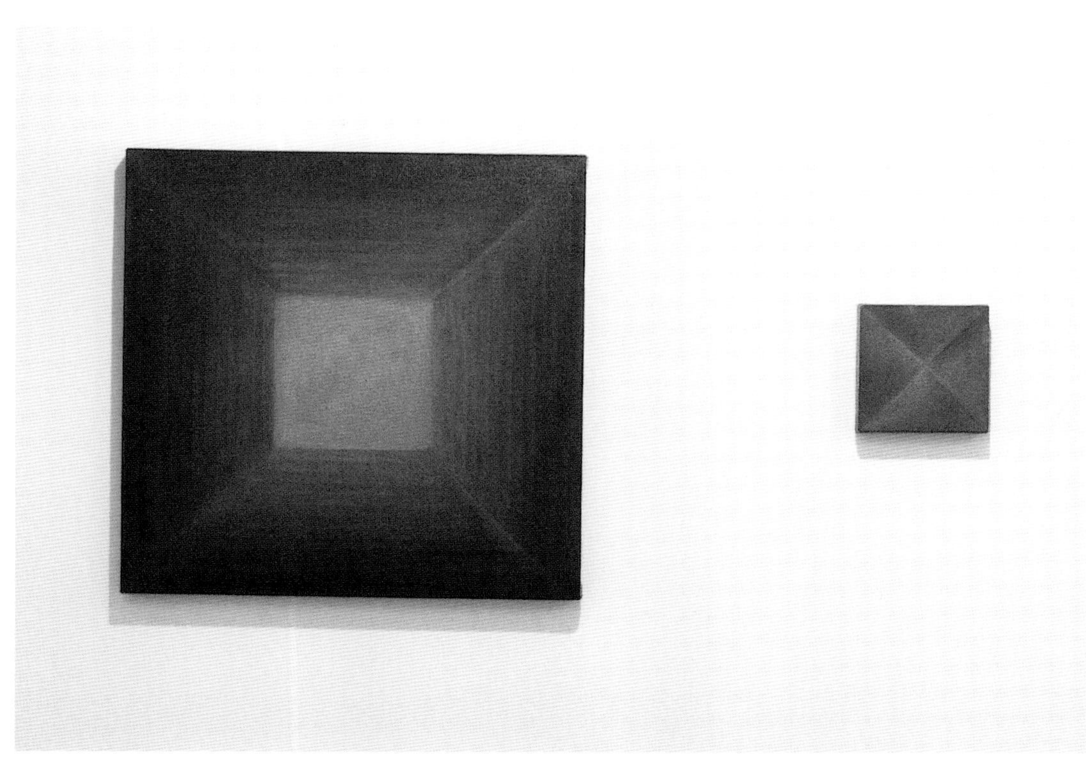

Left: *Unfinished Pyramid,* 1992
Oil on canvas, 35 x 35 inches
Right: *Capstone,* 1992
Oil on canvas, 10 x 10 inches

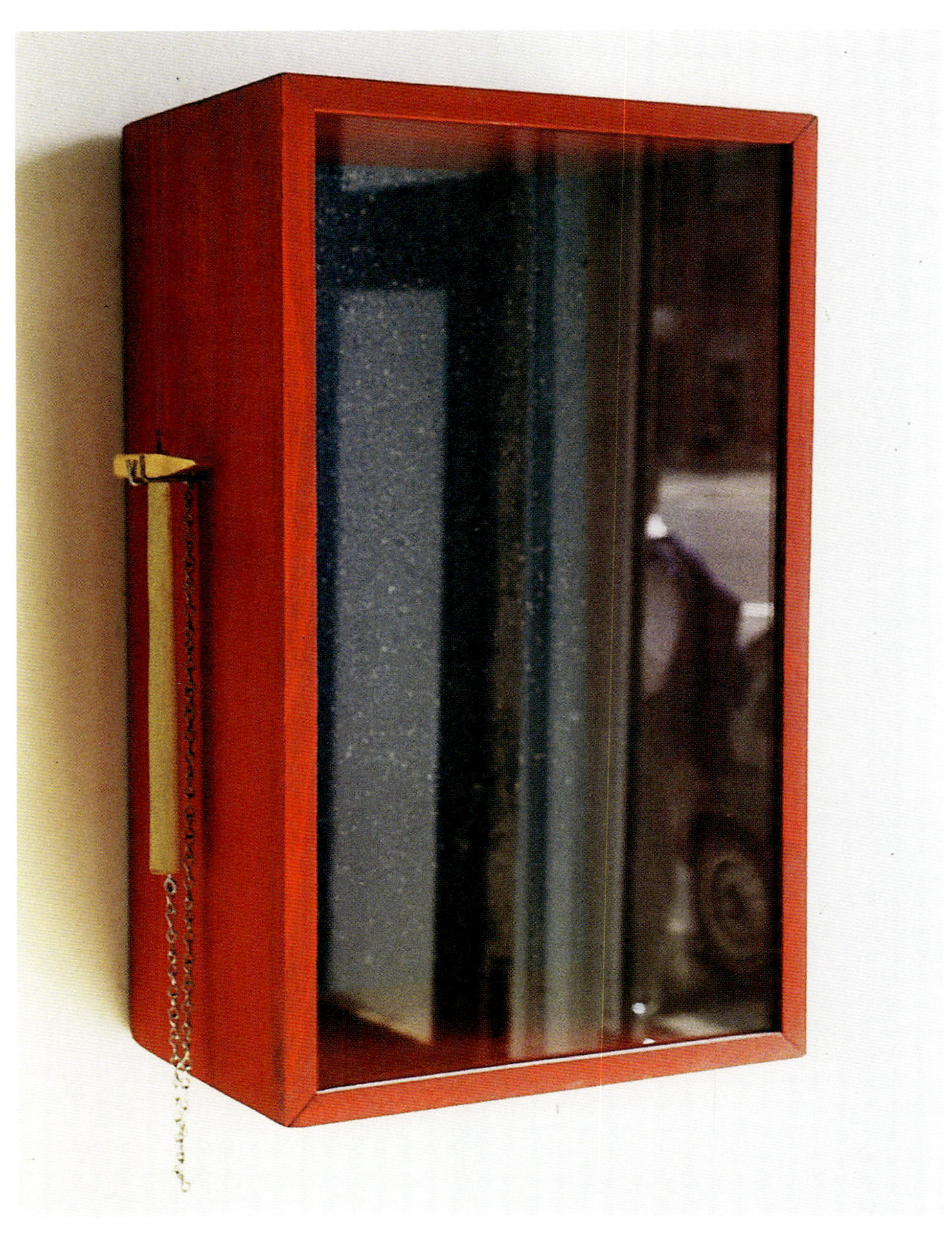

Hidden Entrances, 1994
Hammer, wood, glass, oil, and gold leaf
18 x 12 inches

Hidden Entrances, 1994
Oil on canvas
49 x 36 inches

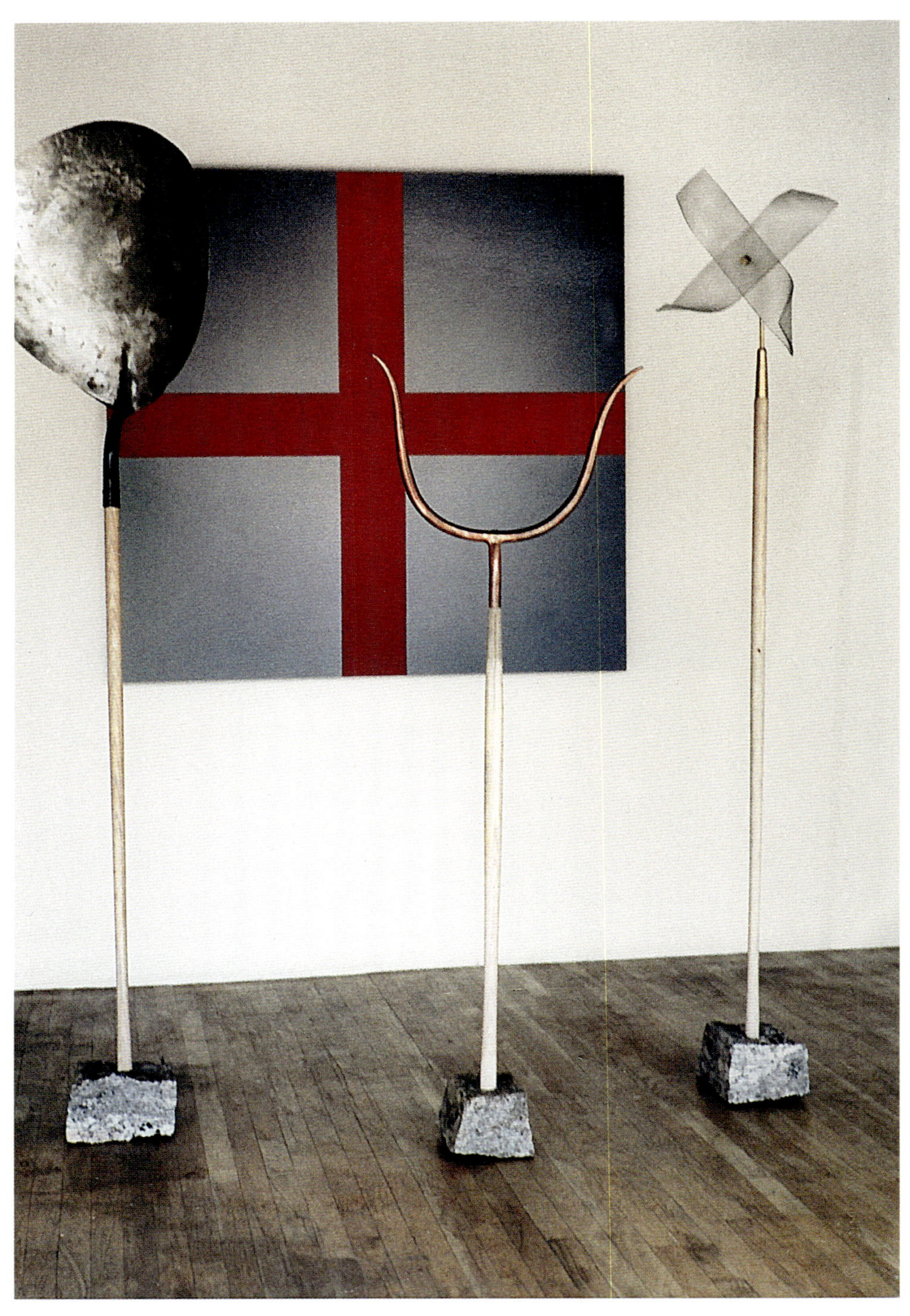

Vertical Minute, 1995
Annika Sundvik Gallery, New York
Installation view

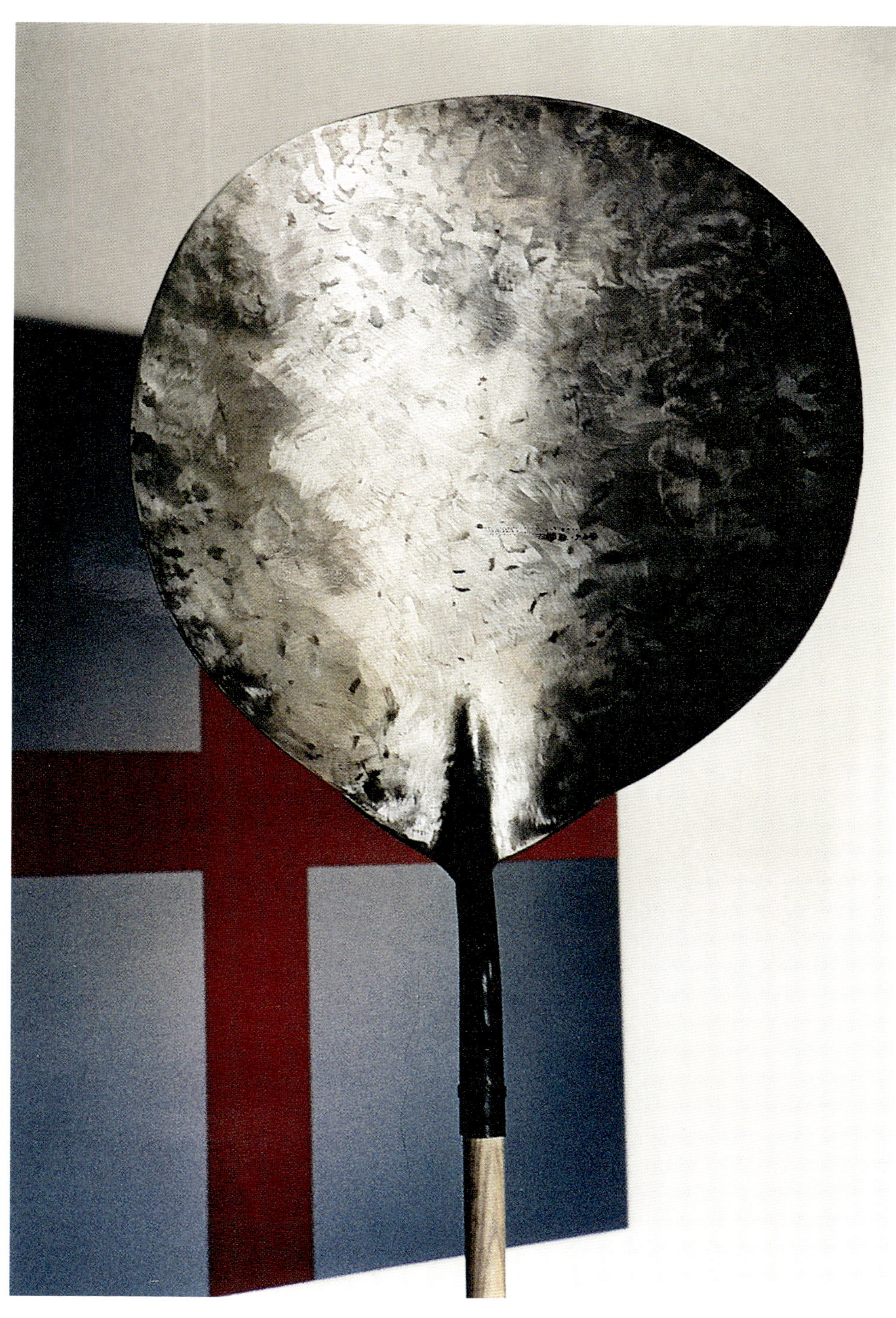

Vertical Minute, 1995
Steel and wood
77 x 22 inches

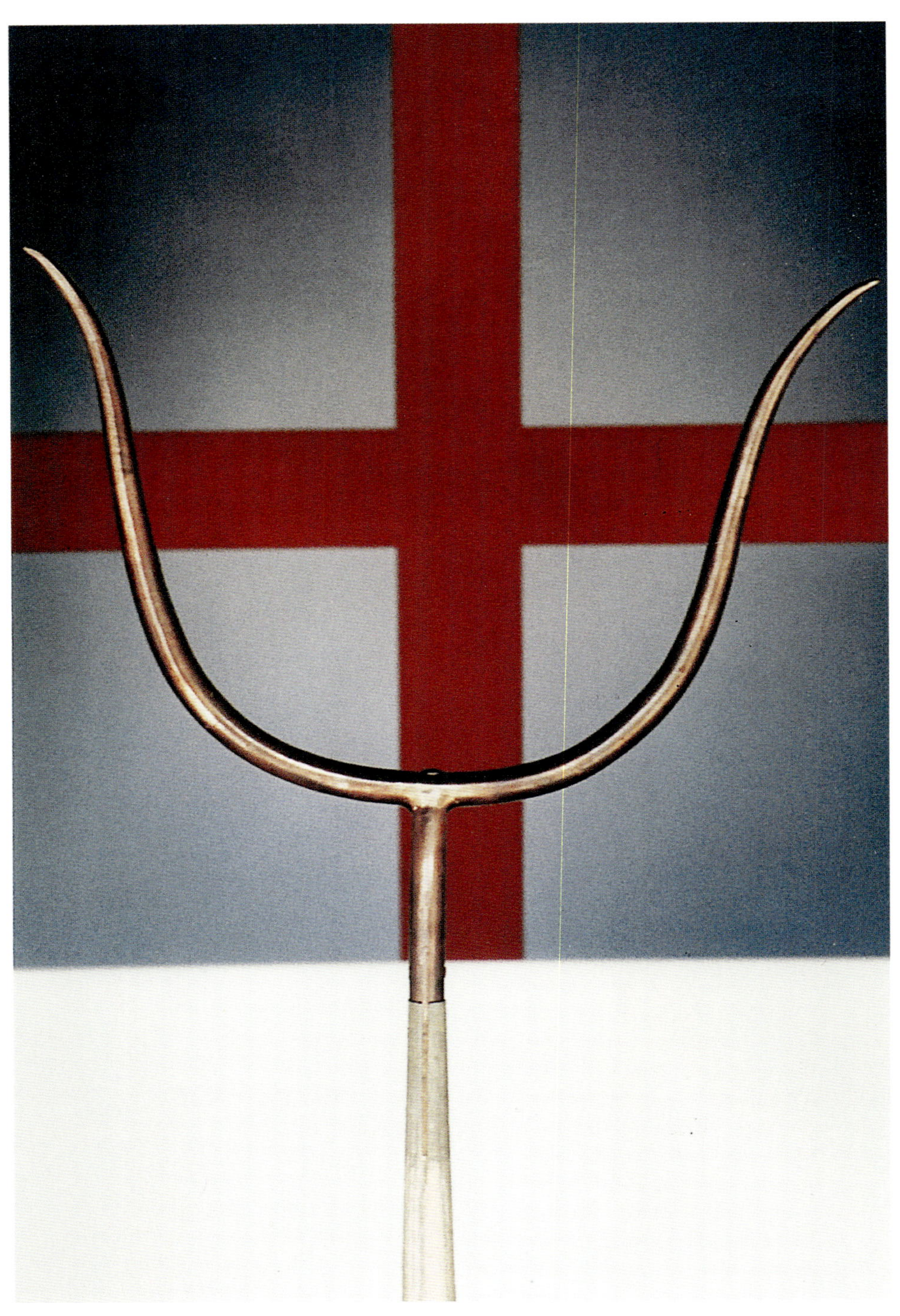

Vertical Minute, 1995
Copper and wood
66 1/2 x 22 inches

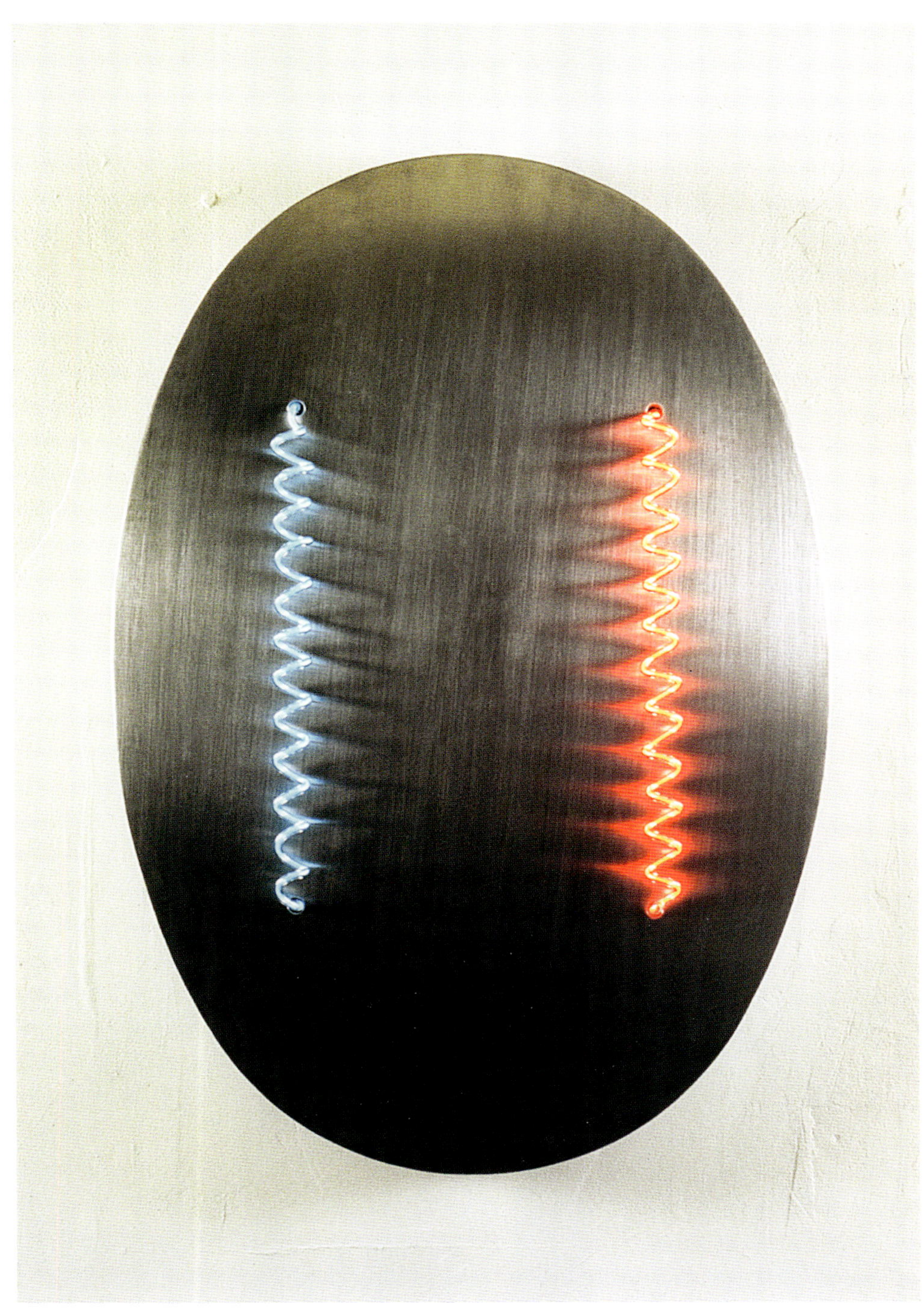

Geologic, 1996
Steel, argon, and neon
24 x 35 inches

Path of the Arrow, 1996
Acrylic on canvas
59 x 47 inches

Phthonos, 1996
Acrylic on canvas
36 x 54 inches

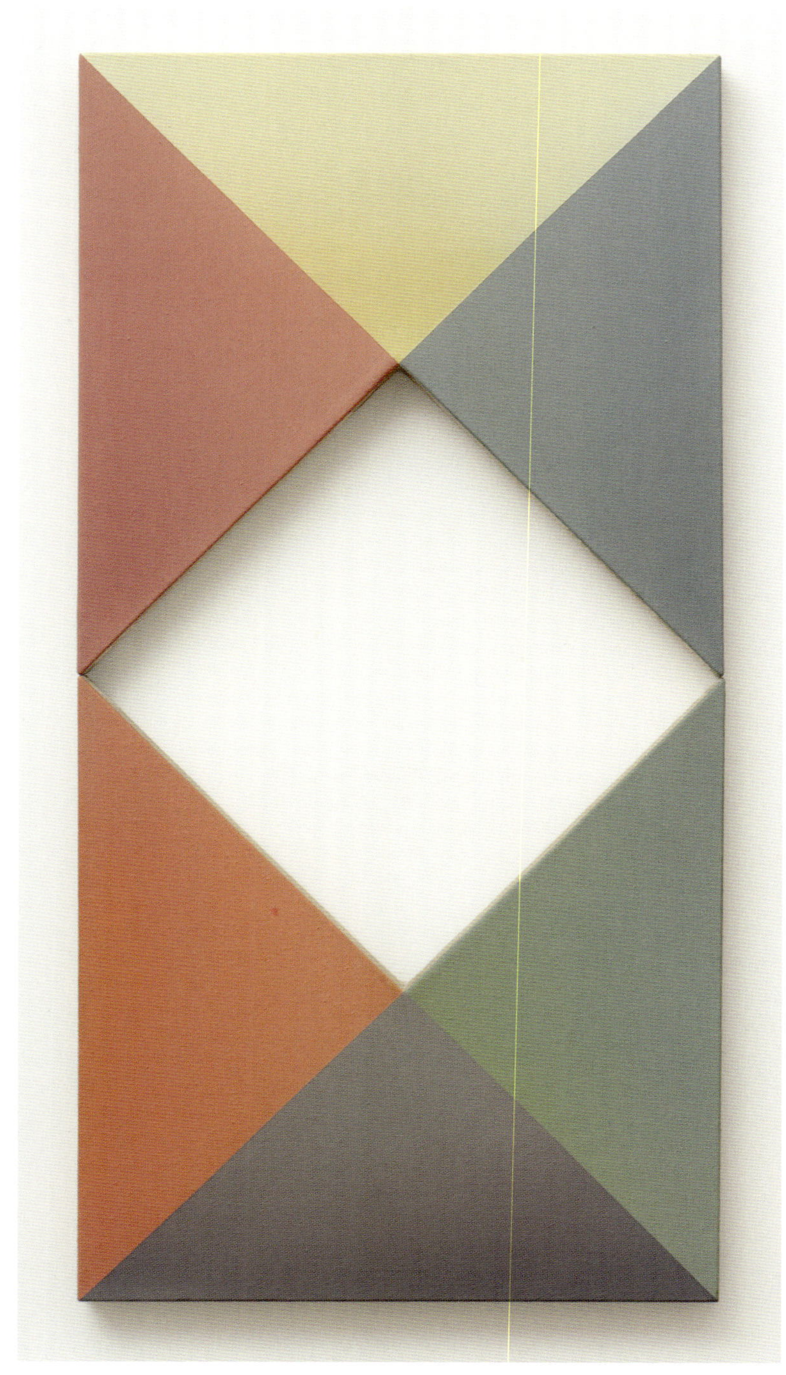

Gate, 1996
Acrylic on canvas
18 x 36 inches

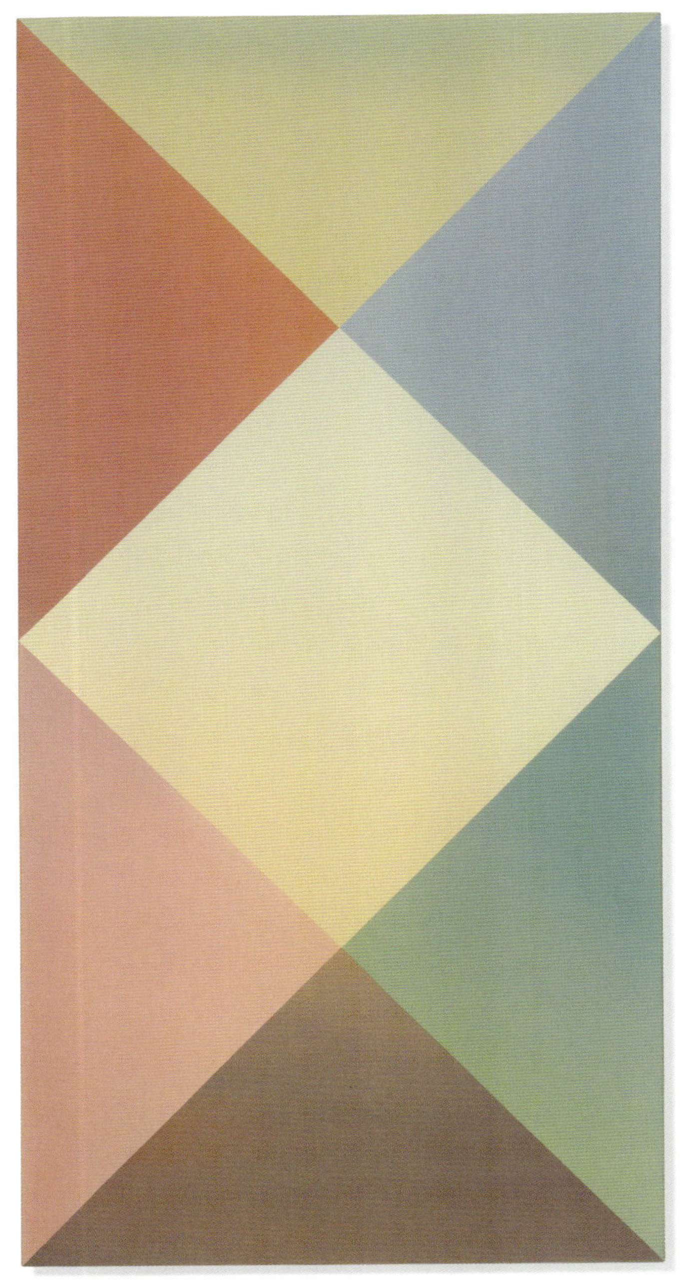

Krana, 1996
Acrylic on canvas
18 x 36 inches

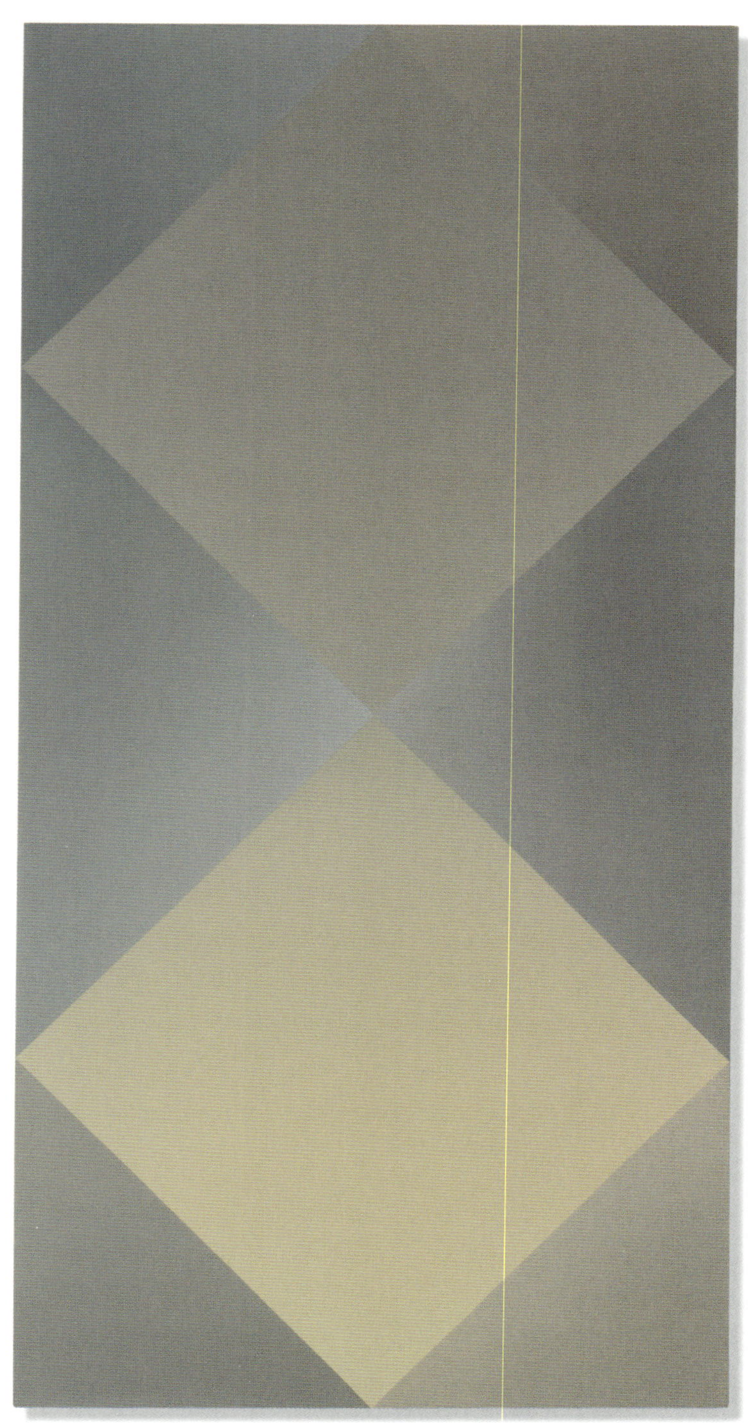

Throne, 1996
Acrylic on linen
51 x 25 1/2 inches

Sounding, 1996
Acrylic on linen
35 x 24 inches

Magneto, 1996
Acrylic on linen
12 3/4 x 12 3/4 inches

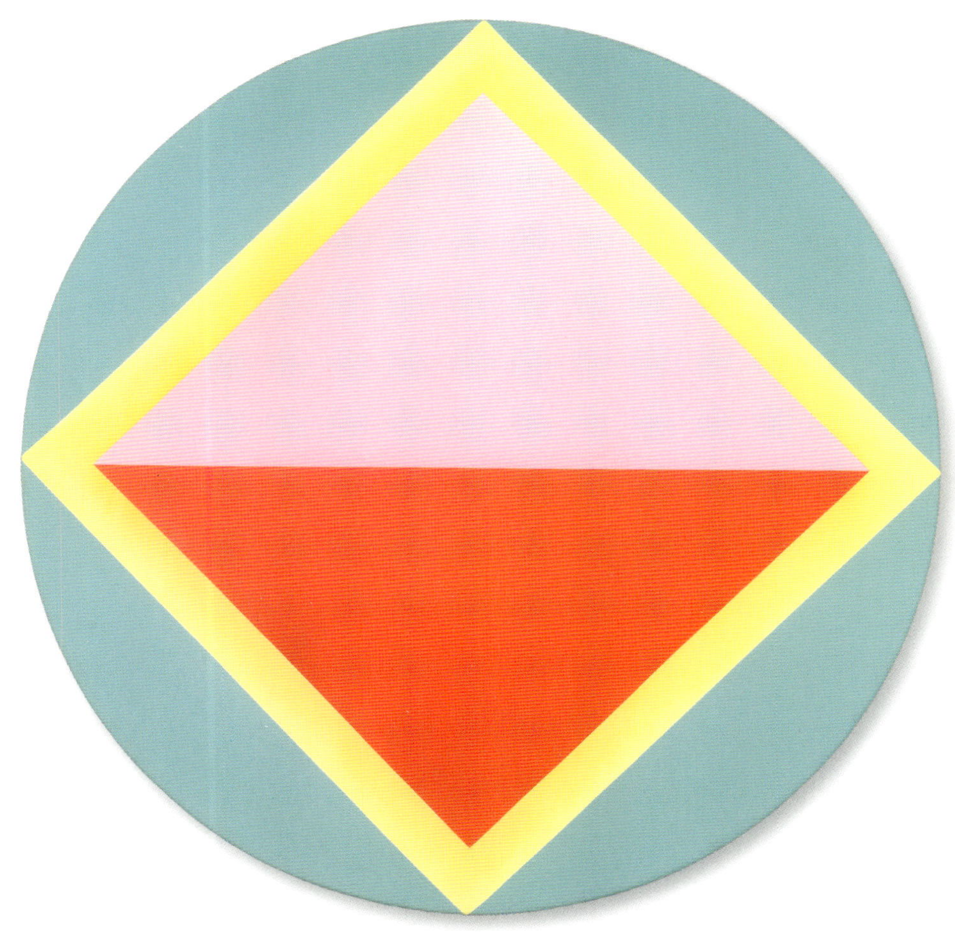

Easy Life Charm, 1996
Acrylic on linen
18 inch diameter

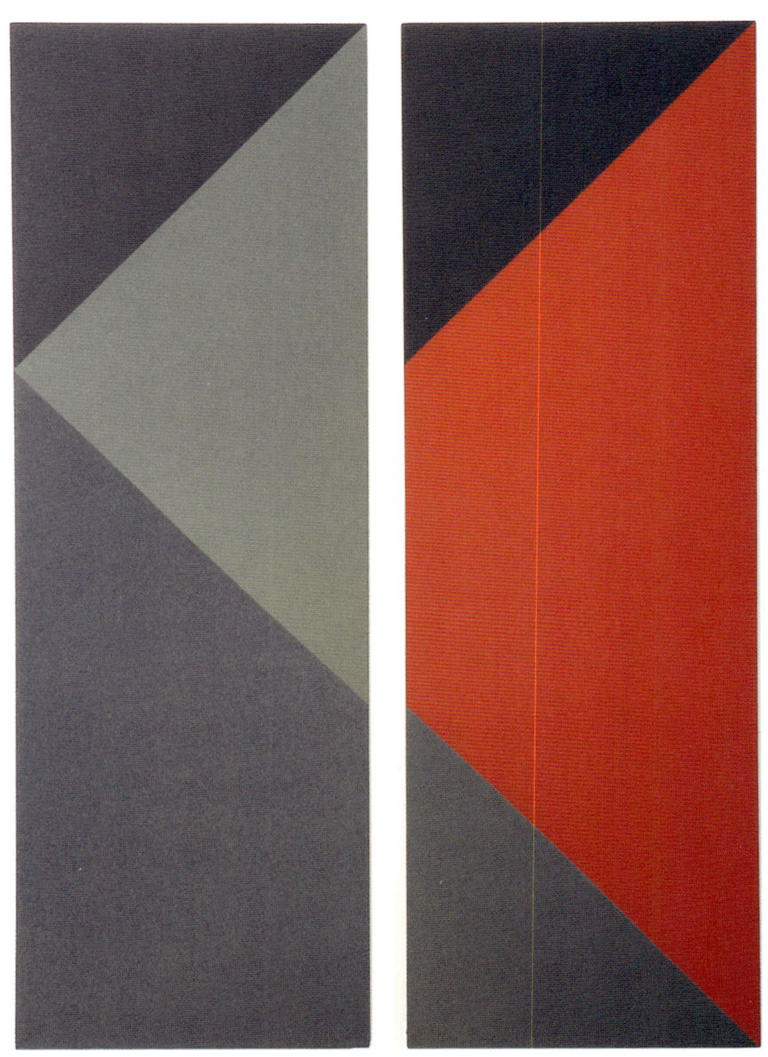

Resh, 1997
Acrylic on canvas
2 panels, 48 x 17 inches each

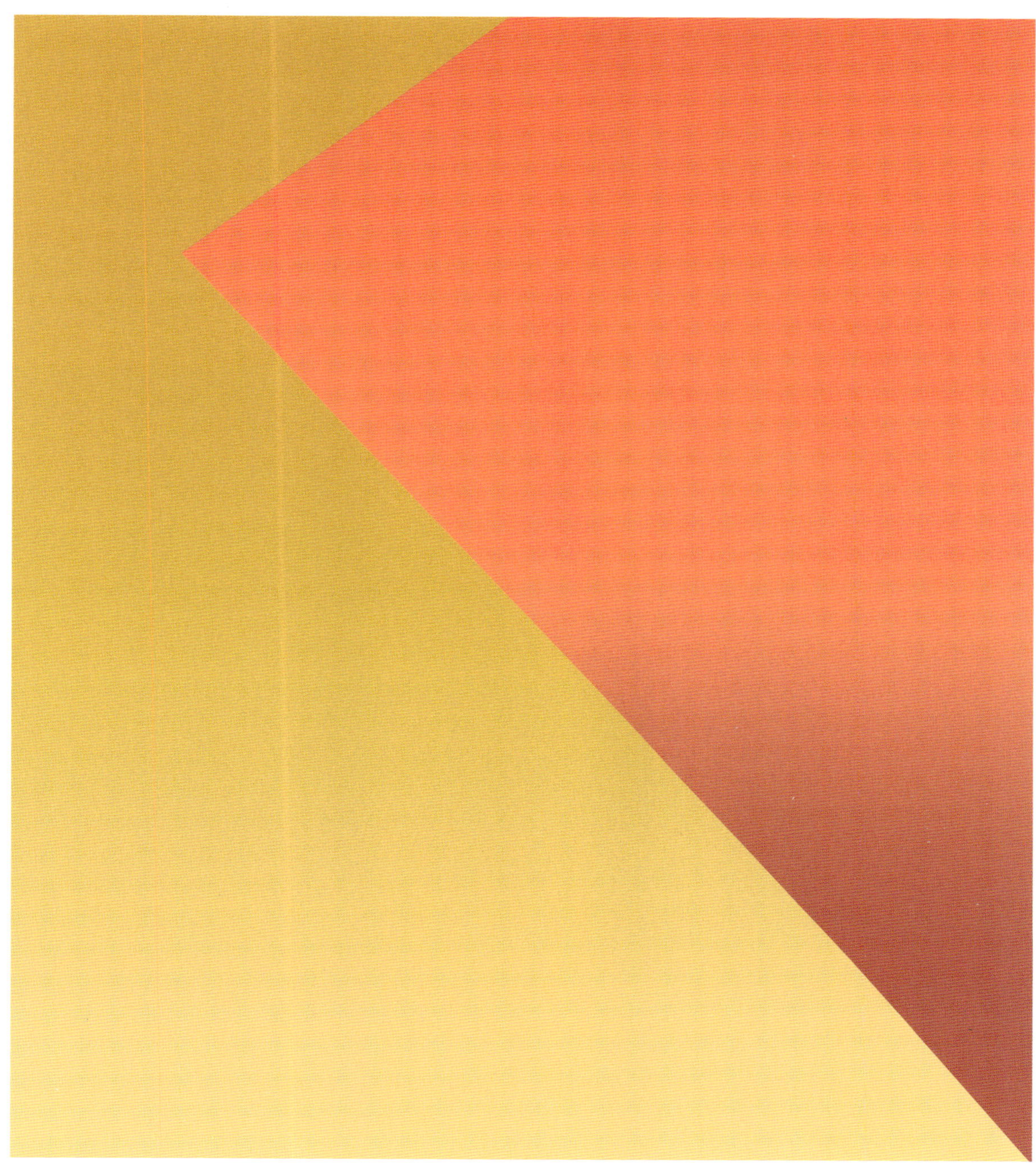

Nakiel, 1997–1999
Acrylic on canvas
56 x 66 inches

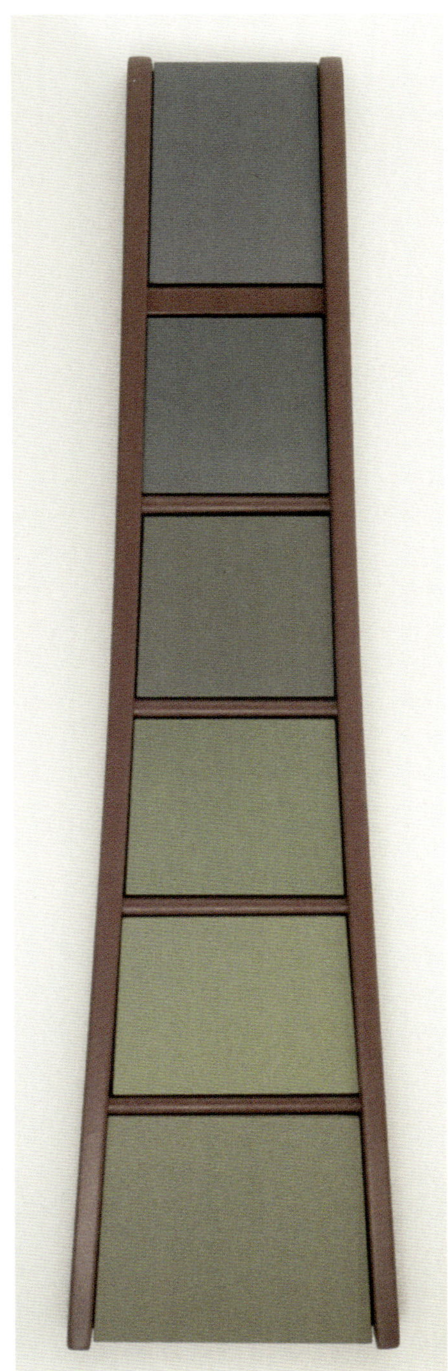

Minium, 1997–1999
Lacquer, acrylic, wood, and canvas
72 x 17 x 3 inches

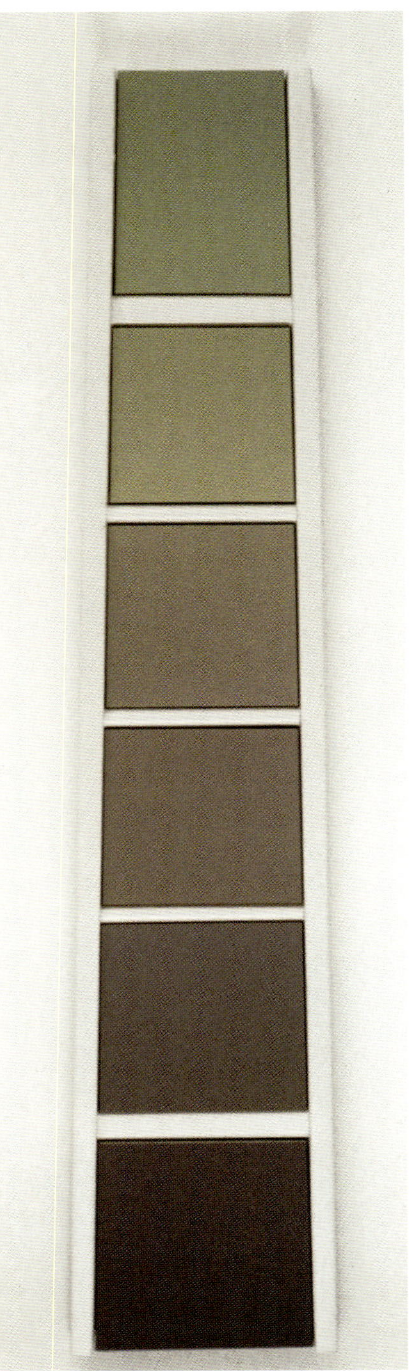

Pearl, 1997–1999
Lacquer, acrylic, wood, and canvas
72 x 15 x 3 inches

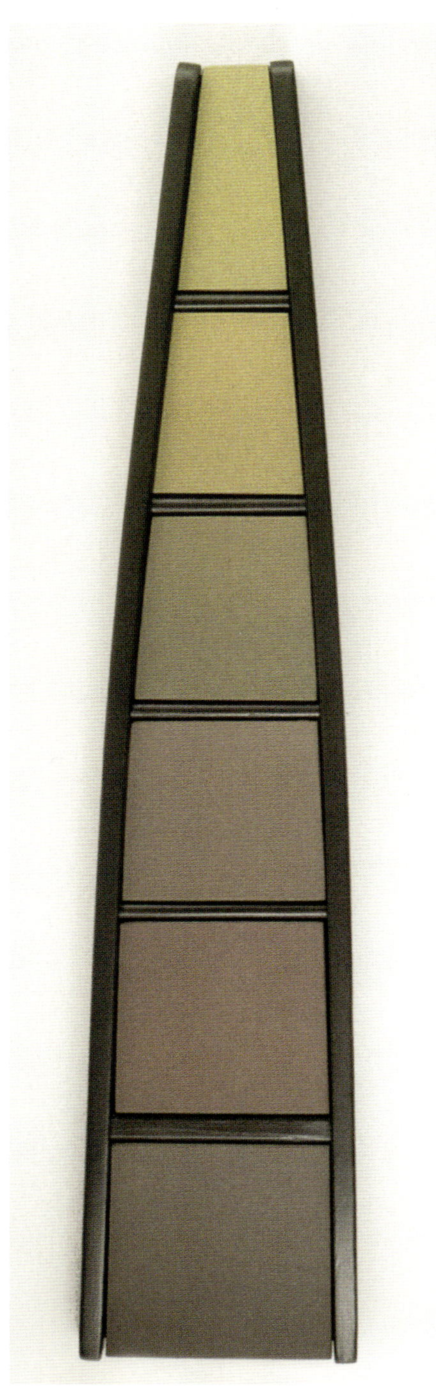

Iron Glimmer, 1997–1999
Lacquer, acrylic, wood, and canvas
72 x 15 x 3 inches

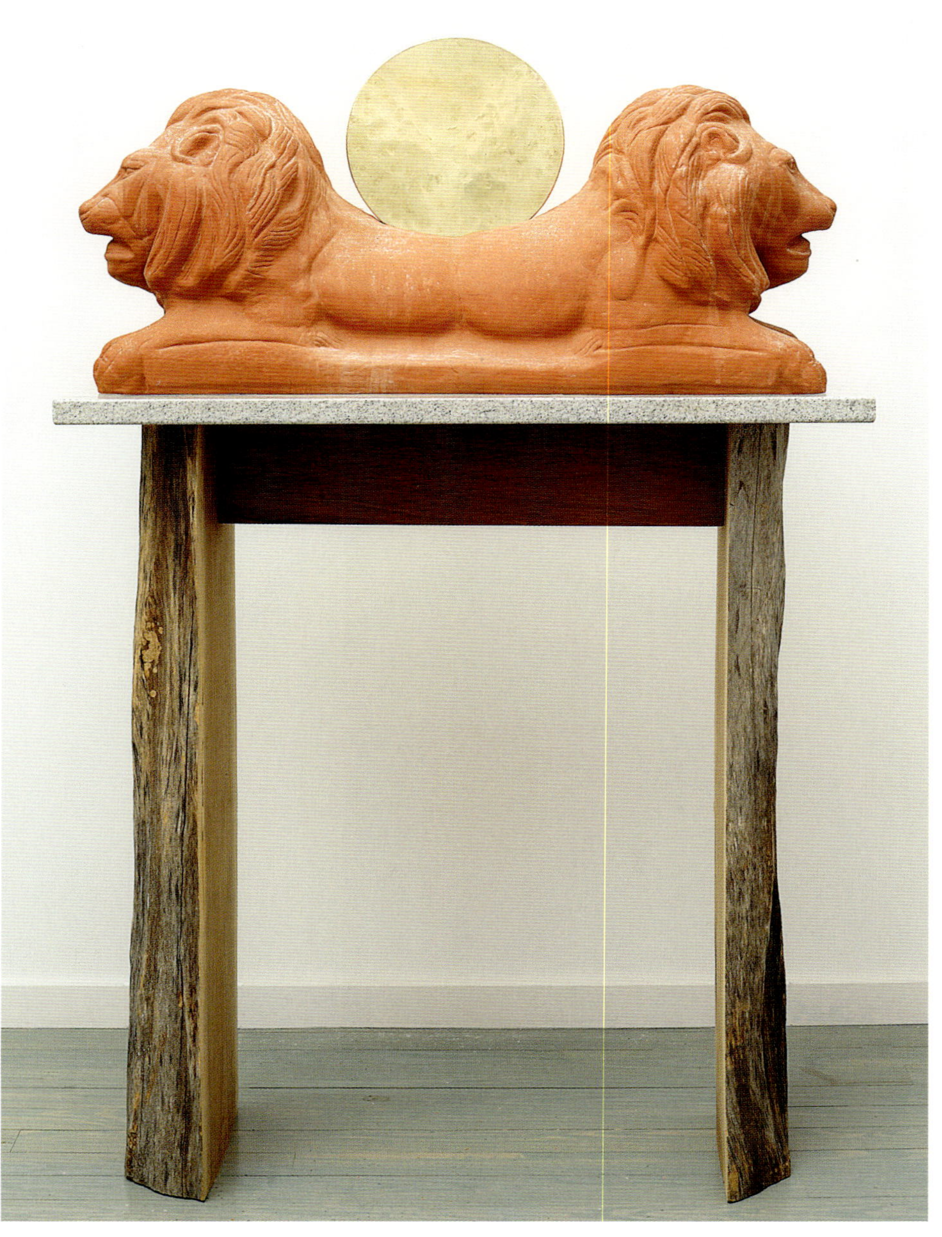

Lionheart, 1997–1999
Clay and brass
57 x 36 x 15 inches

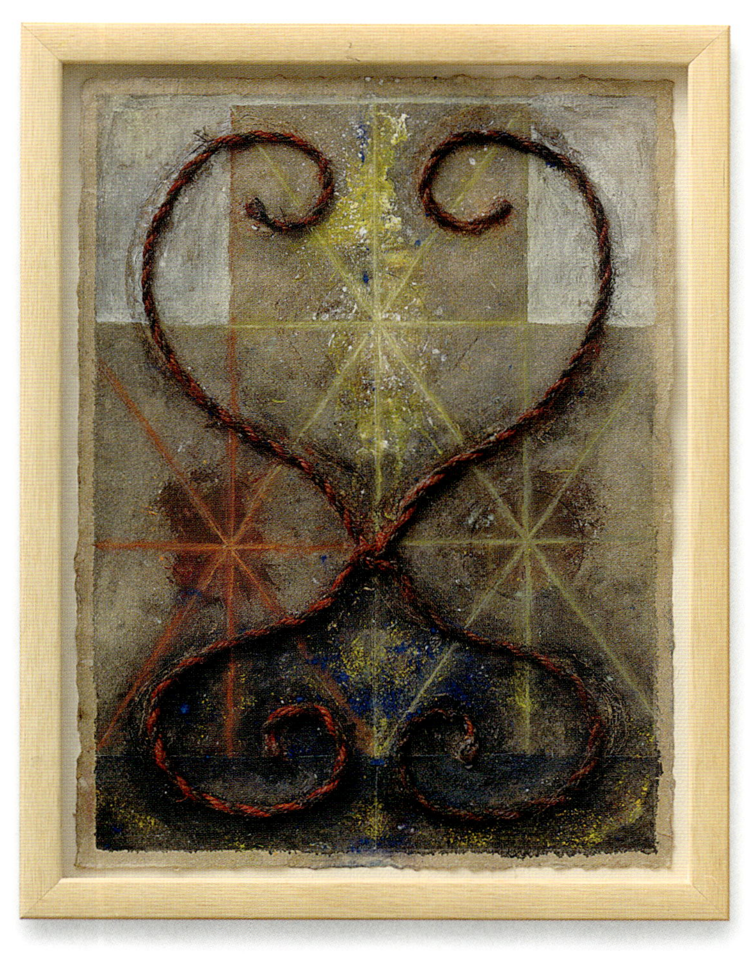

Magistral, 1998
Mixed media
15 1/4 x 11 inches

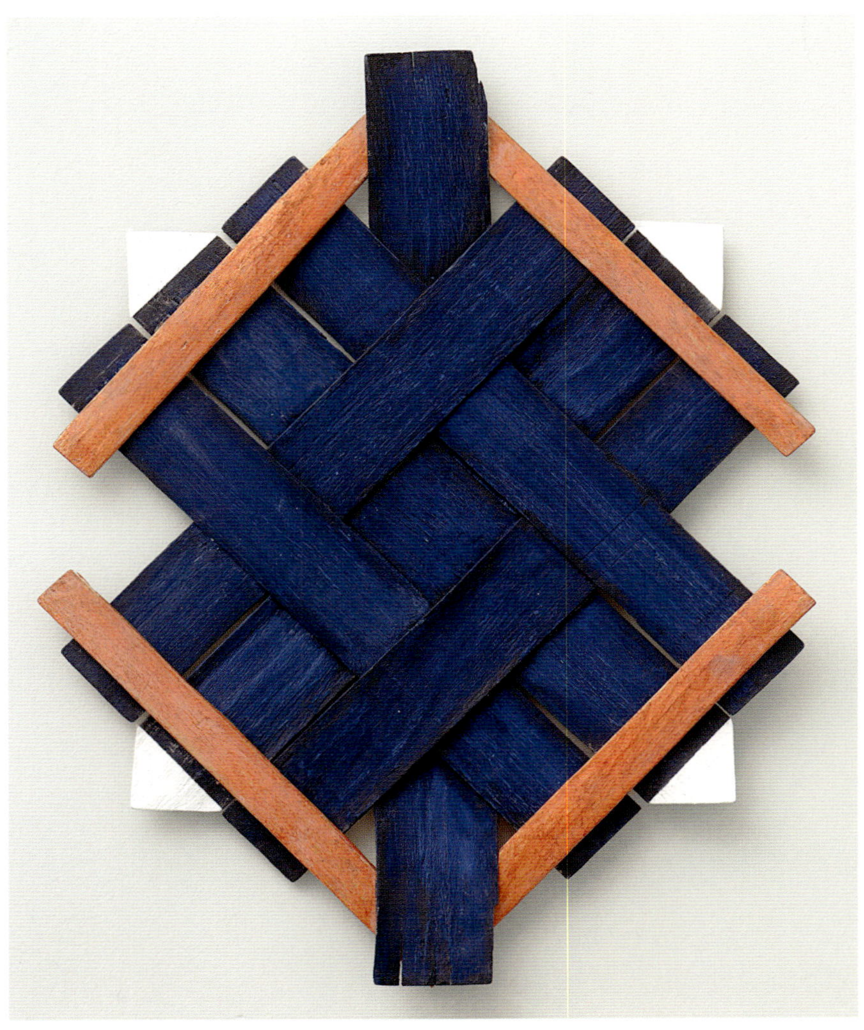

Untitled, 1998
Oil on wood
19 x 14 3/4 inches

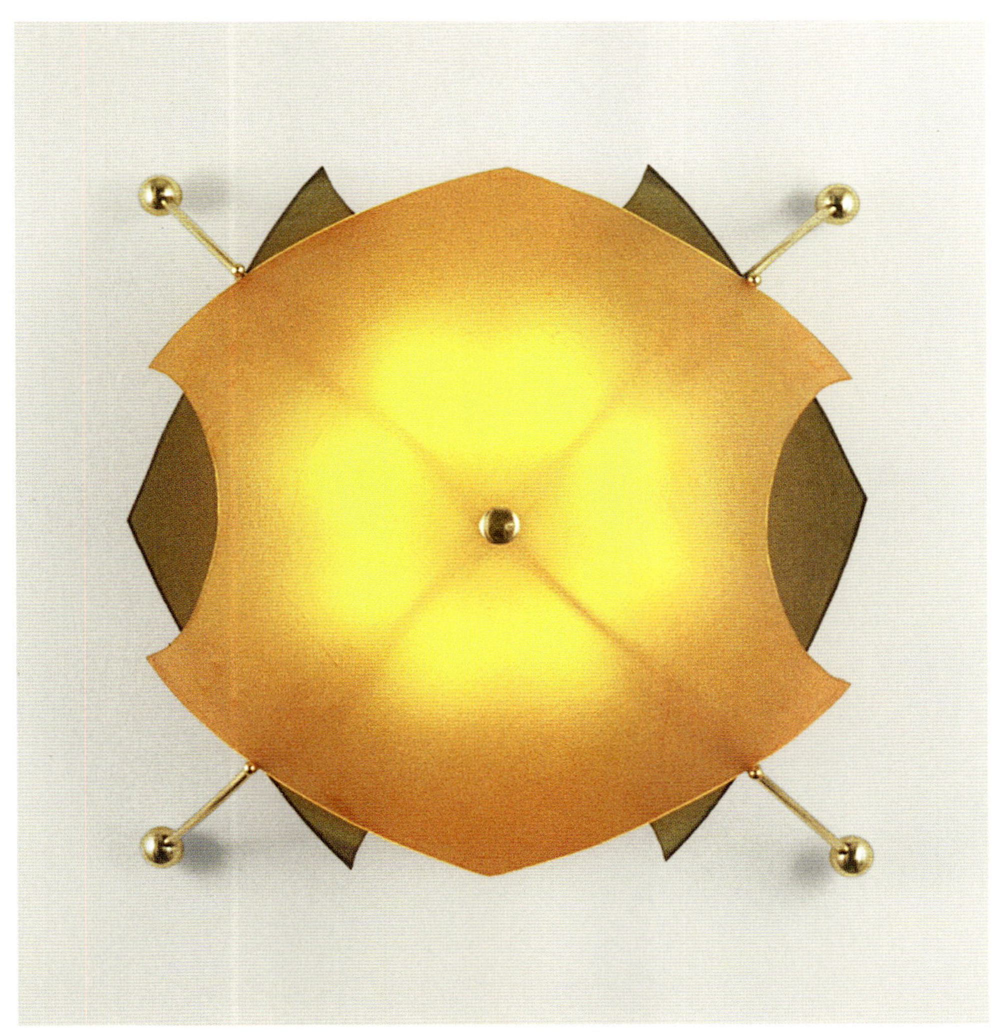

K-4, 1999
Glass, brass, and K-4
17 x 17 inches

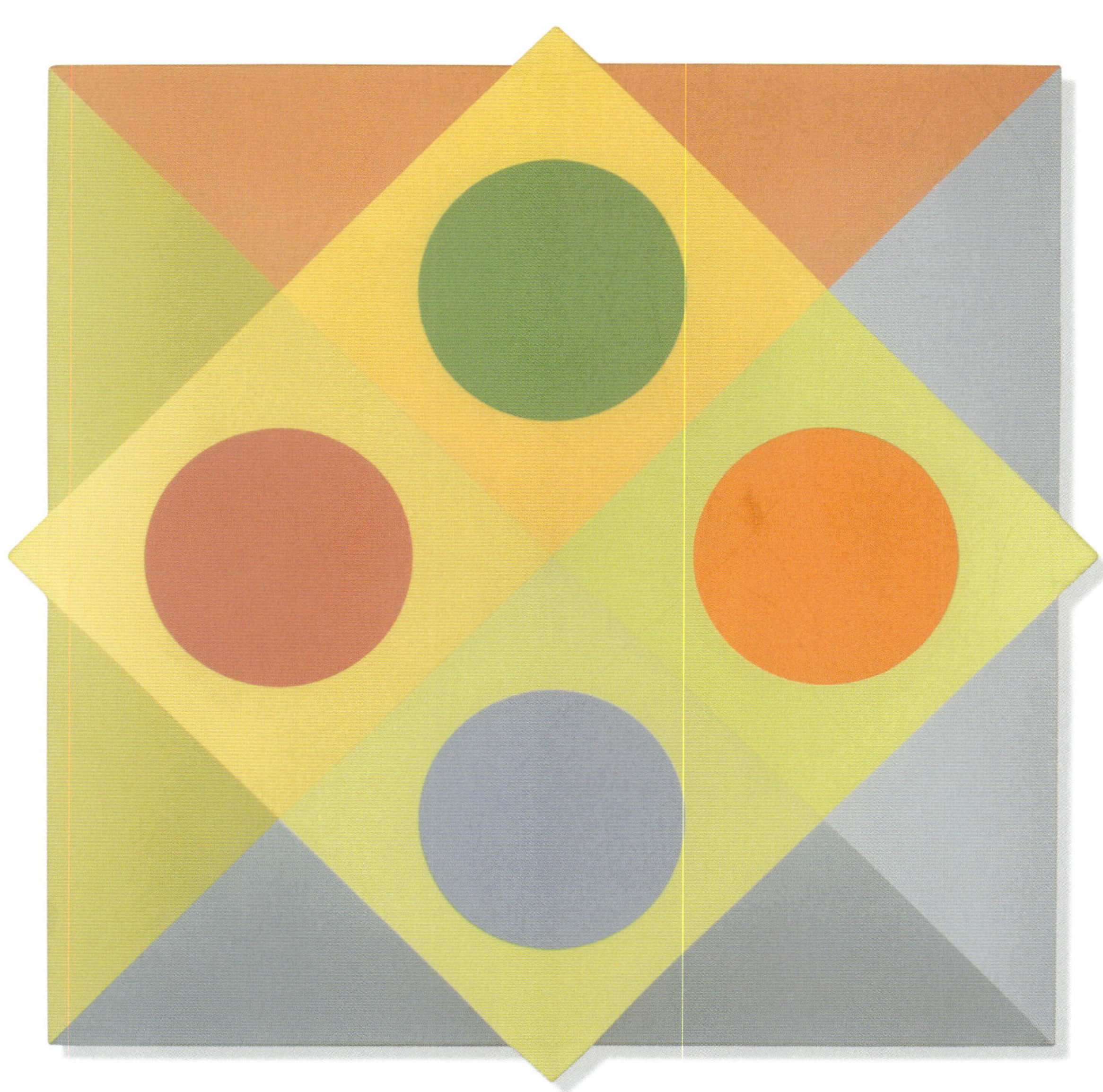

Cameo, 1999
Acrylic on canvas
28 x 28 inches

Khet, 1999
Plaster, encaustic, and linen
34 x 34 inches

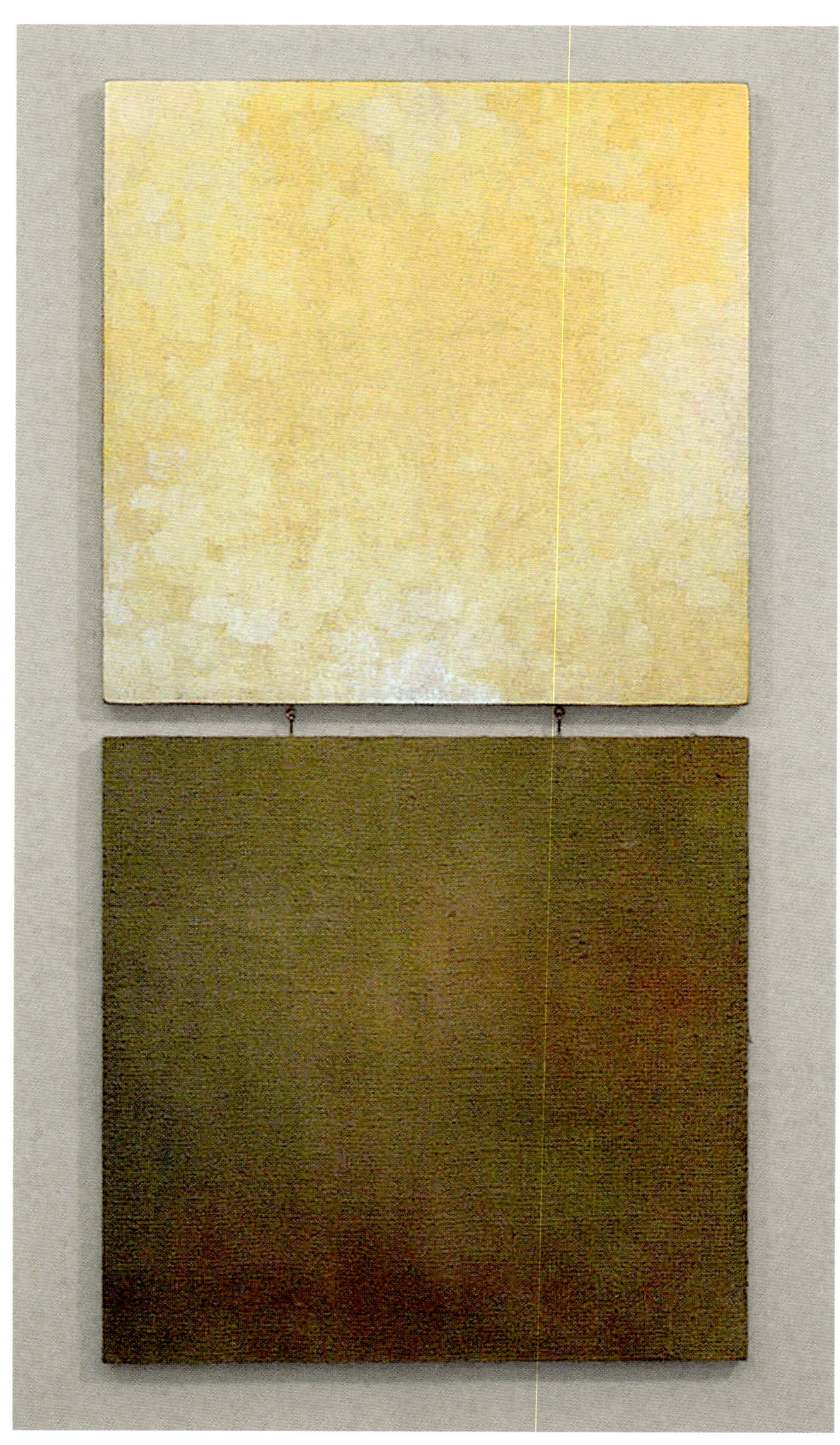

Hook-Up, 2001–2002
Encaustic, gold leaf, burlap, and wood
39 x 19 inches

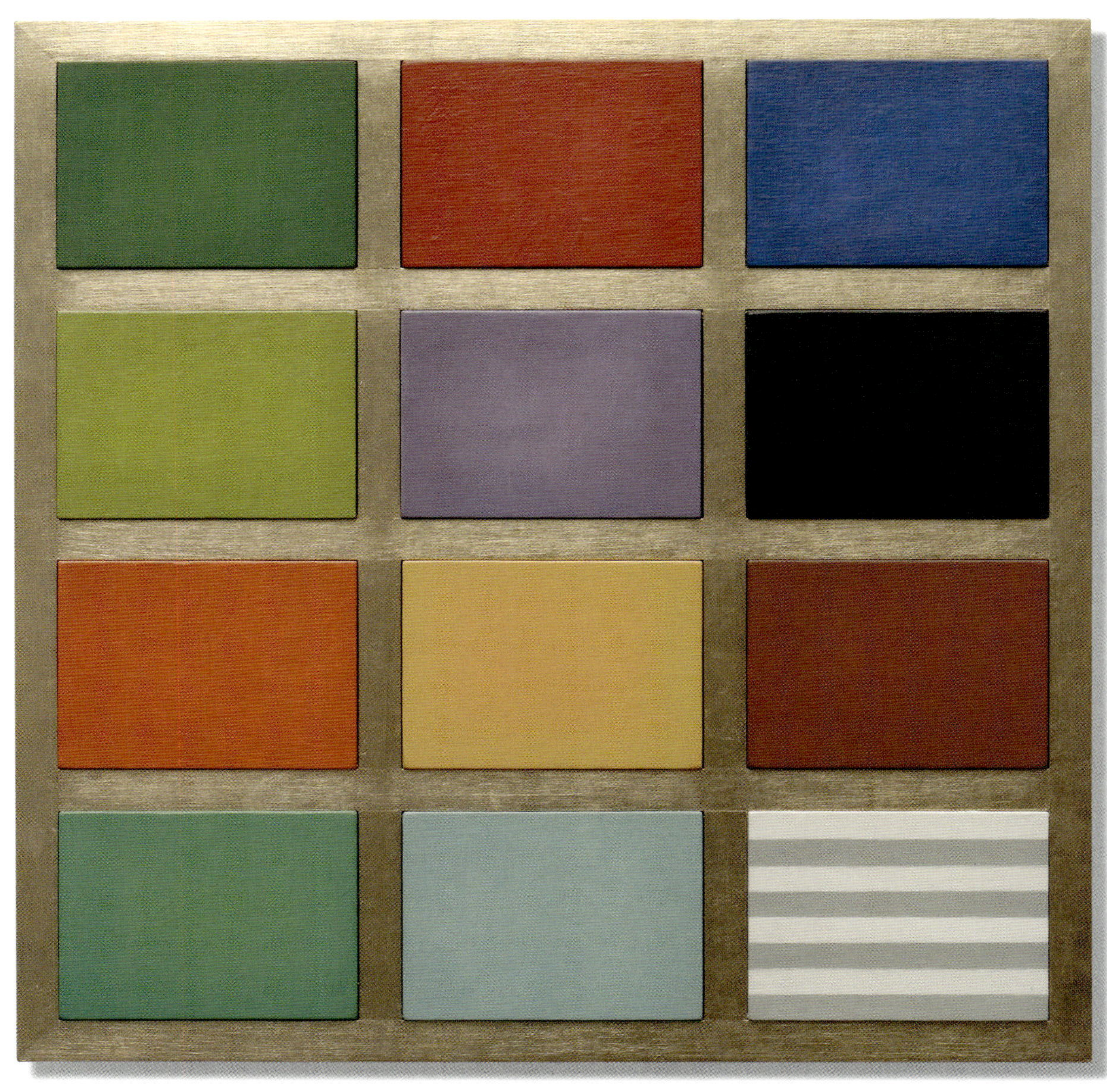

Adamas, 2002–2003
Oil, linen, gold leaf, and wood
25 x 25 inches

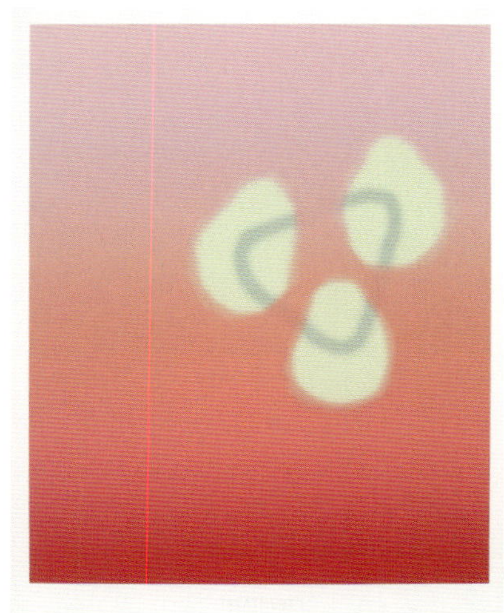
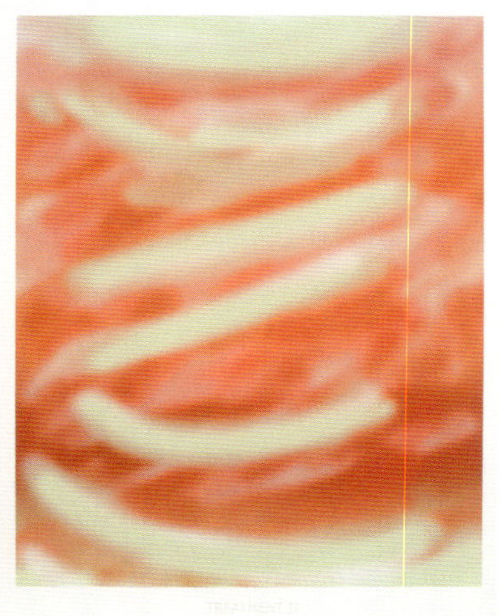

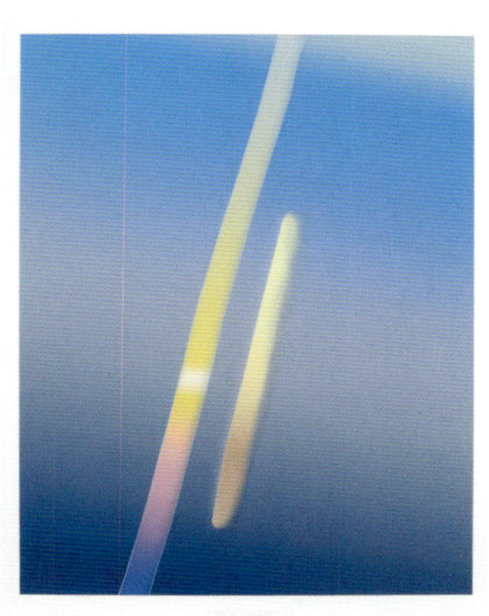
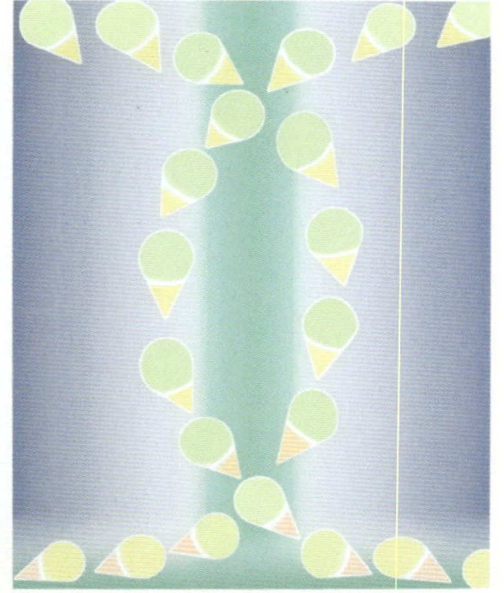

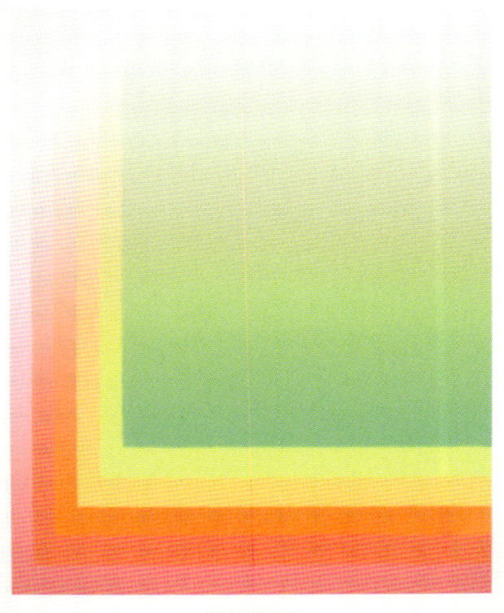

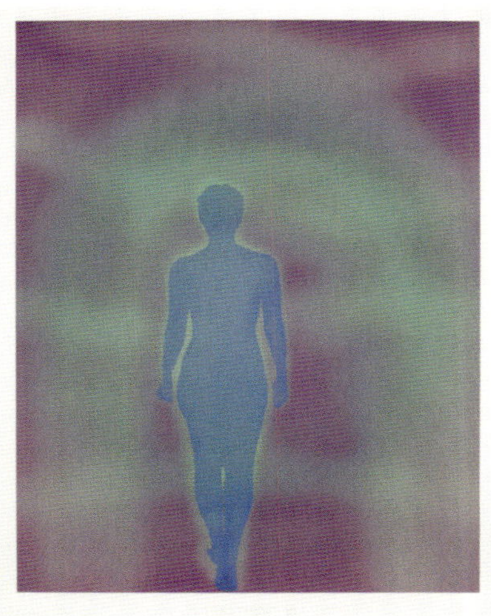
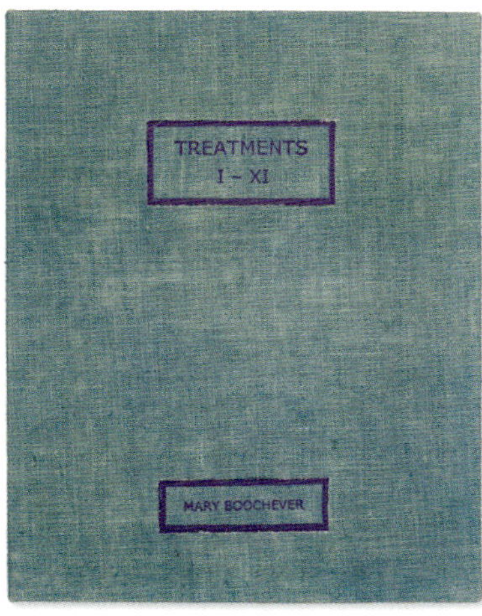

Treatments I – XI, 2003
Archival Ink-jet prints on
Epson Enhanced Matte paper
Signed and numbered on back
Edition of three
Linen-bound box

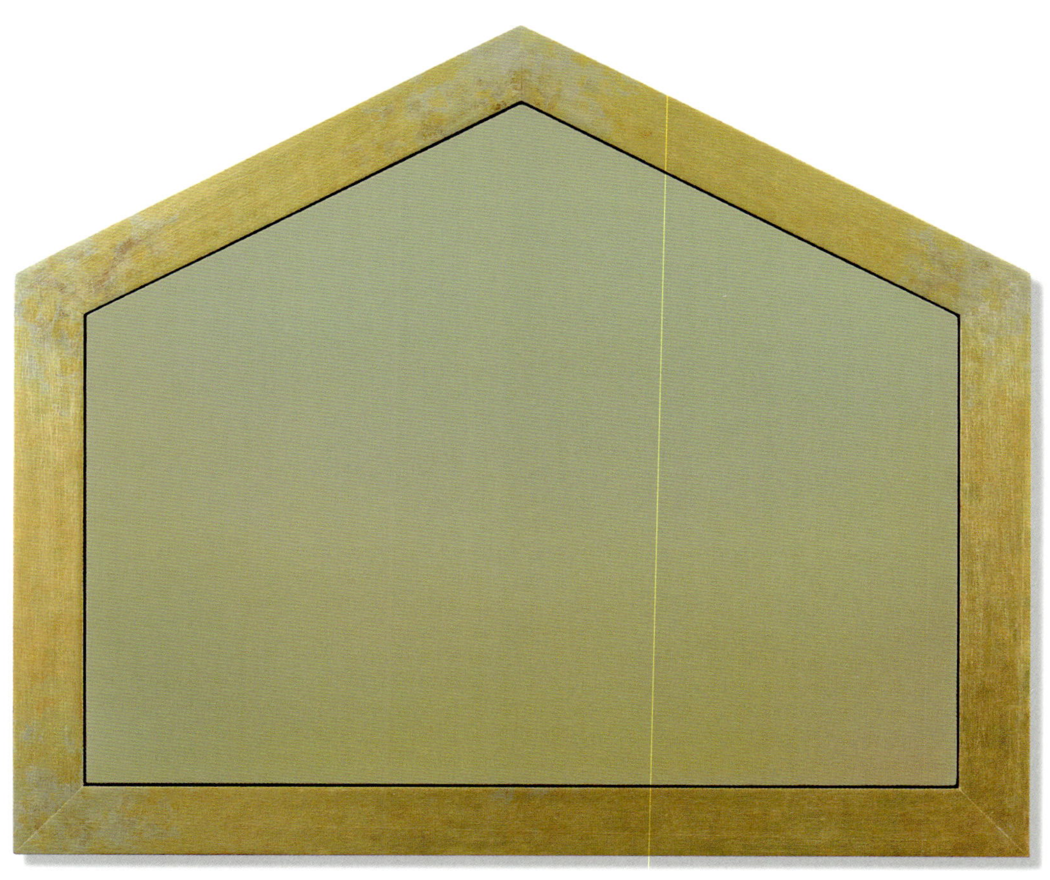

Lux Interna, 2003
Oil, linen, gold leaf, and wood
27 x 32 inches

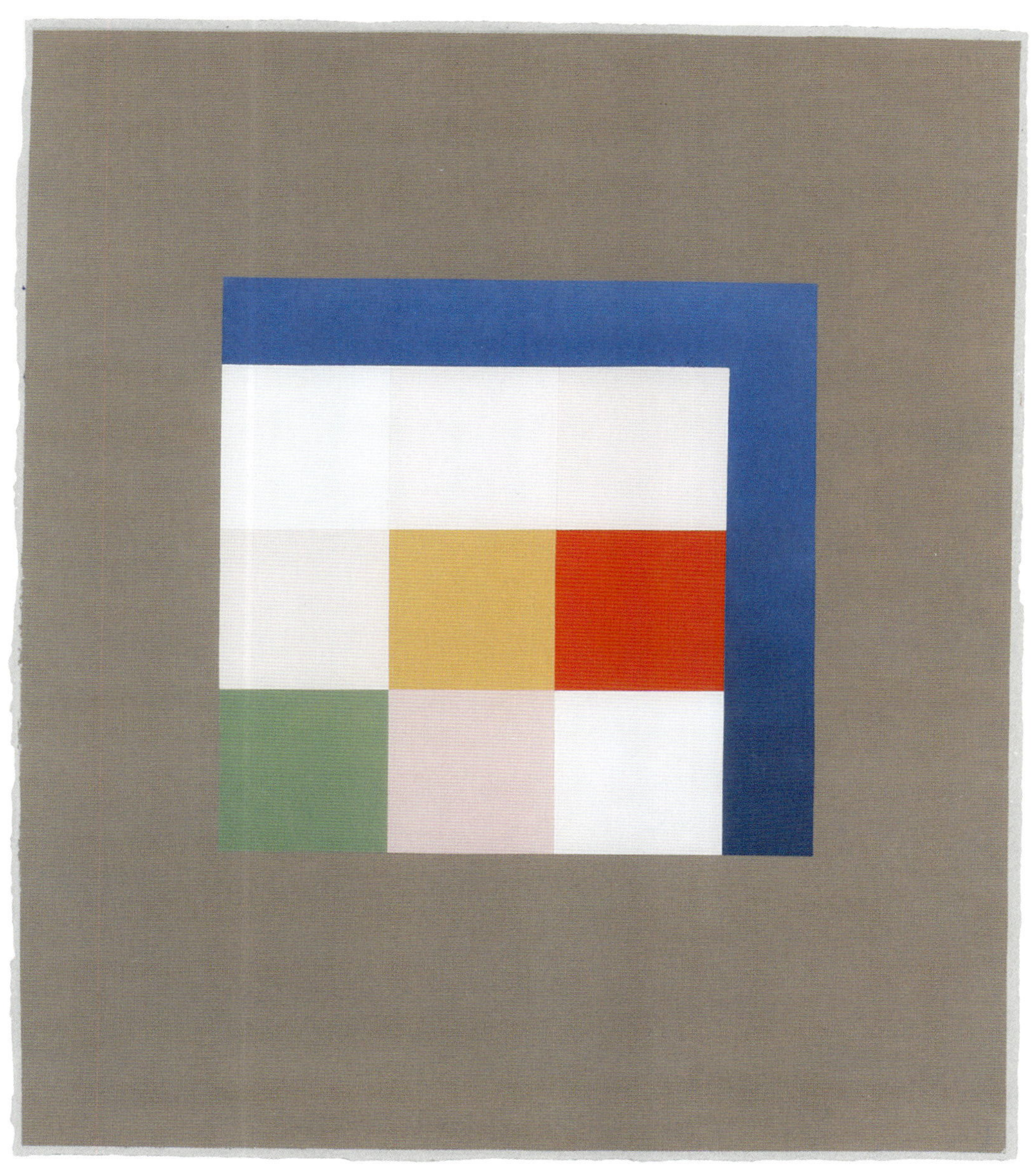

Khar, 2006
Gouache on paper
19 3/4 x 16 3/4 inches

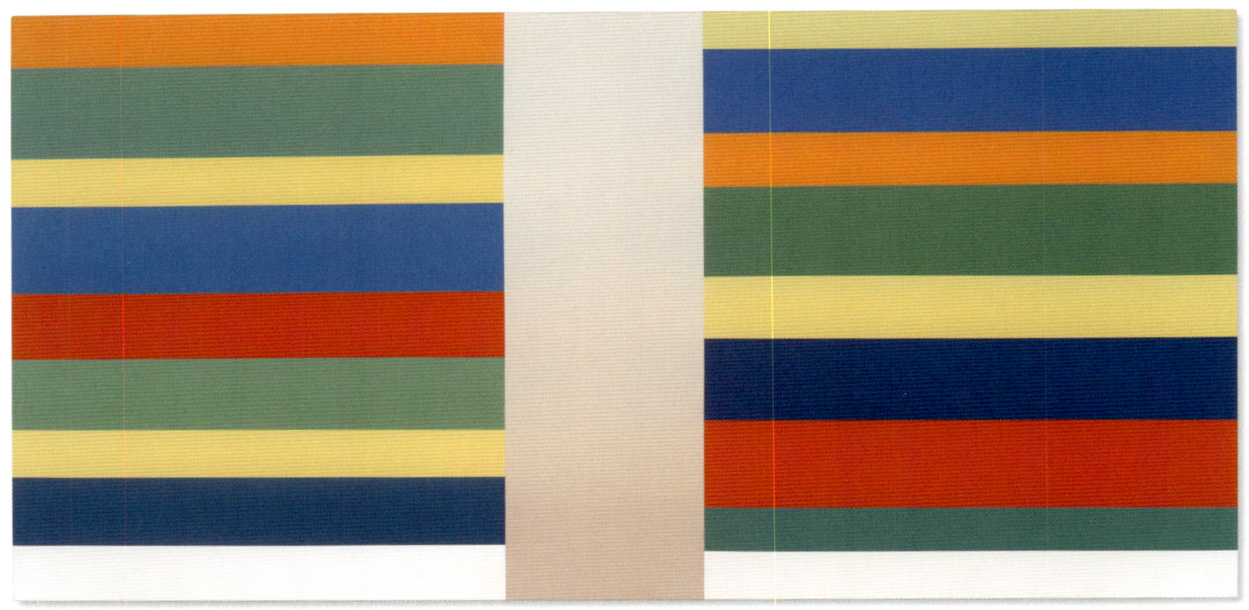

Unhell 1, 2006
Pigments and acrylic on canvas
36 1/2 x 75 inches

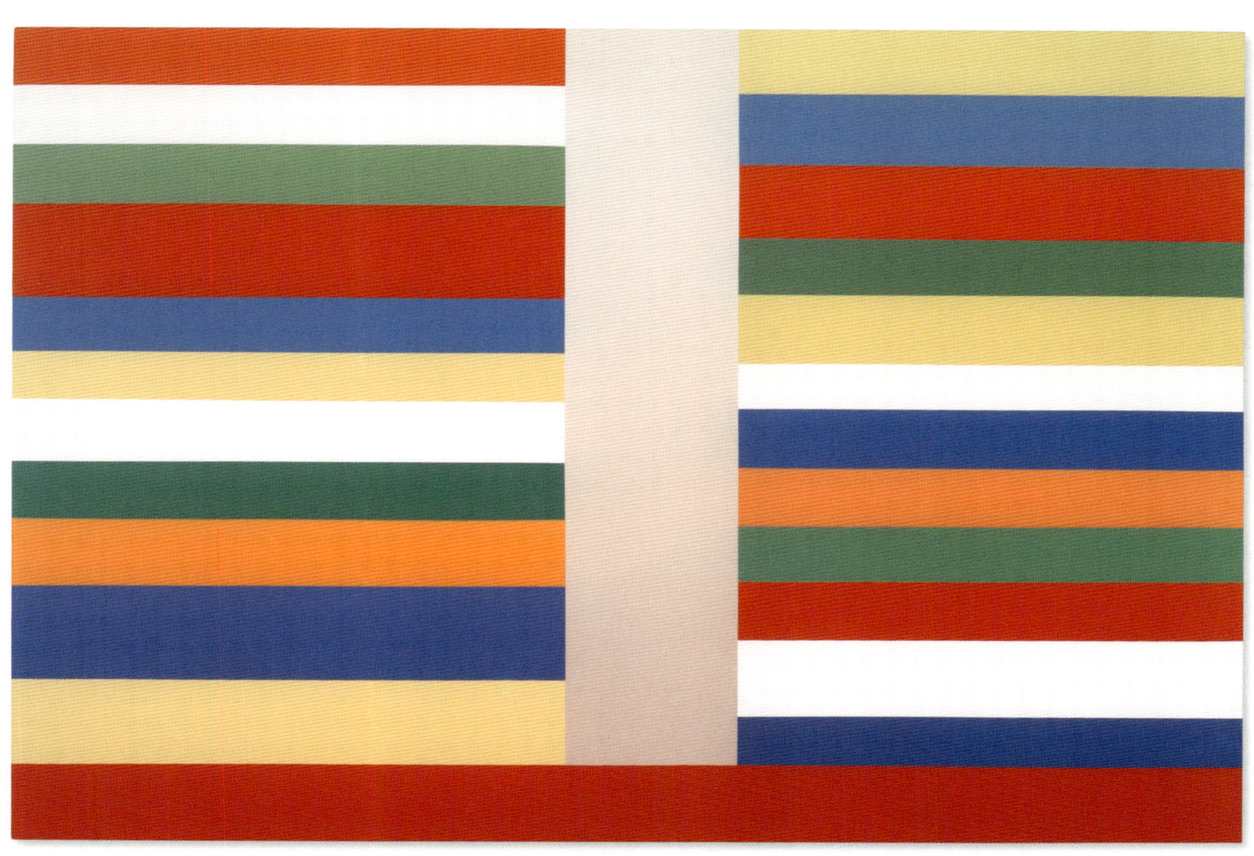

Unhell 2, 2006
Pigments and acrylic on canvas
38 x 57 inches

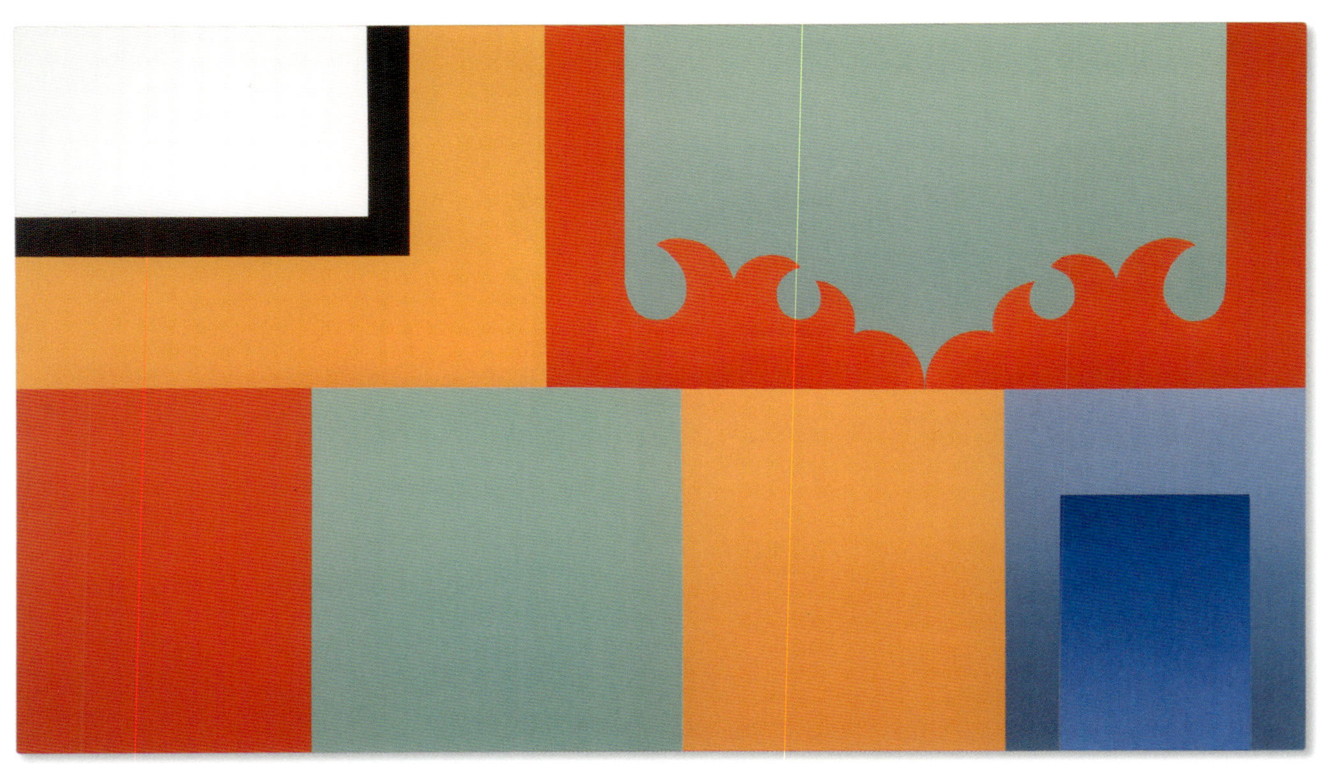

L.A.W., 2006
Pigments and acrylic on canvas
34 1/2 x 59 inches

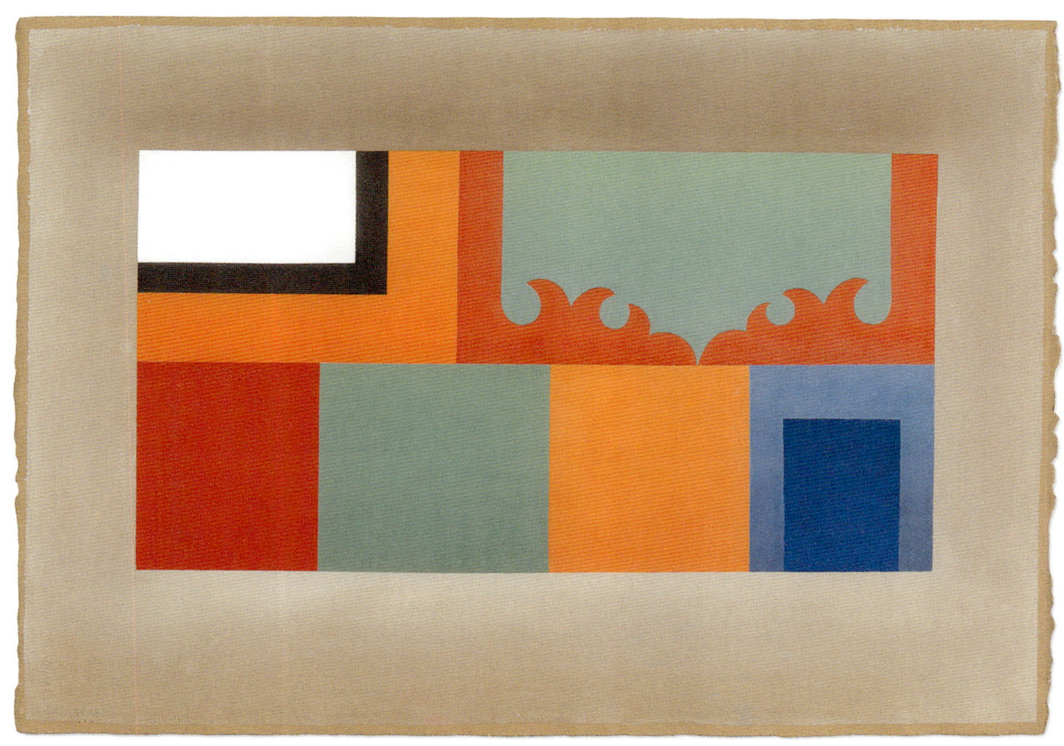

L.A.W., 2006
Gouache on paper
15 1/2 x 22 inches

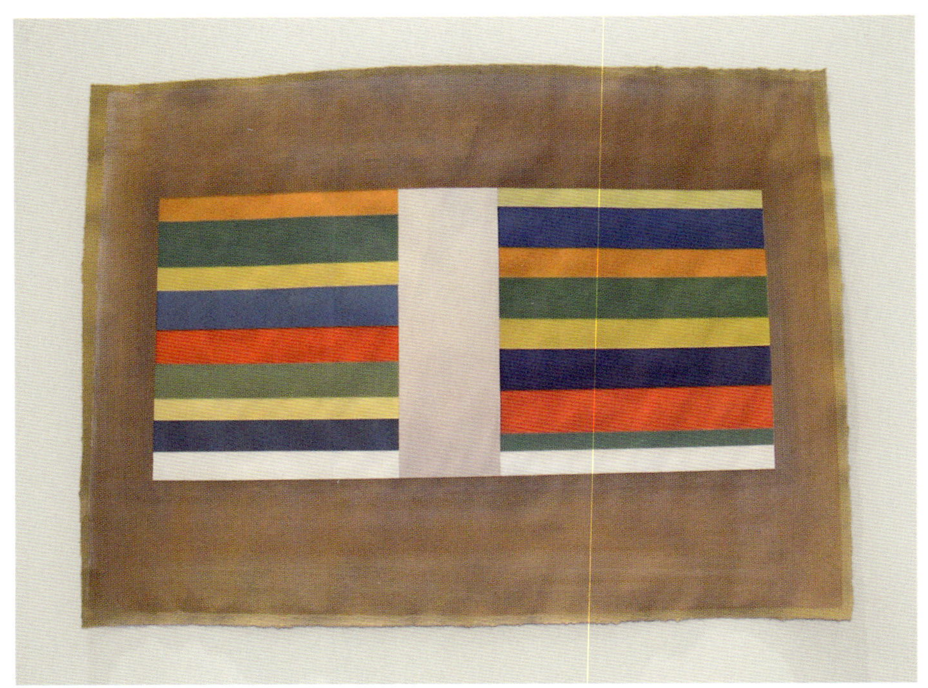

Unhell 1, 2006
Gouache on paper
19 x 24 1/2 inches

126

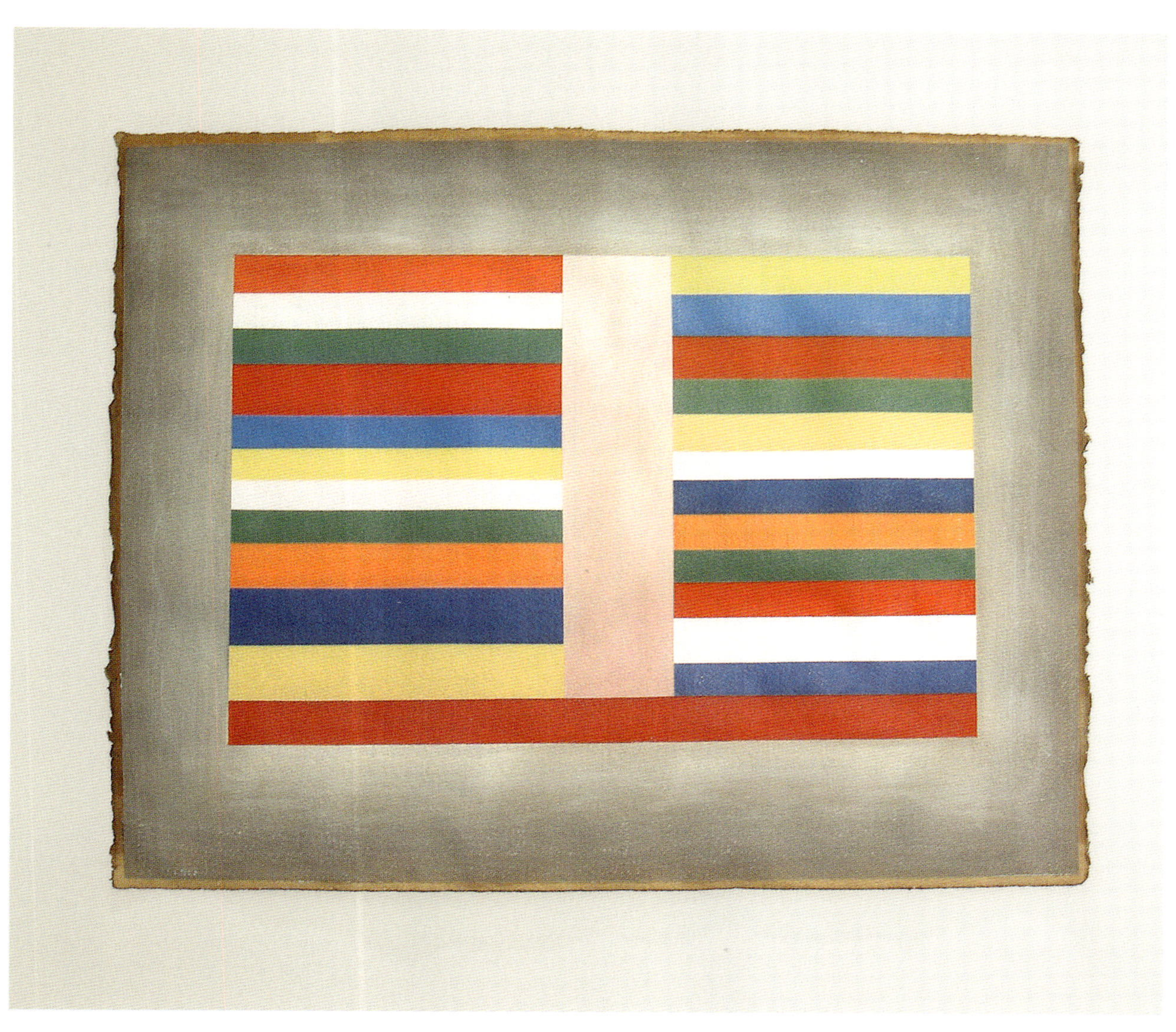

Unhell 2, 2006
Gouache on paper
21 x 26 inches

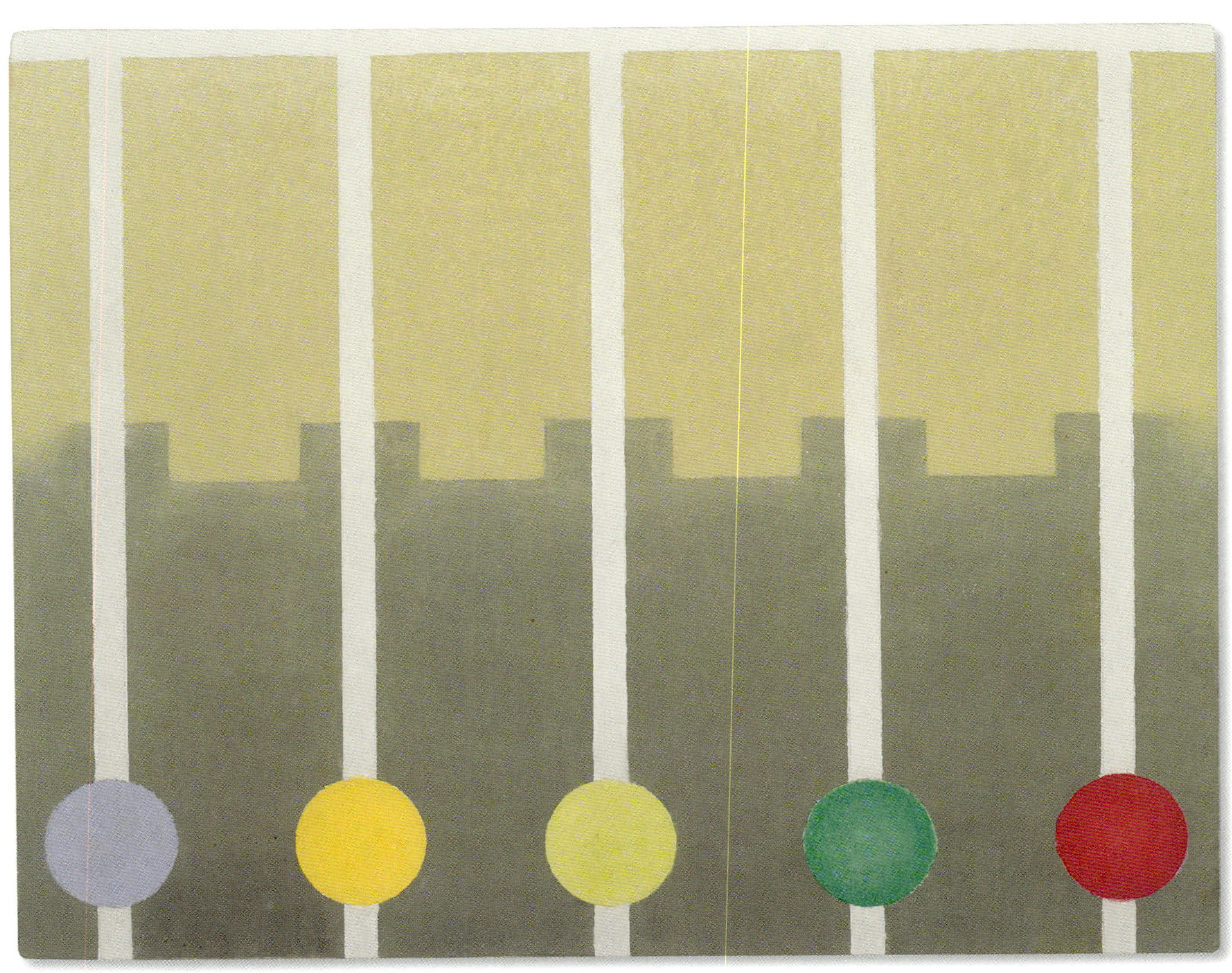

Sub Station, 2009
Oil on wood
8 x 10 inches

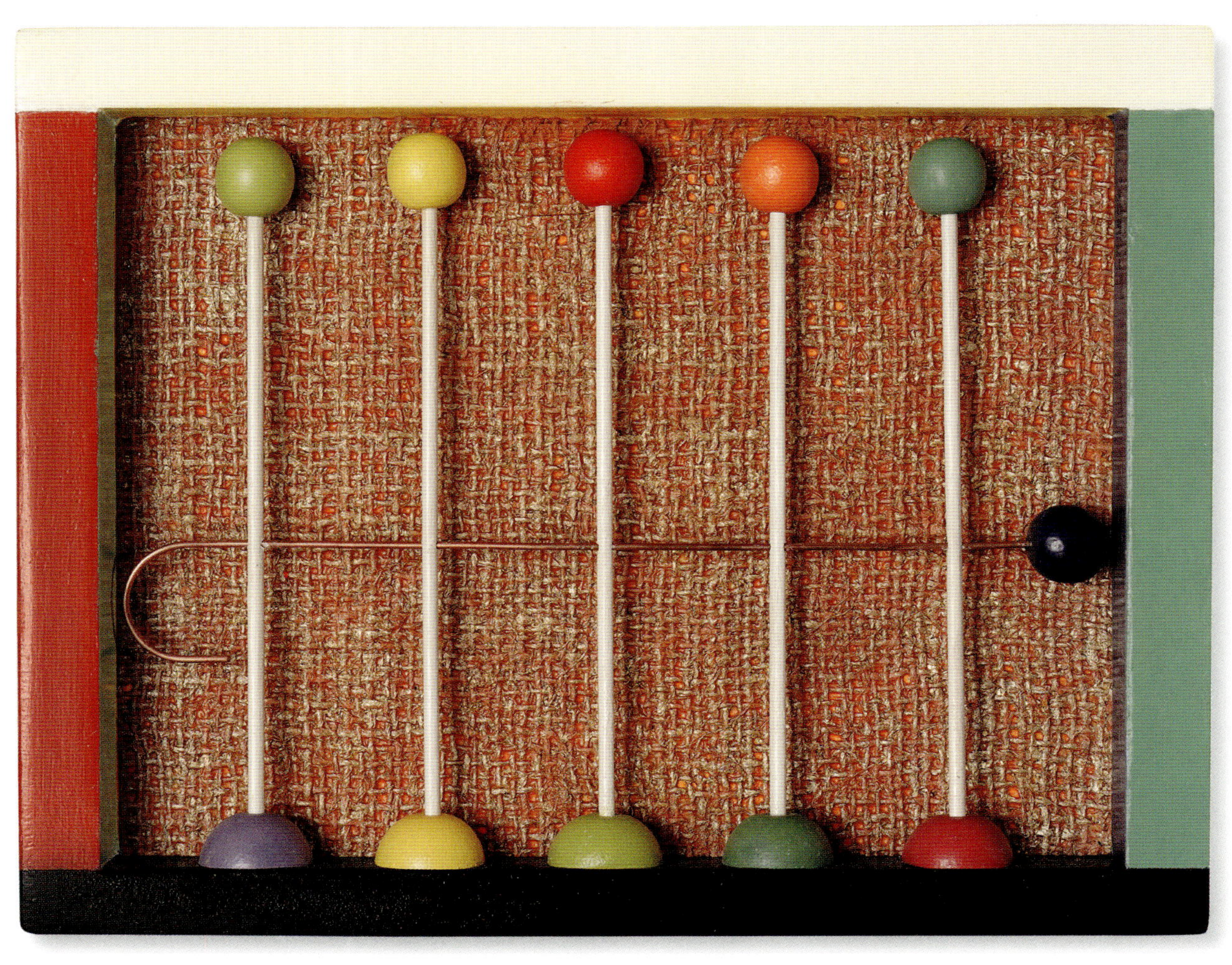

Taction, 2009
Pigment, oil, wood, encaustic, and copper wire
8 x 10 x 1 1/2 inches

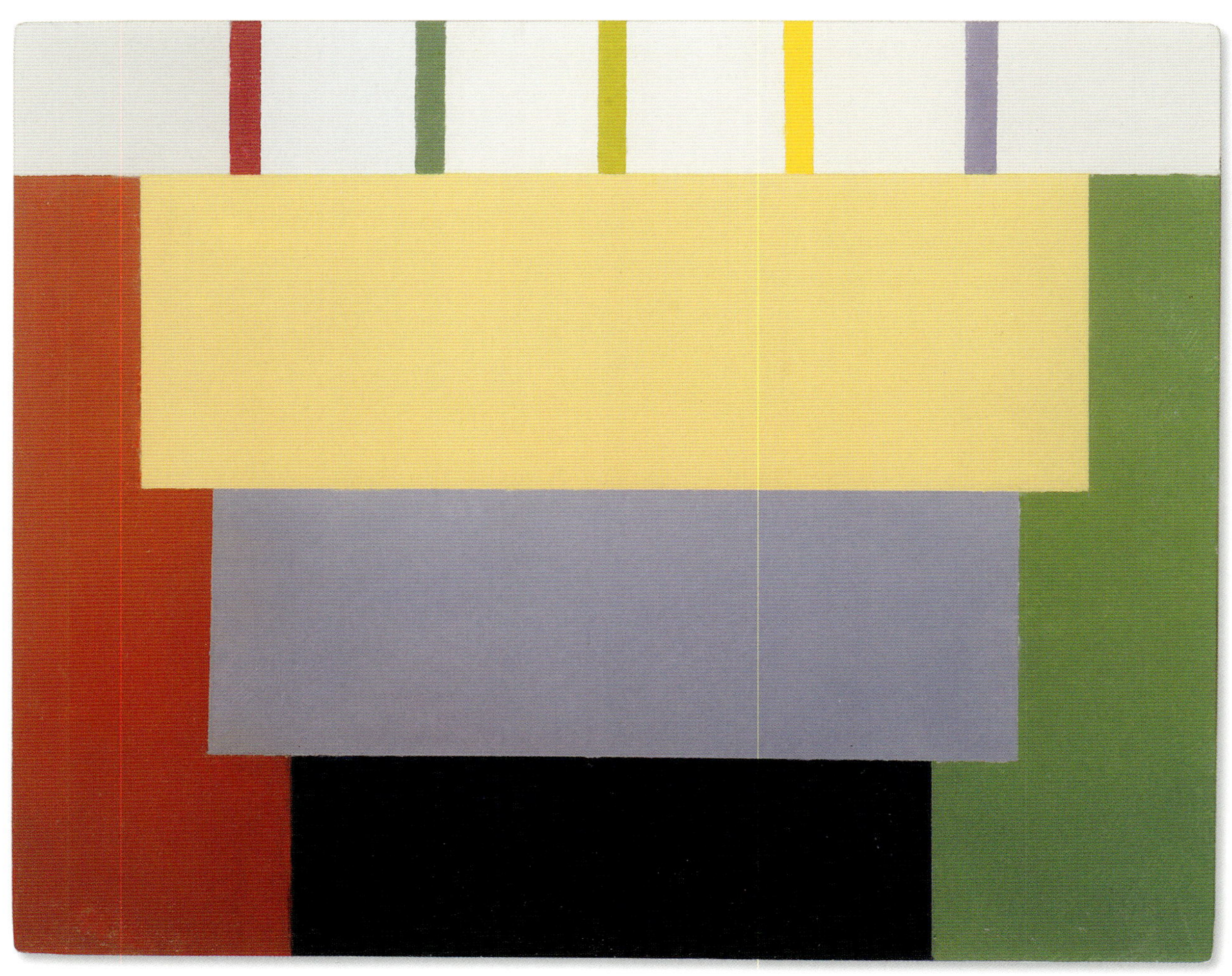

Sakti, 2009
Oil on wood
8 x 10 inches

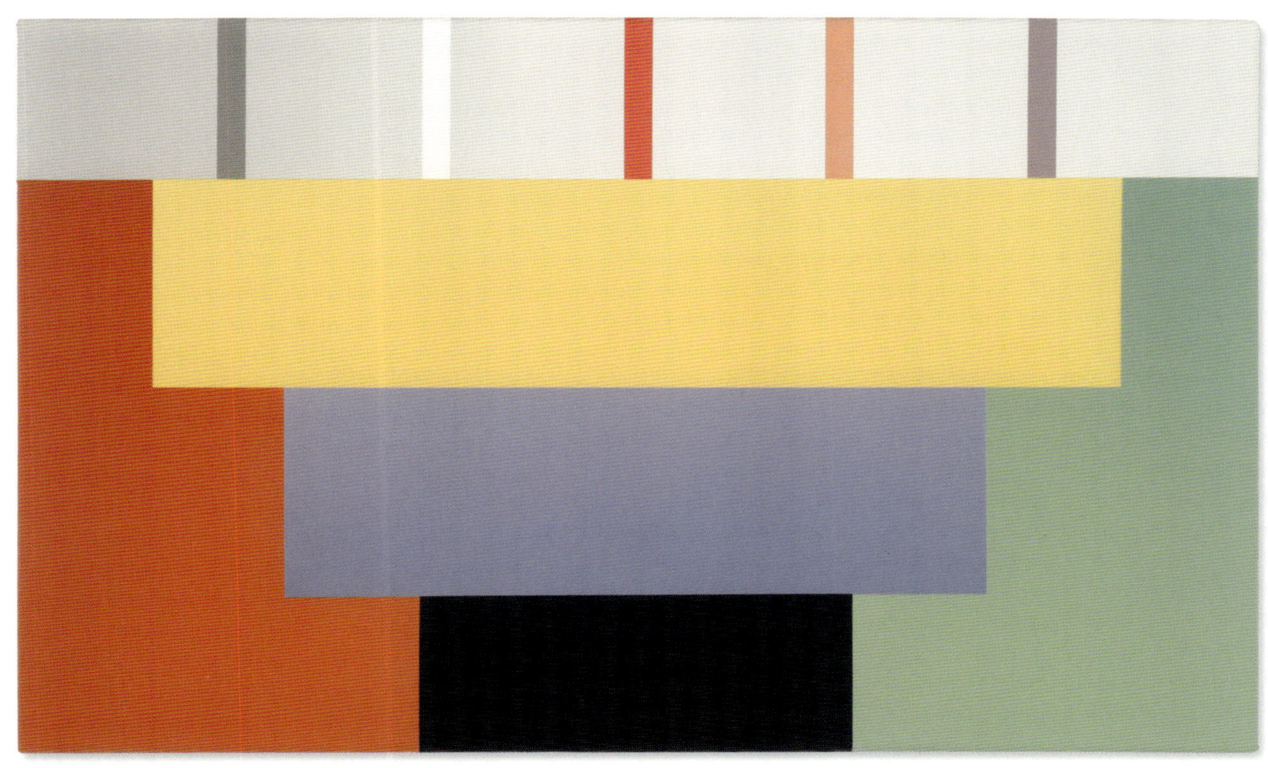

Sakti, 2010
Pigment and acrylic on canvas
14 x 23 inches

Inner Landscape 2, 2012
Pigments and acrylic on canvas
72 x 43 inches

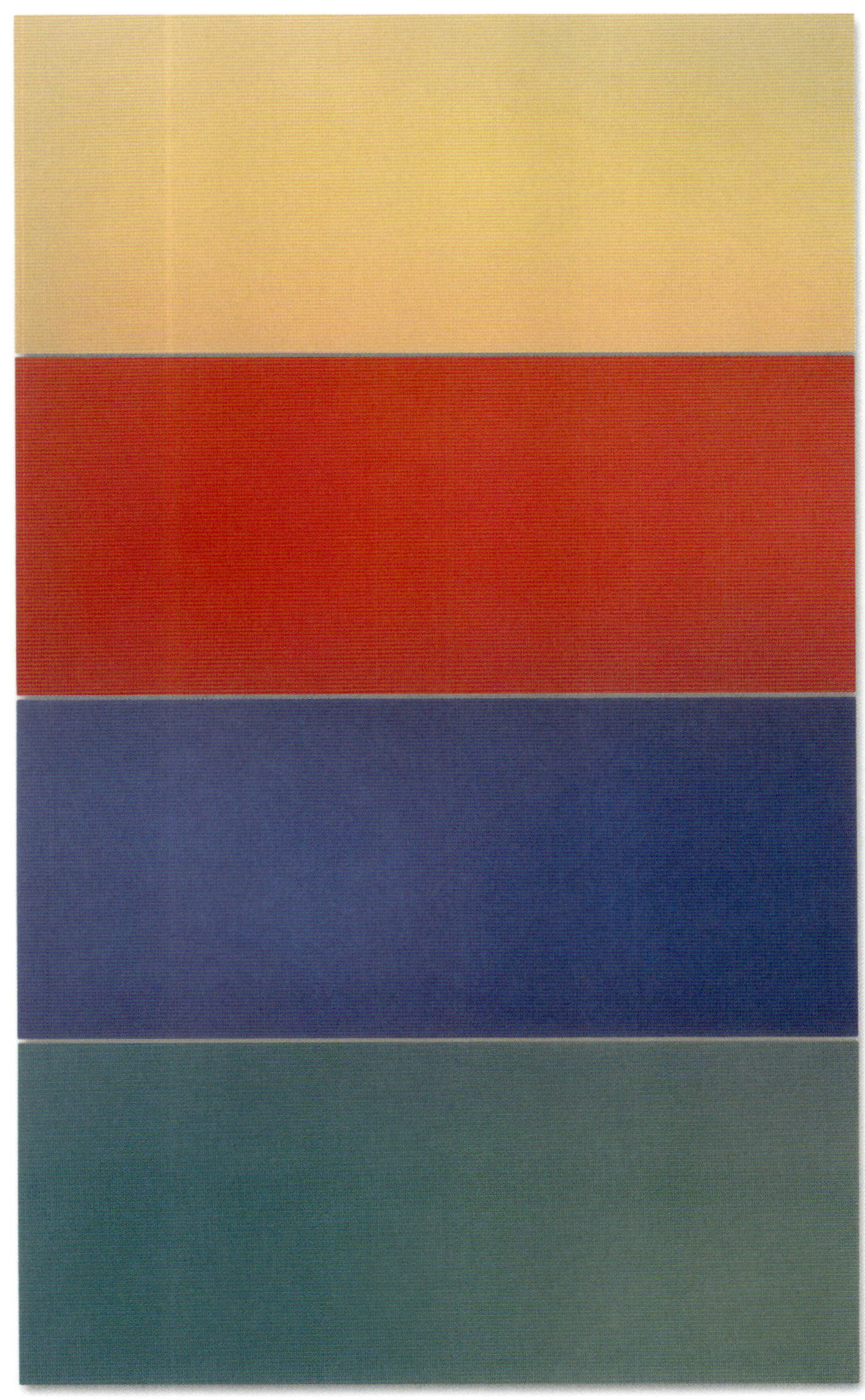

Inner Landscape 1, 2012
Pigments and acrylic on canvas
120 x 72 inches

DISCONNECTED THOUGHTS

JEREMY GILBERT-ROLFE

When my second collection of essays was published in 1995 one of the reviewers complained that whereas the first collection, published ten years earlier, had contained essays about known heavies like Brice Marden, the second didn't talk much about persons of that public stature but rather about artists who were relatively unknown, like Chris Haub and Mary Boochever. He did not seem to want to derive from that the obvious implication, that the writer had decided that Brice Marden was no longer all that interesting, but Mary Boochever was. Of course Marden continues to make works at which we should all look, but by the end of the seventies he seems to me to have turned all that was profound and complex in the works he had made before that into a kind of style, having to do with all the things that good painting is supposed to be. I have, generally speaking, not found this very exciting. Boochever's work ranges from the extremely quiet to the totally nuts, and I find it constantly exciting. Her work is never about good painting and always about what painting could do. She makes works which are so simple and straightforward that one wonders both why they work and why she thinks she can get away with it. And others that go straight to a quite complicated idea about the body and thinking, which is in my view what the most exciting painting usually does (Manet, Mondrian, Pollock, are who come to my mind, I don't know who's in hers, almost certainly artists from Asia as much as from elsewhere, with Rudolf Steiner sitting on a cloud nearby).

I recently had the opportunity to write about Boochever's work as part of an essay about geometric abstraction. I think she takes the spirit of early abstraction in the sorts of directions it implicitly and in some cases explicitly wanted to go. In this sense she's quite a traditional artist but at the same time also one who has no difficultly in thinking in terms which are not restricted by culture. The universal aspirations of early abstraction are realized in her work on a day-to-day basis. The works I wrote about for the essay about geometric abstraction were derived from an Asian diagram about the connection between the extremities of the body and its interior, and it was both straightforward to compare her work with others whose sources were quite different and at the same time clear to see that her idea of what painting can be and do was and is one that cannot be contained, and therefore not explained, by recourse, for example, to an idea of 'good painting' or any other explanation or interpretation which begins with style or a restricted notion of the history of art.

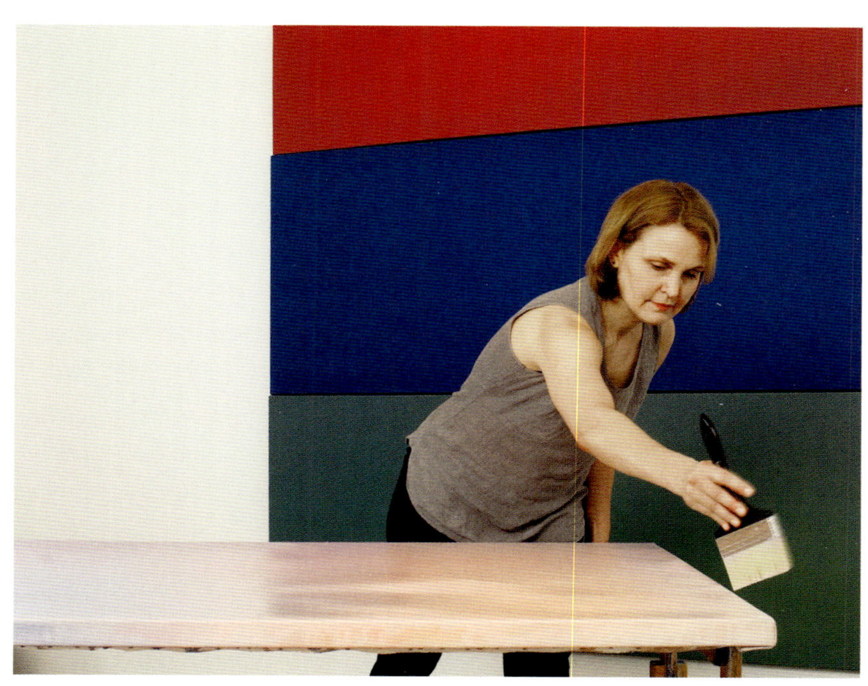

In developing her own color language, Mary Boochever has
explored sources as diverse as the Kabala and Goethe's Color
Theory. Boochever's paintings, sculptures, and installations draw
the viewer into the immediacy of the color experience. Born into a
Washington, D.C., Foreign Service family in 1954, she later studied at
the Akademie der Bildenden Künste in Munich, Germany, under Mac
Zimmerman, Günther Fruhtrunk, and Paul Meyer-Speer. Relocating
to New York City in 1978, she taught at the School of Visual Arts and
guest-lectured at Yale University. After moving to Long Island in 1993
she taught at Suffolk Community College in Riverhead and Lacoste
School of the Arts in France. The artist has shown extensively in
galleries and museums in the U.S. and Europe. She currently lives
and works in Sag Harbor, New York.

www.maryboochever.com

ABOUT THE ARTIST

INDIVIDUAL EXHIBITIONS

2006 *Unhell*, Genovese/Sullivan Gallery, Boston

1999 *Ex Fabrica*, Genovese/Sullivan Gallery, Boston

1996 *Entelechy*, Genovese Gallery, Boston

1995 *Vertical Minute*, Annika Sundvik Gallery, New York

1994 *Hidden Entrances*, Annika Sundvik Gallery, New York

1993 Genovese Gallery, Boston

1992 Daniel Newburg Gallery, New York

1990 Daniel Newburg Gallery, New York

1987 Daniel Newburg Gallery, New York

1982 PS1, Queens, NY, 'Special Projects'

SELECTED GROUP EXHIBITIONS

2012 Ille Arts, Amagansett, New York

2009 *The Big Show*, Silas Marder Gallery, Bridgehampton, NY

2004 *Orbiting Abstraction,* Surface Library, East Hampton, New York

Dense, Genovese/Sullivan Gallery, Boston

All That Glitters, Islip Art Museum, Islip, New York

2003 *Treatments I-XI*, Genovese/Sullivan Gallery, Boston

2000 Malca Fine Art, New York

1999 *The Ninth Triennial*, Fuller Museum of Art, Brockton, Massachusetts

Contemporary Relics, William King Regional Arts Center, Abingdon, Virginia

1998 *Faculty Show*, Lacoste School of the Arts, France

1996 *Celebrating the Permanent Collection*, Part I, Rose Art Museum,

Brandeiss University, Waltham, Massachusetts

She Said, Genovese Gallery, Boston

Annika Sundvik Gallery, New York

1992 *JFK, Myth and Denial*, B4A Gallery, New York, Curated by Kevin Teare and Renee Fotouhi

1991 *Shooter's Hill*, AC Project Room, New York

Daniel Newburg Gallery, New York

1990 *Painting the Dematerialized Ego*, Genovese Gallery, Boston

Grids, Vrej Boghoomian Gallery, New York

Nonrepresentation, Security Pacific Corp., Los Angeles

The Fifth Essence, Gracie Mansion Gallery, New York

Abstract Painting, Lawrence Oliver Gallery, Philadelphia

Specific Metaphysics, Sandra Gehring Gallery, New York

1989 *Riscos*, Machado de Castro National Museum, Coimbra, and Museum de Aveiro, Portugal

Body Fragments, Shea & Becker Gallery, New York

Methods of Abstraction, Gallery Urban, New York

Nonrepresentation (The Show Of The Essay), Curated by Jeremy Gilbert-Rolfe,

Anne Plumb Gallery, New York

Speed Art Museum, Louisville, Kentucky

Sightings: Drawings with Color, Pratt Institute, New York, Curated by Max Gimblett

and Eleanor Moretta

1988 *An Unjaded Taste*, Bruce Museum, Greenwich, Connecticut

1987 *D'Ornamentation*, Daniel Newburg Gallery, New York, Curated by Paul Groot

1986 *Stairwell Installation*, White Columns, New York

Distances, Chapelle de la Salpêtrière, Paris, France

1985 *Logosimuli*, Daniel Newburg Gallery, New York, Curated by Alan Jones

1980 *New York*, Galerie Felix Handschin, Basel, Switzerland

1978 *Junger Western '77'*, Recklinghausen Museum, Germany

SELECTED BIBLIOGRAPHY

2012 Jeremy Gilbert-Rolfe, *New Directions in Geometric Abstraction*, University of Nebraska Press

2004 Cate McQuaid, "Dense," *The Boston Globe*, March 19

Helen A. Harrison, "The Allure of Gold and Glitter," *The New York Times*, January 4

2003 Cate McQuaid, "Mary Boochever, Treatments I – XI," *The Boston Globe*, December 19

1999 Mark Valentine, "Gallery Exhibitions," *South End News*, October 21

1996 Christopher Millis, "Art," *South End News*, November 21

1995 David Shapiro, "Mild Steel," catalogue essay for Annika Sundvik Gallery

Jeremy Gilbert-Rolfe, *Beyond Piety*, Cambridge University Press

1992 Cate McQuaid, "On The Street – Mary Boochever," *The Boston Phoenix*, February 21

1990 Cate McQuaid, "Painting the Ego," *South End News*, October 3

Terry R. Myers, *Arts Magazine*, September

Jeremy Gibert-Rolfe, "The Current State of Nonrepresentation," *Vision Magazine*, spring

1988 Jeremy Gilbert-Rolfe, "Art Pick of the Week: Solid Abstraction," *LA Weekly*, January 15

Jeremy Gilbert-Rolfe, "Nonrepresentation in 1988: Meaning-Production Beyond the Scope of the Pious," *Arts Magazine*, May, pp. 30–39

Jeremy Gilbert-Rolfe, "Beyond Absence: Mary Boochever and Moira Dyer Return a Notion of Being to Abstraction," *Arts Magazine*, October

Donald Kuspit, "Sightings, Drawings with Color," catalogue essay for Pratt Institute, New York

1987 Amelia Jones, *Artweek*, Los Angeles, December 20

ABOUT THE WRITERS

JEREMY GILBERT-ROLFE

Jeremy Gilbert-Rolfe (born UK, 1945) is a painter who also writes about art and related topics. His work has been exhibited in New York, where he has been represented by Alexander Gray since 1970, and may be found in public collections including the Albright-Knox Museum, Buffalo; MoCA, Los Angeles; and MoCA, Miami. In 2010 he and Rebecca Norton formed the collaboration Awkward x 2 to make paintings together and otherwise produce collective work. Gilbert-Rolfe is the author of two collections of essays (the second of which contains a reprint of his 1986 essay about Mary Boochever), a book about beauty and the sublime, and another written together with Frank Gehry. He has written numerous essays for journals and catalogues. His work has received several awards over the years, including a Guggenheim Fellowship for painting, NEA Fellowships for both painting and criticism, and the CAA's Frank Jewitt Mather Award for Criticism. He has lived in California since 1980, where he teaches in and is chair of the graduate program in art at Art Center, Pasadena.

PHILIP VANDERHYDEN

Artist Philip Vanderhyden lives and works in New York. Born in Wisconsin in 1978, he earned a BFA in painting from the University of Wisconsin in 2001 and an MFA from Northwestern University in 2004. Vanderhyden has exhibited extensively nationally, and his work has been reviewed in *Art in America, Artnet* and *Artslant,* among other publications. He recently concluded a solo exhibition of his work at Andrew Rafacz Gallery in Chicago, and he curated the retrospective of Pictures Generation artist Gretchen Bender.

DAVID SHAPIRO

Poet David Shapiro (born 1947) grew up in Deal, New Jersey, in an artistic family. Trained as a classical violinist, he played with a number of orchestras. Shapiro also came to poetry early, publishing his first collection of poems, *January* (1965), when he was 18. Shapiro's subsequent volumes of poetry include *Poems from Deal* (1969), *A Man Holding an Acoustic Panel* (1971), *The Page-Turner* (1972), *Lateness* (1977), *To an Idea* (1983), *House (Blown Apart)* (1988), *After a Lost Original* (1994), and *New and Selected Poems (1965–2006)*. The author of studies on artists such as Jim Dine, Jasper Johns, and Piet Mondrian, Shapiro has taught at Columbia University, Brooklyn College, Princeton University, and the Cooper Union School of Architecture. He is a tenured professor of art history at William Paterson University.

SUSAN L. STOOPS

Susan L. Stoops, Curator of Contemporary Art at the Worcester Art Museum since 1999, was appointed Interim Chief Curator in 2012. She is an authority on international art of the past decade with a special interest in feminist practices. Recent exhibitions include projects with Carrie Moyer, Charline von Heyl, Rona Pondick, Chen Qiulin, Yun-Fei Ji, Martha Rosler, Louise Bourgeois, David Thorpe, Lily van der Stokker, Tony Feher, and Jim Hodges. From 1984–1999, Stoops served as Curator at the Rose Art Museum, Brandeis University, where she organized *More Than Minimal: Feminism and Abstraction in the '70s* (1996). Stoops received a BFA from Syracuse University and a MA in Art History from the University of Massachusetts, Amherst.

ACKNOWLEDGEMENTS

I wish to express my warm appreciation to family, friends, colleagues, and collectors, who have greeted this project with enthusiasm. I am grateful to the essayists Jeremy Gilbert-Rolfe, David Shapiro, Susan Stoops, and Philip Vanderhyden for their insightful contributions; to Kevin Smith for his elegant book design; and to my publisher Guiseppe Liverani of Charta for his vision and engagement in the realization of this book. I thank John Battle, Hisao Hanafusa, David Mastney, Will Paulson, Clayton Orehek, and Frank Scafuri for lending their skills and expertise to my projects.

For their counsel and encouragement, I wish to thank Max Gimblet, Matt Jones, and Kevin Teare.

This book is lovingly dedicated to my husband, Kevin Teare.

COLLECTORS

Rob Barnard

Adam Baumgold

Sue and Joe Berland

Carol and John Boochever

Kathleen and David Boochever

Karen and Steve Bristing

Robin Bruch

Camellia Genovese and David Sullivan

Barbara Kirshenblatt-Gimblett and Max Gimblett

Les Greenberg

Donath Heppeler

Siena and Frederic Ossorio

Larry Mangel

Will Paulson

Nancy Traversy and Martin Lueck

Catherine Rich

Brunhilde Schütz

Michelle Schwarz

Calixte and Chris Stamp

Terence Stamp

Johanna Stella

Craig Stockwell

Sue and David Wahr

New York Public Library

De Cordova Museum

Rose Art Museum

Design
Kevin Smith

Editorial Coordination
Filomena Moscatelli

Copyediting
Charles Gute

Copywriting and Press Office
Silvia Palombi

Promotion and Web
Elisa Legnani

Distribution
Anna Visaggi

Administration
Grazia De Giosa

Warehouse and Outlet
Roberto Curiale

Cover
Foundation, 1990

Photo Credits
Gary Mamay: pages 8,12, 33, 55, 56, 57, 58, 59, 60, 61, 62, 63, 64, 66, 67, 68, 69, 70, 73, 74, 76, 82, 84, 85, 86, 100, 101, 102, 103, 104, 105, 108, 109, 110, 111, 112, 114, 115, 117, 118, 119, 120, 121, 122, 123, 124, 125, 126, 127, 128, 129, 130, 131, 132, 133, 136. Lee Panich: page 75. Leslie Rose: cover, page 72.

We apologize if, due to reasons wholly beyond our control, some of the photo sources have not been listed.

Edizioni Charta srl
Milano
via della Moscova, 27 - 20121
Tel. +39-026598098/026598200
Fax +39-026598577
e-mail: charta@chartaartbooks.it
www.chartaartbooks.it

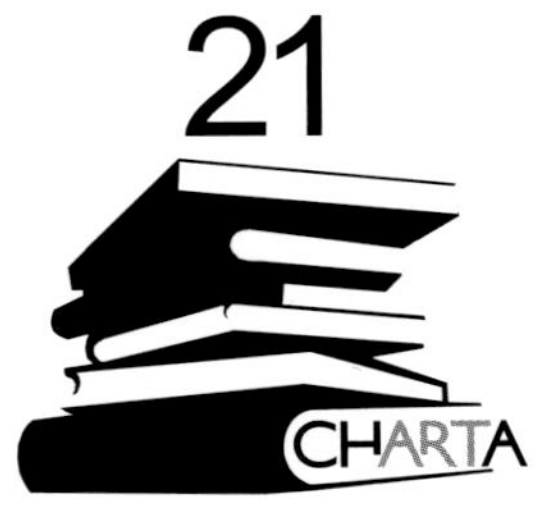

To find out more about Charta,
and to learn about our most recent
publications, visit
www.chartaartbooks.it

Printed in March 2013
by Bianca & Volta, Truccazzano (MI)
for Edizioni Charta